QUINOA
REVOLUTION

QUINOA
REVOLUTION

Over 150 Healthy, Great-Tasting Recipes Under 500 Calories

PATRICIA GREEN & CAROLYN HEMMING

PENGUIN
an imprint of Penguin Canada

Published by the Penguin Group

Penguin Group (Canada), 90 Eglinton Avenue East, Suite 700, Toronto, Ontario,
    Canada M4P 2Y3
Penguin Group (USA) Inc., 375 Hudson Street, New York, New York 10014, U.S.A.
Penguin Books Ltd, 80 Strand, London WC2R 0RL, England
Penguin Ireland, 25 St Stephen's Green, Dublin 2, Ireland (a division of Penguin Books Ltd)
Penguin Group (Australia), 250 Camberwell Road, Camberwell, Victoria 3124, Australia
    (a division of Pearson Australia Group Pty Ltd)
Penguin Books India Pvt Ltd, 11 Community Centre, Panchsheel Park,
    New Delhi – 110 017, India
Penguin Group (NZ), 67 Apollo Drive, Rosedale, Auckland 0632, New Zealand
    (a division of Pearson New Zealand Ltd)
Penguin Books (South Africa) (Pty) Ltd, 24 Sturdee Avenue, Rosebank,
    Johannesburg 2196, South Africa

Penguin Books Ltd, Registered Offices: 80 Strand, London WC2R 0RL, England

First published 2012

1 2 3 4 5 6 7 8 9 10 (CR)

Copyright © Carolyn Hemming and Patricia Green, 2012

Food photography by Ryan Szulc
Food styling by Nancy Midwicki
Prop styling by Madeleine Johari

Manufactured in the U.S.A.

Library and Archives Canada Cataloguing in Publication

Green, Patricia
Quinoa revolution : over 150 healthy, great-tasting recipes
under 500 calories / Patricia Green & Carolyn Hemming.
Includes index.

ISBN 978-0-14-318378-5

1. Cooking (Quinoa). 2. Cookbooks. I. Hemming, Carolyn. II. Title.
TX809.Q55G74 2012   641.6'31   C2012-903281-6

Visit the Penguin Canada website at www.penguin.ca

Special and corporate bulk purchase rates available; please see
www.penguin.ca/corporatesales or call 1-800-810-3104, ext. 2477.

ALWAYS LEARNING   PEARSON

FEB 15 2014

This book is dedicated to every single one of our fellow quinoa lovers, especially fans and readers of *Quinoa 365: The Everyday Superfood*. Thank you for your questions, requests and absolute passion about quinoa.

ALSO BY
Patricia Green & Carolyn Hemming

Quinoa 365: The Everyday Superfood

CONTENTS

PREFACE

SINCE our first book, *Quinoa 365: The Everyday Superfood*, was released in early 2010, people have been sharing their quinoa stories with us, writing to tell us how quinoa is transforming their lives. Parents. Spouses. Whole families. Athletes. Weight-loss dieters. Vegetarians. Cancer survivors. Diabetics. Heart patients. People with food allergies. Those who are gluten-intolerant. Everyone seems to have a story about how they first learned about quinoa, how they're now eating it, what they love about quinoa and how it is revolutionizing their life.

Many of you wrote to share your experiences—"I've lost 15 pounds"... "I've now got energy to exercise"... "I don't feel the need to snack like I used to"... "Gluten-intolerance has prevented me from eating great-tasting foods for years. Now I can't believe I can even eat delicious chocolate cake!"... "I've improved my personal best triathlon time!" And we've heard funny stories too, such as, "The quinoa baking tasted so good my husband snatched it to take to poker night."

Today it seems quinoa is talked about everywhere. Television talk shows, radio, blogs, celebrities. Oprah recommends quinoa. Martha Stewart cooks with quinoa. Dr. Oz says to cleanse with quinoa. It is a common subject in books such as *The 150 Healthiest Foods on Earth: The Surprising, Unbiased Truth about What You Should Eat and Why*; *Food Synergy: Unleash Hundreds of Powerful Healing Food Combinations to Fight Disease and Live Well*; *Power Aging*; *101 Foods That Could Save Your Life!*; *Conscious Health: A Complete Guide to Wellness through Natural Means*; *What Your Doctor May Not Tell You about Diabetes*; and *Get Balanced: The Natural Way to Better Health with Superfoods*.

More than ever, people are being watchful of unwanted processing of and chemicals in their food, choosing to be consciously aware of everything they are putting into their mouths. Increasing numbers of people are keeping close track of their nutrition to ensure they're being calorie-smart and their bodies are getting the minerals and vitamins they need to stay healthy and prevent illness and disease. (With closer attention being paid to calories and nutritional content, we have added those values to each recipe in this book.)

The rising sales of quinoa have also brought attention to ensuring that nobody suffers any negative consequences from the increased demand. Sustainable, fair-trade growing programs now exist, and we have seen first-hand in Bolivia the positive results of quinoa farming. There, quinoa farming has given many farm families a sense of pride, allowing them to support each other as well as their communities.

Amid environmental concerns, quinoa has re-emerged as a practical alternative to other popular crops that can't be successfully grown in difficult conditions. It can be grown in adverse conditions with relatively little water, such as the high, rocky plateaus of Bolivia. Crops are rotated to maintain the integrity of the soil, and llamas are used to feed on quinoa stalks and further fertilize the soil.

So whether we consume quinoa for weight loss, gluten-intolerance, a vegetarian diet, allergy control, disease prevention, overall great health or any of its other numerous advantages, the positive outcomes of using this powerhouse superfood are extensive and far reaching. With even more recipes, we hope to bring the benefits of quinoa nutrition to your table and inspire you to find many delicious ways to revolutionize your health. As always, we're open to hearing your feedback, ideas and great stories of your quinoa adventures.

INTRODUCTION
Revolutionizing Health & Fitness with Quinoa

By Laurie A. Scanlin, Ph.D., & Claire Burnett, MS

QUINOA boasts the highest nutrition profile of all grains (because it's not a grain!) and is the fastest to cook, a prerequisite for almost everyone these days. Most important, whether nutritious food is eaten for boosting health, preventing illness, reaching top athletic performance or for pure pleasure, it should taste good. This book takes a step further into the full advantages of quinoa with recipes for delicious, easy-to-make dishes that nourish. Carolyn and Patricia combine quinoa's appealing taste, versatility and light texture with a variety of fresh vegetables, fruits, legumes, nuts, healthy oils and lean proteins in over 150 tasty recipes, all under 500 calories per serving.

Quinoa's long list of distinguishing traits means there are many benefits to incorporating it into any lifestyle. Dedicated athletes are using it pre and post workout, vegetarians eat it as a source of non-animal protein, those with celiac disease benefit from its being gluten-free, those looking to detoxify or lose weight eat it because of its antioxidants, rich fiber, lean protein and complex carbohydrates. Diabetics, heart patients, those healing from cancer and those who simply choose quinoa as a dietary staple for overall improved health all benefit from quinoa. There is no question quinoa has the power to help many on a large scale and to completely revolutionize what we eat.

Unlike most of today's highly refined crops that have been genetically engineered or selectively bred and monocropped, quinoa does not require this. It is naturally genetically complex. One advantage of its genetic complexity is its ability to withstand harsh climates, where other crops fail to grow at all. The extreme mountain terrain where quinoa thrives is as rugged and hardy as quinoa is—which translates into superior nutrition. And that nutritional powerhouse explains why quinoa started to gain attention and began to be exported from South America over thirty years ago.

Awareness of this superfood continues, and in 2011 alone, the market for quinoa rose 40 percent, as everyone from health-conscious consumers to athletes added quinoa to their diets.

QUINOA'S STRUCTURE

In order to better understand this superfood, it's helpful to know what quinoa *is* rather than what it is not. Although it looks like a cereal grain, quinoa is not a grain. True cereal grains, such as wheat, corn, barley and rice, are seeds of the single-leaf grass family (or monocotyledons). Quinoa is a seed of the double-leaf vegetable family (or dicotyledons). Specifically it is the seed of a broad-leaf plant in the family Chenopodiaceae, which also includes spinach and beets. Quinoa's difference from cereal grains is significant when it comes to superior nutrition and hypoallergenic proteins. Quinoa seeds consist of three basic parts: an outer pericarp, or bran layer; an internal perisperm, a mass of storage tissue that provides carbohydrates and energy; and a large embryo, or germ (the equivalent of an egg yolk). Quinoa germ is high in albumin protein. Similar to the way egg albumin whitens, during cooking the germ "sprouts" from the seed and becomes visible as a white spiral around each cooked seed. These three basic components give quinoa its distinguishing nutritional traits that fit the special dietary needs of so many consumers.

ULTRAMETABOLISM, DETOXIFICATION, VEGAN DIETS & WEIGHT LOSS

Listening to your body's needs, in combination with being educated about food, can go a long way in reaching an optimal body weight and maintaining energy balance. A fundamental step in weight loss is detoxification, eliminating foods that prevent weight loss (empty calories from sugars and refined grains that are stripped of vitamins and minerals, processed foods and foods that we tend to eat in excess). Removing foods from the diet even for a short time, such as favorite foods eaten too often, can detoxify the system and reboot the metabolism. Foods that make us feel bloated or sluggish (such as wheat- or soy-based foods that may be hard to digest or cause inflammation, saturated fat from rich meats and dairy, and fried foods) can negatively affect our metabolism and contribute to chronic health problems. The focus of detox is replacing foods that prevent weight loss with those that cleanse, renew energy and optimize the metabolism so it works as it was originally designed to.

Quinoa is on the list of foods to enjoy for ultrametabolism in Dr. Mark Hyman's series of *UltraMetabolism* books, and in his book *The Conscious Cook*, Tal Ronnen, who once prepared vegan meals for Oprah, makes it a top choice as part of a vegan cleanse. Quinoa is a good source of vegan protein, calcium, B vitamins and iron for renewed energy. It contains both types of dietary fiber: insoluble fiber that helps to curb appetite, and soluble fiber, prebiotic nutrients that fuel the healthy microflora in the intestinal tract, resulting in increased nutrient absorption and improved gut and immune health. High-protein diets have proven to be more effective in promoting weight loss than conventional high-carbohydrate, low-fat diets. The essential amino acid profile, digestibility and bioavailability of quinoa protein are noteworthy. Quinoa protein is the nutritional equivalent of whole milk protein, which is rare for a plant source of protein. For example, rice is limited in lysine, making its protein quality inferior, whereas quinoa has 65 percent more lysine than white rice and 56 percent more than brown rice. Quinoa can restart your metabolism to help you achieve your weight-loss goals and, as part of a sound diet, can improve your long-term health.

QUINOA & EXERCISE

There are many reasons to choose quinoa as an energy source, whether you are just beginning a workout routine or you are an elite competitor. Today, top athletes, from runners and swimmers to road cyclists and triathletes, are consuming quinoa as a daily staple or as a gluten-free option to wheat-based foods. Wheat-based foods such as pasta have been a traditional energy source for athletes, but many of today's top athletes are finding they perform better without wheat. Specifically, some are experiencing increased mental clarity, a reduced bloated or heavy feeling and fewer stomach problems. In people who are sensitive to gluten, the body's defenses end up attacking the nutrient-absorbing cells in the intestine, causing inflammation and a bloated feeling. In a vicious cycle, this inflammation contributes to a reduction in nutrient absorption and may lead to serious malnourishment. This is, of course, of heightened concern for athletes.

Gluten is not the only culprit to blame for inflammation in the intestinal tract and reduced nutrient absorption. Inflammation can be caused by food allergens, sensitivities to food or hard-to-digest food proteins. For those with a food allergy, milk and soy are among the top eight allergens, and some soy-based foods may contain inhibitors (such as trypsin) that actually block protein from being fully digested. Similarly, cereal grains contain anti-nutrients, which are known to impair nutrient absorption (which is why they are avoided in some diets, such as the paleo diet). As quinoa is the seed of a vegetable and not a cereal grain, it does not contain gluten proteins and so does not ignite an inflammatory response. Furthermore, although quinoa is primarily recognized for its balanced amino acid composition (rare for plant-based proteins), it contains proteins that are easy to digest.

Whether for everyday workouts or for bodybuilding or endurance athletics, adding quinoa to a sound diet aimed at avoiding foods that may increase inflammation and reduce nutrient absorption can be extremely effective in enhancing performance.

Exercise & Meal Timing: When to Eat Quinoa

Depending upon your workout goals, quinoa can be a key staple both before and after exercise.

Before your workout

Finding the right pre-exercise meal relies on timing, easy digestibility, balancing calorie intake and managing hunger. A pre-workout meal consumed three hours before competition or two hours before training has been found to work well. Insulin levels can spike an hour or so after eating, causing a dip in blood sugar and leading to a hypoglycemic state known to athletes as "bonking." Proper meal timing combined with choosing foods with higher protein and healthy fat and a lower glycemic index is ideal. Foods with a glycemic index of 55 or lower (ranked on a scale of 1 to 100) help to stabilize blood sugar while providing slow-release energy to maintain a steady state through exercise. A cup (250 mL) of cooked quinoa has a glycemic index of 53. In addition, "glycemic load" is used to assess the quality of carbohydrates in a food (as indicated by its effect on blood sugar) as well as the quantity of carbohydrates per serving. A cup of cooked quinoa contains 25 grams of carbohydrates and a medium glycemic load of 13. The balance between the quality and quantity of carbohydrates in quinoa makes it an effective energy source that won't cause dramatic fluctuations in blood sugar and will provide consistent slow-release energy. This superior advantage of quinoa stems from the internal perisperm of the seed, which contains microscopic starch granules (fifty times smaller than potato starch!). Finally, a bowl of cooked quinoa is easy to digest before competition or training.

After your workout

The right post-exercise meal contains foods that promote quick recovery. Quinoa has four benefits that are critical to quick recovery after exercise.

Stimulates building and repairing muscle. Quinoa contains the branched-chain amino acids valine, leucine and isoleucine, which stimulate building and repairing muscle. One cup of cooked quinoa has 29 percent more branched-chain amino acids than 1 cup of cooked white rice, and 17 percent more than brown rice. Quinoa is a better choice to complement lean meats (also an excellent source of branched-chain amino acids) following an intense workout.

Prevents muscle and bone loss. Foods that contribute to a net blood alkalinity prevent muscle and bone loss. Quinoa's protein and mineral content give it a net alkaline enhancing effect, sparing bone and muscle loss.

Maintains muscle energy reserves. Starches and sugars maintain muscle glycogen, which is essential for high-level performance. A cup of cooked quinoa offers 30 grams of carbohydrates, both complex and simple, that replenish muscle glycogen stores.

Optimizes immune system function. Micronutrients, including antioxidants, vitamins, minerals and phytochemicals, all promote optimal immune-system functioning. The increased ability to fight off illness improves consistency of training and ultimate performance. Quinoa is a good source of vitamins and minerals (vitamins E, B_2, B_6, folic acid and biotin, calcium, phosphorus, magnesium, potassium, iron, copper, manganese and zinc). Quinoa also contains betalain pigments, which are phytochemicals with antioxidant and anti-inflammatory properties. In addition, quinoa germ contains histidine, an amino acid that plays a significant role in the growth and repair of tissues and is needed for the production of both red and white blood cells. Both types of blood cells are important to athletes in particular, because red blood cells carry oxygen to muscles and other tissues, and white blood cells boost immune health. Rice has previously been recognized as a natural source of histidine, but quinoa is a much better source, containing 57 percent more histidine than white rice and 45 percent more than brown rice.

Quinoa as it pertains to health and wellness fits perfectly with our core competence in quinoa research, food science and human nutrition, as well as our personal lifestyles dedicated to fitness. Try something different from the usual wheat pasta, corn or rice. We encourage you to consider protein-rich quinoa. Because this superfood is so mildly flavored and versatile, you'll find that these nutrient-rich, easy-to-make quinoa recipes will suit your taste and help you achieve your dietary goals whether for health, fitness or overall wellness.

QUINOA REVOLUTION

QUINOA is becoming increasingly popular as an everyday food on the dining tables of all kinds of modern families in a variety of cultural settings. No longer limited to a few similar recipes, it can be found in more than just basic breakfast cereals and side salads. In the last few years we have seen quinoa in everything from our lunch salads, dinner entrées, double-layer cakes, pasta, muffins, soups, bakery bread and smoothies—even our shampoo. "Made with quinoa" is a phrase we are seeing more often as this ancient grain becomes mainstream.

This tiny seed, more than five thousand years old, was once hidden away in the high Andes Mountains of South America, but today it is being included in an increasing number of North American meals, not only pushing aside rice and couscous but sometimes even replacing meat. In 2011, imports of quinoa to the United States increased by an astonishing 39 percent from the previous year. This popularity is the result both of quinoa's versatility in cooking and of the incredible health properties of this superfood.

As a superfood, quinoa boasts an array of exceptional properties even beyond a stellar nutritional profile. For starters, it is vegetarian-friendly, gluten-free and a complete protein. It can help prevent disease, encourage the body to heal and provide vitamins and minerals that nourish. While other superfoods exist, even some with tremendous qualities that may seem comparable, none offers a similar nutritional profile. As well, quinoa is by far the most versatile. It can be used in almost any dish, whereas other superfoods may find a place in only a select number of recipes. Not all superfoods are as adaptable to everyday menus and lifestyles.

VITAMIN & MINERAL CONTENT

Quinoa is a good source of minerals such as iron, phosphorus, magnesium, calcium and potassium. It is also rich in vitamins such as vitamin E, riboflavin and folic acid.

TABLE 1: Vitamin & Mineral Comparison

1 cup (185 g) All cooked	CALORIES (KCAL)	FAT	PROTEIN	CARBOHYDRATES	FIBER	MINERALS (MG) CALCIUM	IRON	MAGNESIUM	PHOSPHORUS	POTASSIUM	SODIUM	VITAMINS THIAMINE B_1 (MG)	RIBOFLAVIN B_2 (MG)	NIACIN B_3 (MG)	VITAMIN B_6 (MG)	FOLATE (MCG)	VITAMIN A (IU)	VITAMIN E (MG)
QUINOA	222	3.6	8.1	3.9	5.2	31	2.8	118	281	318	13	0.2	0.2	0.76	0.23	78	9	1.17
AMARANTH	189	2.92	7	35	3.9	87	3.89	120	274	250	11	0.03	0.04	0.44	0.21	41	0	0.3
BARLEY, PEARLED	228	0.81	4	52	7	20	2.5	41	100	172	6	0.15	0.12	3.82	0.21	30	13	0.02
CHIA SEEDS, DRIED	899	56.9	30.6	78	64	1167	14	620	1591	753	30	1.1	0.3	16.3	—	—	100	0.9
COUSCOUS	207	0.3	7	43	2.6	15	0.7	15	41	107	9	0.12	0.05	1.82	0.09	28	0	0.24
ROLLED OATS	131	2.81	4.7	22	3.1	17	1.66	50	142	130	7	0.14	0.03	0.42	0.01	11	0	15
RICE, BROWN LONG GRAIN	205	1.7	4.8	42	3.3	18	0.78	80	154	80	9	0.18	0.05	2.83	0.27	7	0	0.06
RICE, WHITE LONG GRAIN	240	0.52	4.9	52	0.7	18	2.22	22	80	65	2	0.30	0.02	2.73	0.17	179	0	0.07
TEFF	187	1.2	7.2	37	5.2	91	3.8	92	222	198	15	0.34	0.06	1.68	0.18	33	4	—
WHITE POTATO	174	0.28	3.9	39	3.9	18	1.18	50	139	1006	13	0.09	0.08	2.83	0.39	70	18	0.07

USDA National Nutrient Database for Standard Reference, 2011

VEGETARIAN-FRIENDLY

An ideal non-animal protein source for vegetarians, 1 cup (250 mL) of cooked quinoa provides approximately the same amount of protein as a whole egg. Plus, quinoa's versatility in the kitchen means that vegetarians can find many creative ways to enjoy this protein-rich food.

GLUTEN-FREE

Since quinoa is not a grain, it is not related to wheat and does not contain gluten. For the increasing number of people who are affected by wheat-related allergies, celiac disease, colitis or Crohn's disease, quinoa is an ideal food to eat every day. Gluten has also been thought to be a source of problems for children with autism and attention deficit hyperactivity disorder (ADHD). Quinoa is a reasonable solution for a gluten-restricted diet.

COMPLETE PROTEIN

Quinoa is a complete protein—in other words, it contains all eight essential amino acids. Nothing else needs to be combined with quinoa in order for the body to digest and efficiently use quinoa's energy, vitamins and minerals. Hence, quinoa's high digestibility and protein content allow the muscles to effectively make use of available protein and quickly rebuild lean muscle.

WEIGHT LOSS, HEALTH & FITNESS

Quinoa can assist with weight loss. A complex carbohydrate, quinoa does not quickly convert sugars to fats, thus providing an effective long-term energy source. Lower glycemic index foods such as quinoa take longer to digest and as a result do not promote the spike of insulin levels in the blood that triggers the body to store fat. The complete chemistry was not likely known by the ancient Incas, who worshipped quinoa, but we now know that quinoa can help make us healthy, make us strong and help us reach and maintain personal health and nutritional goals.

BUYING QUINOA

Since the release of *Quinoa 365: The Everyday Superfood* in 2010, quinoa has become more readily available in most major supermarkets in North America. It is no longer restricted to health-food stores or specialty or organic aisles in the grocery store. It can usually be found in the same aisle as rice or couscous, and the growing excitement over this superfood means it can often be found featured on display. It can be purchased in bulk, in boxes or in bags, in a variety of brands. Quinoa seeds are available in white (also known as golden), red and black and are also sold as flakes and flour. Quinoa is often a featured ingredient in many processed foods such as commercial breads, pastas and crackers and even in household cleaning products and soaps.

Increasing demand has meant the cost of quinoa has risen slightly. In 2010 it was $3 to $4 a pound ($6 to $8/kg), and as of the time of writing this book it is almost one dollar more. Yet we now benefit from more brands than ever before, better selection and increased availability of quinoa in stores. Also worth considering is that quinoa expands in cooking to three times or more its original volume, so you are getting more for your money than you would with similar foods that only double in volume at best. Therefore, with quinoa, the nutrition you get for your dollar is more than you would get from, say, rice or pasta. Remember that global food prices are on the rise in general, so quinoa is not alone. Even the cost of rice will likely continue to rise.

USING QUINOA

Quinoa is incredibly versatile in the kitchen. Cooked, it makes a great key ingredient in soups, salads, entrées, baked goods, desserts, breakfast cereal and even baby food. Used raw, quinoa seeds can be ground or sprouted and used in salads, sandwiches or breakfast smoothies, making it especially popular with people who follow a raw-food diet.

Quinoa flour is a smart alternative to many flours that contain gluten or have inferior nutritional profiles. It can be used to improve moistness and can be used alongside other flours. A blend of quinoa flour (or cooked seeds) and a wheat flour, for example, will absorb and hold liquid. This is especially useful in baked goods, where the increased moisture helps to produce a fluffy, soft texture. Various combinations of quinoa flour with other flours such as rice, tapioca, almond, coconut and potato starch allow you to create impressive recipes that meet your specific nutritional requirements and invent new fusions of delightfully complex flavors. Quinoa's easily adaptable flavor is also what adds to its versatility. It is complemented by an endless range of flavors, from vegetables, fruits and meats to simple foods such as butter or toasted ingredients. For example, toasted quinoa flour has an incredible affinity with butter in baked shortbread.

Quinoa seeds and flour can also be used as a thickener. In soups, quinoa seeds added whole to the stock or cooked and then puréed with the stock produce a thick soup that could be mistaken for a heavy cream soup in texture, and without the added fat and calories. Quinoa seeds can also improve the texture of otherwise ordinary dishes, adding dimension and character. See page 3 for basic recipes for using quinoa as a thickener. Good examples of recipes that use it as a thickener include Chipotle Corn Chowder (page 90) and Simple Chicken Pot Pie Stew (page 109).

Quinoa flakes are widely available and can be used as a breakfast cereal, a coating for meats and vegetables, and in baking or as a dessert ingredient. Basic instructions for cooking quinoa flakes are on page 4. Examples of flake recipes are Thai Chicken Fingers (page 78) and Lemon Ginger Blueberry Crisp (page 200).

BABY QUINOA

Less common than regular quinoa but growing in popularity is baby quinoa. Also known as kaniwa or kañawa, baby quinoa is an even smaller seed closely related to quinoa. In South America it grows around Lake Titicaca, in both Peru and Bolivia. Baby quinoa contains no saponin, a break for those who are sensitive to any bitter saponin flavor and dedicated to rinsing their quinoa. This tiny red seed tastes milder and sweeter than regular quinoa, but contains even more protein and fiber. It is great sprouted or cooked together with regular white quinoa. Baby quinoa and regular quinoa cook just the same, 2 cups (500 mL) of water to 1 cup (250 mL) of seeds.

Rinsing Quinoa

Some people prefer to rinse quinoa seeds before cooking. This may help eliminate any bitter flavor that might remain on the quinoa. A slightly bitter taste may occasionally persist, however. The bitterness is caused by saponin, the protective coating of the quinoa seed that works as a natural insecticide and pesticide. Most packaged quinoa has been repeatedly rinsed during processing and does not require further rinsing. However, if you purchase quinoa in bulk, or direct from growers, it may require some rinsing. If you prefer to rinse your quinoa before cooking, see page 6 for complete instructions.

Cooking Quinoa

People new to cooking quinoa often ask us what recipe they should begin with. First recipes usually include simple salad dishes and breakfasts such as Spiced Carrot & Raisin Cereal (page 23) and Greek Quinoa Salad (page 58). But there are really no overly complicated quinoa dishes! The recipes in this book will show you how easy it is to cook with quinoa. We encourage cooks of all levels to be inspired and find even more ways to incorporate quinoa into their daily meals.

Quinoa may more than triple its original volume when cooked. Cooking proportions are the same as those for rice, 2 cups (500 mL) of water for every 1 cup (250 mL) of quinoa seeds. It can be cooked in a variety of liquids, from water to soup stock, fruit juices, various types of milk and more. Our simple method for cooking quinoa in water can be found on page 5. Methods for cooking quinoa in other liquids can be found on pages 7 to 9. Cooked quinoa can be conveniently stored in the refrigerator for up to five days and used in many different and easy meals during the week.

Quinoa can be cooked on the stovetop, in a rice cooker or in a slow cooker. Since quinoa can more than triple in volume when cooked, be sure you use exactly the amount of liquid specified in the recipe you are using. Do not guess! Many people write us to tell us their quinoa didn't cook completely, and it's usually because they didn't add enough liquid. Ratios of uncooked quinoa to water and cooked yields can be found on page 5.

When cooking quinoa with oils, it's best not to use unrefined oils that have a low smoke point (the temperature at which they begin to break down). Oils such as extra virgin olive oil, flaxseed, hemp and walnut are better used in marinades or salads, because the heat of cooking degrades their nutrients and eliminates their essential fatty acids, such as omega-3s, that are so beneficial in the first place.

SUSTAINABILITY & FAIR TRADE

Although grown in various locations around the world, quinoa is primarily produced where it originated, in South America, mainly in Bolivia, Peru and Ecuador. The increasing global demand for quinoa means that these countries are once again producing quinoa much like their ancestors did more than five thousand years ago—and because of it, are able to improve their standard of living.

More and more consumers today want to understand where their food comes from and how it is grown, and they want reassurance that foods are grown in healthy and sustainable environments in which the growers are treated well and trading is fair. Quinoa is no exception. Not only is quinoa healthful and enriching

A NOTE ON NUTRITIONAL VALUES

Nutritional values in this book are always based on the first option provided in the recipe. For instance, if the ingredient option is "vegetable or chicken stock," the nutritional values provided are based on vegetable stock. Also, optional ingredients are not included in the nutritional values. For lower-cholesterol diets, we have provided reduced-cholesterol options for eggs in the recipes along with the normal egg count. For example, a recipe may call for "2 large eggs + 4 large egg whites (or 4 eggs total)," meaning that if you are not on a low-cholesterol diet, you may simply use 4 whole eggs.

for those who eat it, but it is also beginning to have a positive impact on the people who grow it, their communities and the overall environment where it grows.

Quinoa-farming communities throughout South America are continuing to improve their practices for sustainability as they now have increased access to technology and training. In 2011, of all the quinoa grown in Bolivia, Peru and Ecuador, 42 percent was exported to other countries such as the United States and Canada, and 58 percent was consumed locally. This means that many South American farm communities are consuming even more quinoa than they were before, as what was once viewed as a peasant food is now being valued because of its desirability and demand in the North American marketplace, and the world.

In this cookbook you will find simple recipe ideas for quick meal preparation such as breakfasts and salads, along with family meals and ideas for more formal settings. With each recipe we have provided nutritional breakdowns that will help you meet the requirements of your medical, health or fitness goals. Whatever your family's tastes or your personal health demands, we are confident you'll find something to enjoy.

NEED GLUTEN-FREE?

All the recipes in this book can be made gluten-free. If you require your recipes to be gluten-free, always make sure that all the ingredients you use are consistently gluten-free. Each region will have different products available that meet gluten-free standards, including products such as Worcestershire sauce, tamari, oats, buns, sour cream and more.

You Asked Us!

We receive many questions about quinoa, from cooking tips to nutrition. Here are some of the most commonly asked questions and their answers.

Where can I buy quinoa?

You should be able to find quinoa in most major supermarkets across North America. It is usually found near the rice or couscous. Different colors (red, white, black) and types (flakes, flour, seeds) are occasionally kept in the specialty section of the grocery store. If you can't find it, be sure to ask because it may be hiding. Quinoa can also be found in most natural food stores and bulk food stores. It is generally easier to find than you might think.

I have just started using quinoa. What type of recipe should I start with?

The best choice for starting out cooking with quinoa is to use quinoa seeds (rather than flakes or flour). Quinoa seeds are generally the least expensive and will introduce you to the flavor of quinoa. The seeds have the longest shelf life and have the best nutrition, as they have not been processed. The type of recipe to start with is truly up to you, but you will find that soups and stews are easy, along with basic breakfasts and salads. Most people start by using cooked quinoa in recipes where they have traditionally used rice. Quinoa puffs or quinoa sprouts are good options as introductions to quinoa, as their flavor is very mild. Many people find that quinoa flour has a stronger flavor, so we suggest trying it after you have tried a few of the other forms first.

Should you always eat quinoa cooked? Are there any advantages to eating it uncooked?

If you are consuming uncooked quinoa seeds, you can certainly benefit from all of the nutrients, provided that the seeds are cracked or partially ground. This is because the uncooked seed has a shell, or pericarp, that protects it. (During cooking, this shell will soften and break open.) If this shell is still intact when you swallow it, the quinoa seed will simply pass through your body without being digested and without providing you with any of its fabulous nutritional benefits. (The same applies to flaxseeds.) Therefore, we recommend slightly grinding or soaking the seeds before you consume them uncooked.

When you add quinoa to a recipe, should you cook it first?

Not necessarily. If the recipe has sufficient liquid and cooking time, such as chili, then you would add raw (uncooked) quinoa. If the dish requires the quinoa to be cooked separately first, the recipes in this book will tell you so in the instructions.

I already have cooked quinoa in the refrigerator and want to use it in my recipe. How do I know how much cooked quinoa to use in place of the uncooked amount the recipe calls for?

Refer to the cooked yields chart (table 2 on page 5). For instance, if the recipe calls for ⅔ cup (150 mL) uncooked quinoa, that would produce approximately 2 cups (500 mL) of cooked quinoa. Keep in mind, however, that many recipes in this book require the quinoa to be uncooked at first, as it will cook along with the rest of the dish. Timing can also be an important factor in many recipes. For instance, in preparing a soup, you would add *uncooked* quinoa much earlier in the method than you would add *cooked* quinoa. Also, sometimes cooking times of quinoa vary and can be critical in recipe preparation. Some recipes require the quinoa to be cooked extremely fluffy, almost overcooked. Plump or very fluffy quinoa is essential, for example, in purées, soups, baking, puddings, baby foods and sauces. If the quinoa is not cooked enough, you will end up with a purée full of tiny, crunchy seeds rather than a smooth, flawless end result.

Quinoa seeds can sometimes taste bitter. How can I fix this?

If you are noticing bitterness, thoroughly rinse your quinoa before you cook it. For complete instructions, see page 6. Also, if you are extremely sensitive to bitterness caused by the saponin of regular quinoa, you may want to try baby quinoa instead. It is saponin-free. Learn more on page xxiii.

Do I have to rinse quinoa seeds?

No, quinoa seeds do not require rinsing. Any saponin that remains on the seeds has no negative effects on the body. In fact, we do not rinse our quinoa at all. To rinse or not to rinse depends on how sensitive you are to the bitterness. Usually, most traces of bitterness are already rinsed off after the seeds are cultivated and processed or washed. Most of the quinoa that is processed and in the market today requires minimal rinsing, if any (it's already been rinsed so much). If you prefer to rinse, instructions are on page 6. If you are extremely sensitive to bitterness caused by the saponin of regular quinoa, you may want to try "baby quinoa" instead. Learn more on page xxiii.

I like the flavor of cooked quinoa but my kids do not like it. How can I get them to eat it?

Some people don't like the slight bitter flavor in some quinoa, so try rinsing your quinoa thoroughly before cooking with it. For complete instructions, see page 6. Soups, stews , puddings and especially recipes where quinoa is puréed are good ways to introduce quinoa to children. Try the Individual Mighty Meat Loaves on page 143 and Creamy Banana Breakfast Cereal on page 25.

I tried your recipe for sprouting quinoa but nothing happened. Why not?

Occasionally, quinoa seeds just won't sprout. This may be because they have not been soaked long enough, possibly they are old or because of the way they have been handled. We suggest you try again, ensuring all steps are followed closely, or buy a different brand or purchase seeds from a different store.

I cooked the quinoa according to your instructions, but there was still some water left in the bottom of the pot and the quinoa looked partially cooked. What did I do wrong?

Occasionally, quinoa can sometimes cook that way. If the water is still warm, just cover the saucepan and let it sit for another 5 to 10 minutes. If the saucepan has cooled, return it to the burner and bring it to a boil. Then turn the heat off, cover and leave it for another 5 minutes. Check to see if the water has absorbed. If water still remains, replace the cover again and the quinoa should absorb the remaining water.

What is the quickest way to cool cooked quinoa for something like a salad?

Place the saucepan or bowl of hot or warm quinoa in the sink or in a larger bowl with water and ice. It will cool within about 15 minutes. Another option is to spread the cooked quinoa on a baking sheet. This is useful when you are cooking large amounts of quinoa. You can also place the saucepan in the freezer briefly.

I made one of your salad recipes and it tasted great, but I noticed after an hour it tasted as though there was hardly any dressing. What happened?

Most likely the quinoa that you used was still warm. Freshly cooked quinoa, even when only slightly warm, will continue to absorb liquid, including salad dressing. To prevent this, ensure that your cooked quinoa cools before you add sauces or dressings.

The salad I made was great the first day but lost some flavor by the second day. How can I fix it?

If you cooled the quinoa completely before making the salad, it is probably just a matter of making some more dressing. Keep in mind that our recipes are designed to have the most flavor without unnecessary additional calories.

I overcooked my quinoa. What can I do with it?

Don't toss it out! Overcooked or extra-fluffy quinoa is perfect for many recipes. It works great in this book's blender recipes, added to smoothies or cake batters, in scrambled eggs or added to meat loaves, burgers, breakfast cereals or salads during the week. It is fantastic blended into a thick and creamy texture, where it is useful in baby foods, as a soup thickener or as a custard or pudding dessert. Some recipes that can use overcooked quinoa are the Baked Roasted Red Pepper Dip on page 71, Blackberry Brûlée on page 193, and Chocolate Hazelnut Cream on page 196. Examples of recipes that require extra-fluffy cooked quinoa are Chocolate Cream Mini Cupcakes with Avocado Icing on page 179 and Healthy Baked Quinoa Falafels on page 138.

Can I freeze leftover cooked quinoa or cook it and then freeze it for future meals?

Yes, you can. We suggest measuring the cooked quinoa into resealable freezer bags in amounts you would normally use. For best freshness and flavor, we recommend quinoa be frozen for no more than one month.

I don't have the pan size called for in the recipe. Can I use another pan size?

Unless alternative pan sizes are given in the recipe, we don't recommend changing pan sizes. Different pan sizes may dramatically affect the results of your baking. This is especially true in recipes that contain little or no gluten. If you must use a different-sized pan, carefully monitor your baking and adjust cooking times as needed to ensure it cooks properly, as using a different pan size affects rising, and may result in underbaking or overbaking a recipe.

Does quinoa flour have the same nutritional benefits as quinoa seeds?

Yes, quinoa flour has the same nutritional breakdown as regular white quinoa. Nutrition labels on packaged quinoa do not include much of the vitamin and mineral values, so refer to the complete nutritional breakdown on page xx. Keep in mind that over time, flours of all kinds lose nutritional value because they are not whole. Quinoa *seeds*, being whole, retain their nutrients and have a much longer shelf life.

You often use cooked quinoa seeds instead of flour in baking. Can I replace regular flour with cooked quinoa seeds in other recipes?

We do not have a simple formula for using cooked quinoa in baking. It is difficult to find a consistent formula for replacing flour with cooked quinoa because baking chemistry is so recipe-specific. If you are determined to figure it out, the best way is through trial and error for each recipe—as tiresome as that may be.

Quinoa flour can be expensive. Are there any alternatives?

You can certainly grind your own flour to reduce the cost of buying it. We recommend that you test this first in whatever appliance you are using to grind, as different appliances will provide coarse or fine flours. Consider the desired texture when using home-ground flour in recipes, as it may especially affect baking results. Also, some grinding methods can be problematic—for instance, we do not recommend using a standard wheat-flour grinder, because the natural oil in quinoa seeds may permanently damage the grinder. Instructions for how to best grind your own flour can be found on page 3.

If you are looking for quinoa flour at a better price, try to find stores that sell it in bulk and possibly offer it cheaper. If you are not on a gluten-restricted diet, you may also bake with half quinoa flour and half whole wheat or all-purpose flour.

I have purchased both white and red quinoa. Do I cook them both in the same manner and can they be used interchangeably?

You can certainly cook both the white (golden) quinoa and the red quinoa using the same method. Some people prefer to cook red quinoa slightly longer, with a bit more water, to soften the seeds even further. Depending on the recipe, and how the quinoa is to be used, you may choose to cook one color rather than the other. The only difference after cooking is that red quinoa has a slightly different texture, similar to that of wild rice. Deciding whether to use red or white often depends on your personal preference. For example, if you wish to accent a particular dish with color, you may opt for red or black quinoa. If you plan to serve the dish to fussy eaters such as children, you may choose white quinoa.

When I cooked colored quinoa, there was some water left in the bottom of the pot. What should I do?

Sometimes when you cook black or red quinoa, you may find that not all the water in the saucepan has absorbed at the end of the recommended cooking time. If the quinoa has cooked to the desired level, you can drain the water off. If you want to cook the quinoa a little more, while it is still warm simply leave the lid on for 5 more minutes. The quinoa will continue to absorb the remaining water and expand.

What types of recipes work best with black quinoa?

Black quinoa is much the same as white and red quinoa when it comes to taste and flavor. The texture of black quinoa is slightly different from that of white quinoa—it is similar to the texture of wild rice. Choosing a recipe to use with black quinoa is mostly a personal preference. Some people use black quinoa when they want dishes to look different or to add some drama to a dish. It's really up to you when you use black quinoa instead of the other color varieties. Experiment and have fun!

Is it possible, or practical, to cook quinoa in a microwave oven?

Of all the ways to cook quinoa, we don't recommend cooking it in a microwave oven. We've tested cooking it this way, and it just doesn't turn out well or consistently enough. However, feel free to experiment with cooking quinoa in your microwave oven; you may find that with a certain cooking time, power level and amount of water, it works in your microwave.

Reheating quinoa in a microwave is a personal preference. You may even discover that reheating quinoa leftovers is completely unnecessary. Many cooked quinoa dishes do not require reheating and are delicious for lunches. Quinoa salads are a great option to carry with you and eat during your day.

Keep in mind that microwave ovens are suspected of contributing to ill health, as they significantly deplete or modify nutrients in food and are said to create cancer-causing free radicals.

Can you cook quinoa in a rice cooker?

Absolutely! Simply follow the manufacturer's instructions for cooking white rice. However, since quinoa triples or more in volume as it cooks (whereas rice only doubles), make sure there's enough room in your cooker.

Is quinoa good for those with gluten-intolerance?

Yes! Quinoa does not contain gluten. Combined with other gluten-free ingredients, you can make some fantastic gluten-free meals. Every recipe in this book can be made gluten-free. Readers are constantly telling us how these recipes have improved their quality of life and allow them to enjoy their food more than ever before. In some cases those affected by gluten-intolerance have previously felt restricted to less flavorful foods, and have not been able to eat delicious foods for a long time. We have had many people tell us that eating quinoa has put pleasure back into their daily gluten-free menus. If you want extra tips and information, see pages xiii–xviii, where quinoa scientist Laurie Scanlin outlines some of the key benefits of quinoa and reasons to avoid gluten.

I am gluten-intolerant, so if one of your recipes calls for regular all-purpose or whole wheat flour, can I use a gluten-free substitute?

Yes. Many of our recipes work with a variety of gluten-free flours and blends. One type or several types are often used together to achieve a desired result, such as ability to rise, bond and stick together, particular texture and so on. However, this is not stated in each recipe because whether you use all-purpose gluten-free or brown rice flour—or any of the others—may change the flavor and overall outcome of the dish. So experiment with your preferred replacement flour and see how you like the flavor and final result.

I am a vegetarian. Can I benefit from eating quinoa?

Vegetarians can definitely benefit from eating quinoa. Quinoa is a terrific non-animal protein source and provides all eight essential amino acids. Highly digestible and extremely versatile, quinoa allows vegetarians to increase their meal options with healthful nutrients.

Can I eat quinoa if I am on diet?

Yes! Quinoa is a complex carbohydrate, so it provides energy throughout the day, digesting slowly and not causing insulin levels to spike, which is believed to cause fat storage in the body. In the popular points-based weight-loss programs, a serving of 1 cup (250 mL) of cooked quinoa is equal to 3 points. If you want extra tips and information, see pages xiii–xviii, where quinoa scientist Laurie Scanlin outlines some of the key reasons quinoa makes an ideal food for dieting, health and fitness.

Is quinoa good for diabetics?

Quinoa is a great food for diabetics. It has a low glycemic index and is a complex carbohydrate, so sugars digest slowly, maintaining proper blood sugar levels. The complete nutrition of quinoa will also provide many of your daily vitamins and minerals. Ensure you ask your doctor any questions you have about maintaining proper blood sugar levels. If you want extra tips and information, see pages xiii–xviii, where quinoa scientist Laurie Scanlin outlines some of the key reasons quinoa makes an ideal food for dieting, health and fitness.

I'm on a raw-food diet. How can I still benefit from eating quinoa?

You can still enjoy quinoa if you eat raw foods. One option is sprouted quinoa and another is raw, cracked quinoa or quinoa soaked for a short period of time. Sprouted and raw quinoa each contain similar nutrition to cooked quinoa seeds. Quinoa sprouts can be used in shakes and smoothies, salads and sandwiches. (See the quinoa sprout recipe on pages 10 and 11 and recipes that use sprouts such as Carrot & Raisin Sprout Salad on page 52 and Apple Cabbage Sprout Salad on page 46.) (For raw-food recipes, do not toast nuts.) Other alternatives include cracking the raw seeds (see the basic method for cracked quinoa on page 11), grinding them or cooking the seeds for only a few quick minutes. Simply cook the quinoa just long enough to split the outer pericarp (shell), quickly halt the cooking process and cool the quinoa. Then it is ready to add to your meals and recipes.

How does quinoa compare with products that are "enriched" with the same minerals and vitamins?

When products are "enriched," it means that minerals or vitamins are added during the product's processing and either are not natural to the product or were depleted during processing. Quinoa is a complete protein (it contains all eight essential amino acids) and is naturally chock-full of vitamins and minerals—meaning nothing needs to be added! It is simply one of nature's perfectly created nutrient-rich foods.

Can quinoa be grown in North America?

Quinoa prefers a growing climate that is dry, and it grows best where it originated, in South America. Some farmers do grow it in North America, and some do so quite successfully, but not without tackling challenges caused by the differences in climate. There are several commercial growers in Canada and the United States; however, the majority of quinoa comes from South America, where it has been cultivated since the 1500s. Today it is best grown in fair-trade, sustainable programs.

EASY QUINOA
BASICS

EASY QUINOA BASICS

WHETHER you're just starting to cook with quinoa or are experienced with quinoa in the kitchen, this chapter will provide you with a quick reference to all of the quinoa basics—everything from how to use the flour, how to use flakes, different cooking methods, grinding your own flour, sprouting quinoa, to how to cook quinoa in various liquids (which can sometimes be tricky). With plenty of simple solutions, best practices and tips, we've got everything to get you started cooking quinoa and on your way to becoming a polished pro. Soon your friends and family will be asking you for quinoa advice.

THICKENING LIQUIDS WITH QUINOA FLOUR

Quinoa flour is a great option for thickening liquids. It adds a hint of nutty flavor to your dish and holds up well to cooking and freezing. It may separate ever so slightly after sitting in the refrigerator for a few days, but this is solved with a quick stir.

Soup or stew

- Whisk in 2 Tbsp (30 mL) flour for every 1 cup (250 mL) liquid.

Gravy, cheese sauce or pudding

- Whisk in 3 Tbsp (45 mL) flour for every 1 cup (250 mL) liquid.

Cold liquid: To thicken a cold liquid, whisk in the flour until evenly dispersed. Bring the liquid to a boil. Reduce to medium heat and simmer for approximately 3 minutes, stirring constantly until thickened.

Hot liquid: To thicken a hot liquid (which may or may not also contain solids such as meat and vegetables), in a small bowl, whisk the flour into an equal amount of cold liquid (such as water, stock or wine). Stir the mixture into the hot liquid and simmer for approximately 3 minutes, stirring constantly until thickened.

MAKING QUINOA FLOUR

You can easily make your own quinoa flour using a household coffee grinder. If you don't mind a coarser, more rustic grind of flour, this is the best method we've found so far. Use a coffee grinder or mill to grind ¼ cup (60 mL) of quinoa seeds at a time. This type of grinding will result in a consistency slightly smaller than cornmeal. This size of grind is best used in a soup or stew, as a thickener or in any recipe where the ground seeds are able to absorb liquid. Be cautious when using it in baking, as it may make recipes such as cookies or pastry a bit crunchy. We do not suggest using a traditional flour mill to grind quinoa, as the natural oils in the quinoa may permanently damage your expensive grinder.

QUINOA FLAKES

Quinoa flakes are very quick to hydrate and are generally used for breakfast cereals, for baking and as a batter or coating for poultry, fish and other meats. Flakes can also be used as a thickener in a soup or stew or ground into a flour. Flakes may have a bit more nutty flavor to them than seeds, but the taste can complement other flavors quite nicely. If you are adding dried fruit to your recipe, add a couple more tablespoons of boiling water so there is enough liquid available to be absorbed by both the fruit and the quinoa.

BASIC QUINOA FLAKES

½ cup (125 mL) water

¼ cup (60 mL) quinoa flakes

Bring the water to a boil in a small saucepan (or appropriate-sized saucepan if you're making a larger amount). Stir in the flakes and reduce to medium heat. Continue to stir for 2 to 3 minutes, until the flakes have thickened and are tender.

PER SERVING: Energy 110 calories; Protein 4 g; Carbohydrates 21 g; Dietary Fiber 2 g; Fat 2 g; Sugar 0 g; Cholesterol 0 mg; Sodium 260 mg

QUICK & EASY QUINOA FLAKES

No saucepan required! This method is great if you want a quick way to prepare flakes at home, at work or any time you want a portable meal. Perfect for when you go camping!

⅓ cup (75 mL) quinoa flakes

½ cup (125 mL) boiling water

Place the quinoa flakes in a bowl. Pour the boiling water over the flakes. Stir quickly and cover with a plate or piece of foil. Let sit for 8 minutes without removing the cover. Fully cooked quinoa flakes should be tender.

PER SERVING: Energy 140 calories; Protein 5 g; Carbohydrates 28 g; Dietary Fiber 2 g; Fat 2 g; Sugar 0 g; Cholesterol 0 mg; Sodium 340 mg

COOKING QUINOA (SEEDS)

Simmer method

Generally, quinoa cooks in water at a ratio of 2:1, that is, 2 cups (500 mL) of water for every 1 cup (250 mL) of quinoa. Combine the water and quinoa in an appropriate-sized saucepan (for amounts, see table 2 below). Bring to a boil. Reduce heat to a simmer, cover and cook for 15 minutes. Check to see if the quinoa is tender. The quinoa is cooked when the center of the seed is no longer white and is translucent. If the quinoa still has a distinctly white center or if water remains in the bottom of the saucepan (when cooking any color), cover the saucepan and allow the quinoa to sit, off the heat, for 5 more minutes or until all the remaining liquid has been absorbed. Remove the lid and fluff with a fork.

TABLE 2: Amounts to Use for Cooking

SERVING	COOKED YIELD (APPROXIMATELY)	AMOUNT OF UNCOOKED QUINOA & WATER	
		QUINOA	WATER
1	½ cup (125 mL)	2 Tbsp + 2 tsp (40 mL)	⅓ cup (75 mL)
2	1 cup (250 mL)	⅓ cup (75 mL)	⅔ cup (150 mL)
3	1½ cups (375 mL)	½ cup (125 mL)	1 cup (250 mL)
4	2 cups (500 mL)	⅔ cup (150 mL)	1⅓ cups (325 mL)
6	3 cups (750 mL)	1 cup (250 mL)	2 cups (500 mL)

TOASTING QUINOA SEEDS OR FLOUR

Toasting quinoa releases and deepens its flavor, giving it a mild, fragrant aroma that adds another dimension to any dish. (If you are sensitive to any bitter flavor quinoa sometimes has, toasting the seeds first can help to mellow any bitterness.) This technique can be used in almost any recipe in which you might want a toasted flavor. There are two basic methods for toasting quinoa.

Oven method

Preheat the oven to 350°F (180°C). Place the seeds or flour on a baking sheet and bake for 5 to 7 minutes, until fragrant and you smell a "toasted" aroma. Watch closely as it can burn quickly. Toasted flour will be light golden brown, but seeds will not change color much, even when completely toasted.

Stovetop method

Place the quinoa seeds or flour in a large saucepan on medium heat. Stir for 3 to 5 minutes, until fragrant and you smell a "toasted" aroma. Watch closely as both seeds and flour will not change color much and can burn quickly.

RINSING QUINOA

Although generally unnecessary, some people prefer to rinse quinoa before using it. This will remove any remaining bitter flavor that is sometimes present. This bitter taste comes from saponin, a natural protective coating on the seed. Most of this bitterness is removed during commercial processing, when the seeds are thoroughly washed. Still, if you prefer to rinse, these are some of the best methods.

Strainer method

Rinse the quinoa in a fine-mesh strainer under running water or immerse the quinoa in water while in the strainer and use your hand to swish the quinoa around, then rinse. Continue immersing and rinsing until you've satisfied yourself that the bitter flavor is gone.

Soak-and-rinse method

Rinse the quinoa in a fine-mesh strainer under running water. Place the quinoa in a glass bowl or jar, cover with water and put in the refrigerator for at least 1 hour or overnight. (Be sure to use glass. Plastic can harbor micro-organisms that affect sprouting; metal can affect chemistry.) Remove from the refrigerator and rub the quinoa seeds together in the water. Rinse under running water in the mesh strainer once more. (Note: If your seeds are left overnight to soak, there is a chance that they may sprout slightly. However, small sprouts should not affect your cooking too much. In fact, your living quinoa sprouts are even more nutritious than you may have expected!)

Stocking method

Place the quinoa in a new piece of pantyhose or a knee-high stocking and tie the open end securely. Immerse in a bowl of water and soak for 5 to 20 minutes—the shorter time if you're not as concerned about the bitter flavor, and the longer time if you are sensitive to the bitter flavor. Rub the quinoa seeds together in the stocking. Rinse the stocking under cold running water. Repeat until you've satisfied yourself that the bitter flavor is gone.

COOKING QUINOA IN LIQUIDS

This section accommodates those who have dietary restrictions or are creating or adapting their own quinoa recipes. These basic recipes can easily be doubled, tripled or more. When using colored quinoa in these recipes, note that it may require a few extra minutes of cooking time to absorb all the liquid after being removed from the heat.

STOCK (VEGETABLE, CHICKEN OR BEEF)

MAKES 1½ CUPS (375 ML) OR 2 SERVINGS

1 cup (250 mL) vegetable, chicken or beef stock

½ cup (125 mL) quinoa

Combine the stock and quinoa in a medium saucepan. Bring to a boil, then reduce to a simmer. Cover and cook for 17 minutes. Remove from the heat. Check to see if the quinoa is cooked (the center of the seed should be translucent and all the water should have been absorbed). If it needs a few more minutes, just replace the lid and let it rest for another 5 minutes, until all remaining liquid is absorbed. Fluff with a fork and serve.

PER SERVING (sodium-reduced vegetable stock): Energy 160 calories; Protein 6 g; Carbohydrates 29 g; Dietary Fiber 3 g; Fat 2 g; Sugar 1 g; Cholesterol 0 mg; Sodium 70 mg

TOMATO JUICE

MAKES 1¾ CUPS (400 ML) OR 2 SERVINGS

1 cup (250 mL) tomato juice

½ cup (125 mL) water

½ cup (125 mL) quinoa

Combine the tomato juice, water and quinoa in a medium sauce-pan. Bring to a boil, then reduce to a simmer. Cover and cook for 15 minutes. Stir quinoa, cover again and cook for another 15 minutes. Remove from the heat and check to see if the quinoa is cooked (the center of the seed should be translucent and all the water should have been absorbed). If not, replace the lid and let sit for another 5 minutes. Fluff with a fork and serve.

PER SERVING (sodium-reduced tomato juice): Energy 180 calories; Protein 7 g; Carbohydrates 32 g; Dietary Fiber 3 g; Fat 2 g; Sugar 4 g; Cholesterol 0 mg; Sodium 15 mg

APPLE, ORANGE OR PINEAPPLE JUICE

MAKES 1½ CUPS (375 ML) OR 2 SERVINGS

1 cup (250 mL) apple, orange or pineapple juice

⅓ cup (75 mL) water

½ cup (125 mL) quinoa

Combine the juice, water and quinoa in a medium saucepan. Bring to a boil, then reduce to a simmer. Cover and cook for 25 minutes. Remove from the heat and let sit, covered, for another 5 minutes. Fluff with a fork and serve.

PER SERVING (unsweetened apple juice): Energy 210 calories; Protein 6 g; Carbohydrates 41 g; Dietary Fiber 3 g; Fat 2 g; Sugar 12 g; Cholesterol 0 mg; Sodium 10 mg

ALMOND MILK (SWEETENED OR UNSWEETENED)

MAKES 1½ CUPS (375 ML) OR 2 SERVINGS

1 cup (250 mL) almond milk

½ cup (125 mL) water

½ cup (125 mL) quinoa

Combine the milk, water and quinoa in a medium saucepan. Bring to a boil, then reduce to a simmer. Cover and cook for 20 minutes, stirring occasionally. Remove from the heat and let sit, covered, for another 5 minutes. Fluff with a fork and serve.

PER SERVING (unsweetened): Energy 180 calories; Protein 7 g; Carbohydrates 28 g; Dietary Fiber 3 g; Fat 4 g; Sugar 0 g; Cholesterol 0 mg; Sodium 95 mg

SOY MILK (SWEETENED OR UNSWEETENED)

MAKES 1½ CUPS (375 ML) OR 2 SERVINGS

1 cup (250 mL) soy milk

½ cup (125 mL) quinoa

Combine the milk and quinoa in a medium saucepan. Bring to a boil, then reduce to a simmer. Cover and cook for 25 minutes, stirring occasionally. Remove from the heat and let sit, covered, for 5 minutes. Fluff with a fork and serve.

PER SERVING (unsweetened): Energy 200 calories; Protein 10 g; Carbohydrates 29 g; Dietary Fiber 3 g; Fat 4 g; Sugar 0 g; Cholesterol 0 mg; Sodium 45 mg

LIGHT COCONUT MILK

MAKES 1½ CUPS (375 ML) OR 2 SERVINGS

1 cup (250 mL) light coconut milk

½ cup (125 mL) quinoa

Combine the milk and quinoa in a medium saucepan. Bring to a boil, then reduce to a simmer. Cover and cook for 15 minutes. Remove from the heat and let sit, covered, for another 5 minutes. Fluff with a fork and serve.

PER SERVING: Energy 240 calories; Protein 6 g; Carbohydrates 29 g; Dietary Fiber 3 g; Fat 11 g; Sugar 0 g; Cholesterol 0 mg; Sodium 20 mg

TABLE 3: Cooking Quinoa in Various Liquids—Yields

	WATER	STOCK	TOMATO JUICE	FRUIT JUICE	ALMOND MILK	SOY MILK	COCONUT MILK
COOKING TIME (MINUTES)	15	22	35	30	25	30	20
½ CUP (125 ML) UNCOOKED	makes 1½ cups (375 mL)	makes 1½ cups (375 mL)	makes 1¾ cups (400 mL)	makes 1½ cups (375 mL)	makes 1½ cups (375 mL)	makes 1½ cups (375 mL)	makes 1½ cups (375 mL)

QUINOA IN A RAW-FOOD DIET

People who eat raw foods have several options for incorporating quinoa into their diets. Sprouting is extremely popular with raw-food eaters, and it certainly provides a good dose of nutrition. There are extraordinary benefits to eating the enzyme-rich, super nutrition of sprouted quinoa. Eating quinoa uncooked or raw increases the ways you can add it to your daily meals, and in the raw form it is extremely portable because it does not require refrigeration. Sprouted and raw quinoa both contain the same great foundation of nutrition found in cooked quinoa seeds.

Sprouting Quinoa

Quinoa sprouts are a great way to grow your own local produce at any time of the year. It is becoming increasingly popular to eat raw, sprouted foods that are full of enzymes and rich in vitamins and minerals. Quinoa sprouts can be eaten as a nutritious snack all on their own, used in cold recipes such as salads or used as a sandwich topping. Recipes that feature sprouted quinoa are Blueberry Sprout Smoothie on page 31, Green Veggie Super Shake on page 32, Apple Cabbage Sprout Salad on page 46, and Carrot & Raisin Sprout Salad on page 52.

For sprouts, use organic quinoa when possible, as it has been handled in a manner that reduces the risk of contamination. Cleanliness when sprouting is important in eliminating any chance of contamination, which may occur with any kind of sprout. Quinoa is one of the quickest-sprouting seeds, rapidly germinating in two to 4 hours. Quinoa sprouts are best when eaten small because they have more crunch and stay fresh longer. Sprouts that are grown for a longer time are larger, softer in texture and deteriorate more quickly.

Distilled water

½ cup (125 mL) quinoa

Wash your hands thoroughly. Place the quinoa in a clean glass or ceramic casserole dish with a lid (do not use plastic, which can harbor residual bacteria that may contaminate your sprouts). (You can also use a sterilized mason jar, with the opening covered with cheesecloth and an elastic band.) Pour in enough distilled water to cover the quinoa, stir with a clean spoon and soak for 40 minutes at room temperature.

Using a fine-mesh strainer, drain the seeds. While the seeds are in the strainer, rinse them with more distilled water. Rinse the casserole dish with distilled water. Return the wet quinoa to the casserole dish and cover with the lid, leaving a slight opening for air circulation. Place in the refrigerator or a cool, dark location. Repeat rinsing every 8 to 10 hours until the quinoa has sprouted to the desired length; it will be ready to eat anytime after about 8 hours.

Store the sprouts in a glass or ceramic (not plastic or metal) container in the refrigerator with the lid open slightly to allow for air circulation. Use sprouts within 3 days. Do not eat them if they have any odor or visible mold, which can result from lack of air, not enough rinsing or being sprouted in too warm an environment. The final quantity of sprouts will depend on the duration the sprouts are grown: the longer they're grown, the bigger they'll be.

Cracked or Raw Quinoa

Similar to flaxseeds, uncooked quinoa is protected by a pericarp. If this shell is still intact when you swallow it, the quinoa seed will simply pass through your body without being digested. However, raw quinoa seeds can still provide fantastic nutrition if cracked or partially ground before you ingest them.

Quinoa can be ground slightly in a blender, food processor or coffee grinder. It is then ready to be added to your recipes. Even easier, you can place raw quinoa seeds in a resealable plastic bag and gently crack them by rolling over them with a rolling pin. You can add ground or cracked quinoa seeds to breakfast cereals, shakes, salads, desserts and more.

REVOLUTIONIZE
BREAKFAST

REVOLUTIONIZE BREAKFAST

WE seem to have less time than ever these days, but now you can start loving your mornings again! This chapter is sure to bring you back to life with quinoa recipes so enticing and energizing you will start to look forward to breakfast. With solutions for busy schedules and restricted diets, we have uncomplicated recipes you can make often and grab when you're heading out the door. When you're getting your family ready for the day, breakfast needs to be quick and easy, yet nutritious and delicious enough to make breakfast worth eating! Extra-quick recipes include Grab & Go Breakfast Cereal (page 24) and Anytime Breakfast Bars (page 34).

Quinoa will give you that extra boost you need to get through a busy morning, whatever it is you do. It's hard enough to get the required amount of daily vegetables, so why not start in the morning? With quinoa you can load up on extra antioxidants, energy, fiber, nutrients and protein, even before noon. Try Green Veggie Super Shake (page 32) and Orange Ginger Quinoa Breakfast Cereal (page 29).

For those mornings where peace and relaxation are in the plans, and you're up for something extra tasty, several recipes are delicious enough for dessert, like Red Velvet Waffles (page 18) and Apple Pie Pancakes (page 16). For an extra-special breakfast, try Vanilla Crème Crêpes with Fresh Strawberries (page 20).

Whether you're feeding a family, entertaining or cooking for one, quinoa breakfasts offer something a bit different, with the complete nutritional elements to feed the body. Now that is worth getting out of bed for!

Apple Pie Pancakes 16

Carrot Cake Pancakes 17

Red Velvet Waffles 18

Vanilla Crème Crêpes
with Fresh Strawberries 20

Apricot Matcha Breakfast Porridge 21

Baked Vanilla Bean Quinoa 22

Spiced Carrot & Raisin Cereal 23

Coconut Omega-3 Cereal 23

Creamy Chocolate Breakfast Cereal 24

Grab & Go Breakfast Cereal 24

Creamy Banana Breakfast Cereal 25

Hot Pistachio Cereal with
Greek Yogurt & Honey 27

Hot Cinnamon Zucchini Breakfast 28

Orange Ginger Quinoa Breakfast Cereal 29

Strawberry Rhubarb Breakfast 30

Blueberry Sprout Smoothie 31

Sunshine Sprout Smoothie 31

Green Veggie Super Shake 32

Chocolate Hazelnut Bars 34

Cranberry Coconut Bars 34

Dark Chocolate Cherry Bars 35

Date and Walnut Bars 35

Maple Pecan Granola 36

Peanut Butter & Tomato Sprout Toast 37

Quinoa Mushroom Omelet 38

Smoked Gouda & Onion Omelet 39

Sunday Brunch Casserole 40

Traditional Breakfast Sausage Rounds 41

APPLE PIE PANCAKES

**MAKES 18 PANCAKES,
SERVING 6**

2 ⅔ cups (650 mL) quinoa flour

¼ cup (60 mL) organic
cane sugar or white sugar

2 Tbsp (30 mL) baking powder

½ tsp (2 mL) salt

1 tsp (5 mL) cinnamon

½ tsp (2 mL) nutmeg

2 ½ cups (625 mL) buttermilk

2 large eggs

2 Tbsp (30 mL) vegetable oil

1 tsp (5 mL) pure vanilla extract

1 ½ cups (375 mL) peeled
and diced apples

A nutritious breakfast that could easily double as dessert. Warm, spicy apples fill these velvety soft buttermilk pancakes, with every serving containing 25 percent of your daily value of iron and 40 percent of your calcium. Top these pancakes with caramel sauce and pecans for an extra-special treat.

Combine the flour, sugar, baking powder, salt, cinnamon and nutmeg in a large bowl. In a medium bowl, whisk together the buttermilk, eggs, oil and vanilla; stir in the apples. Add the buttermilk mixture to the flour mixture and combine well.

Lightly grease a large skillet or spray with cooking oil and place on medium-high heat. When the skillet is hot, spoon the batter into the pan to make 4-inch (10 cm) rounds. When a few bubbles form on the top, flip the pancakes and cook for 30 seconds more or until the center springs back when gently pressed. Serve hot with butter and maple syrup.

PER SERVING: Energy 390 calories; Protein 14 g; Carbohydrates 58 g; Dietary Fiber 8 g; Fat 12 g; Sugar 17 g; Cholesterol 70 mg; Sodium 320 mg

Want something different? Try birch syrup. It has a slightly spicy caramel flavor that is unique and delicious. It is a little more expensive than maple syrup, at an average of $22 per ½ cup (125 mL), but this is because producing it is a bit trickier. It is made in Canada, Alaska, Russia, Ukraine and Scandinavian countries. It is worth the treat!

CARROT CAKE PANCAKES

Breakfast that tastes like dessert! These golden pancakes are packed with carrots, raisins and pineapple along with the goodness of quinoa. Tasty topped with maple syrup, or step it up with freshly whipped cream.

Measure the flour, sugar, baking powder, salt, cinnamon and nutmeg into a large bowl. Mix well. In a medium bowl, whisk together the milk, eggs and applesauce. Stir in the carrots, pineapple, raisins and pecans. Add the milk mixture to the flour mixture and stir just until blended.

Grease a large skillet or spray with cooking oil and place on medium heat. When hot, pour scant ¼-cup (60 mL) portions of batter into the pan. The pancakes will be ready to flip when you first see bubbles and the underside is lightly golden brown. Watch them carefully, as they brown quickly. Flip and cook the pancakes for another 30 seconds, until the center springs back when pressed. If the pancakes buckle when you slide the spatula under them, lightly oil the pan again for the next batch. Serve with maple syrup.

PER SERVING: Energy 250 calories; Protein 9 g; Carbohydrates 38 g; Dietary Fiber 6 g; Fat 8 g; Sugar 12 g; Cholesterol 65 mg; Sodium 240 mg

SERVES 6

1½ cups (375 mL) quinoa flour

1 Tbsp (15 mL) organic cane sugar or white sugar

3½ tsp (17 mL) baking powder

½ tsp (2 mL) salt

1½ tsp (7 mL) cinnamon

½ tsp (2 mL) nutmeg

1 cup (250 mL) 1% or 2% milk, buttermilk or soy milk

2 large eggs, beaten

¼ cup (60 mL) applesauce

1 cup (250 mL) shredded carrots

⅓ cup (75 mL) crushed pineapple, drained well

⅓ cup (75 mL) seedless raisins

¼ cup (60 mL) chopped toasted pecans

To toast nuts, preheat the oven to 350°F (180°C). Spread the nuts on a baking sheet and toast in the oven, stirring once if necessary, for 5 to 7 minutes, until fragrant and lightly toasted.

RED VELVET WAFFLES

SERVES 5

WAFFLES

2 to 3 small red beets, unpeeled

2 cups (500 mL) water

2 cups (500 mL) quinoa flour

¼ cup (60 mL) unsweetened
    cocoa powder

3 Tbsp (45 mL) organic
    cane sugar or white sugar

4 tsp (20 mL) baking powder

¼ tsp (1 mL) salt

2 large eggs, beaten

1¼ cups (300 mL) 1% or 2% milk

¼ cup (60 mL) vegetable oil

1 tsp (5 mL) pure vanilla extract

LEMON CREAM CHEESE TOPPING

(OPTIONAL)

½ cup (125 mL) light cream cheese

½ cup (125 mL) low-fat plain yogurt

1 Tbsp (15 mL) pure maple syrup

½ tsp (2 mL) grated lemon zest

¼ tsp (1 mL) pure vanilla extract

Shhh. No one will guess these velvety waffles are sweetened with nutritious puréed red beets. Extra-delicious served with the optional Lemon Cream Cheese Topping.

For the waffles, in a medium saucepan, bring the beets and water to a boil. Lower heat to medium and simmer the beets until tender. Remove beets from the pot, reserving the red cooking water. Rinse beets under cool water and gently remove the skin with your fingers. (You may want to wear rubber gloves!) Chop beets into large chunks and place in a food processor. Process until smooth. Set aside to cool.

Combine the flour, cocoa, sugar, baking powder and salt in a large bowl. In a medium bowl, whisk together the eggs, milk, oil, vanilla, ¼ cup (60 mL) of the puréed beets and 1 cup (250 mL) of the reserved beet cooking water. Add the beet mixture to the flour mixture. Blend well and set aside.

For the lemon cream cheese topping, in a medium bowl, whip the cream cheese, yogurt, maple syrup, lemon zest and vanilla until smooth. Set aside.

Grease or lightly spray a waffle iron with cooking oil and preheat it. Pour the batter onto the waffle iron according to the manufacturer's instructions and close. Remove the waffles when the lid lifts open easily, after 5 to 6 minutes. Serve waffles with lemon cream cheese topping (if using) or butter and maple syrup.

Waffles will keep in the refrigerator for up to 2 days in a sealed container. Reheat in a toaster or toaster oven.

PER SERVING: Energy 390 calories; Protein 12 g; Carbohydrates 49 g; Dietary Fiber 8 g; Fat 17 g; Sugar 11 g; Cholesterol 75 mg; Sodium 200 mg

VANILLA CRÈME CRÊPES WITH FRESH STRAWBERRIES

MAKES 12 (6-INCH/15 CM) CRÊPES, SERVING 6

CRÊPES

⅓ cup (75 mL) quinoa flour

¼ cup (60 mL) brown rice flour or whole wheat flour

2 tsp (10 mL) cornstarch

2 large eggs

2 large egg whites

1 cup (250 mL) 1% or 2% milk

FILLING

3 cups (750 mL) low-fat plain thick Greek yogurt

⅓ cup (75 mL) pure maple syrup or honey

1½ tsp (7 mL) pure vanilla extract

3 cups (750 mL) sliced fresh strawberries

Easy to make and even easier to eat, this nutritious breakfast will satisfy breakfast eaters of any age. Vanilla crème, made with thick Greek yogurt, is wrapped in a lightly sweetened crêpe with fresh strawberries.

For the crêpes, stir together the quinoa flour, rice flour and cornstarch in a medium bowl. Add the eggs, egg whites and milk. Whisk until smooth.

Heat a lightly oiled 6-inch (15 cm) skillet on medium-high heat. Pour 2 Tbsp (30 mL) of batter into the center of the pan; quickly tilt the pan in a circular motion to spread the batter over the bottom. Flip the crêpe when the edges begin to curl, after about 30 to 45 seconds. Cook the other side for another 30 seconds, then remove from the pan. Place the hot crêpe on a plate and cover with foil. Repeat with the remaining batter.

For the filling, mix together the yogurt, maple syrup and vanilla.

Place a crêpe on a plate and spoon ¼ cup (60 mL) each of filling and strawberries in the center. Fold sides over. Serve garnished with additional strawberries, if desired.

PER SERVING: Energy 250 calories; Protein 16 g; Carbohydrates 36 g; Dietary Fiber 3 g; Fat 5 g; Sugar 22 g; Cholesterol 70 mg; Sodium 105 mg

APRICOT MATCHA BREAKFAST PORRIDGE

Matcha is a finely ground superior green tea from Japan. It is said to be rich in phytonutrients and antioxidants that can be easily absorbed because the powdered leaves are ingested rather than removed after steeping, as with traditional teas. If you are a matcha fan, you will enjoy this delicious combination with apricots and coconut milk.

Bring the water, quinoa, apricots and matcha to a boil in a medium saucepan. Reduce to a simmer, then cover and cook for 20 minutes. Pour in the coconut milk and continue to cook only until heated through. Remove from the heat and stir in the maple syrup and vanilla. Serve.

PER SERVING: Energy 260 calories; Protein 6 g; Carbohydrates 43 g; Dietary Fiber 4 g; Fat 7 g; Sugar 13 g; Cholesterol 0 mg; Sodium 15 mg

SERVES 2

1½ cups (375 mL) water

½ cup (125 mL) quinoa

3 Tbsp (45 mL) diced dried apricots

¾ tsp (4 mL) matcha green tea powder

½ cup (125 mL) light coconut milk

1 Tbsp (15 mL) pure maple syrup

¾ tsp (4 mL) pure vanilla extract

Leftover coconut milk? Measure easy-to-use portions in sealed freezer bags and store in the freezer for up to 3 months.

BAKED VANILLA
BEAN QUINOA

SERVES 4

1 cup (250 mL) water

½ cup (125 mL) quinoa

1 vanilla bean

½ cup (125 mL) whole milk

2 Tbsp (30 mL) unsalted
    butter, melted

¼ cup (60 mL) organic
    cane sugar or white sugar

1 large egg

½ tsp (2 mL) baking powder

½ tsp (2 mL) salt

Fluffy quinoa is baked with whole milk and the natural aromatic goodness of vanilla beans. A superb way to spice up a traditional hot baked breakfast cereal and an impressive brunch dish to serve guests.

Preheat the oven to 350°F (180°C).

Combine the water and quinoa in a medium saucepan. Split the vanilla bean lengthwise, and use the end of a butter knife or small spoon to scrape out the sandy black seeds. Add the seeds and the pod to the pot. Bring to a boil, then reduce to a simmer. Cover and simmer for 15 minutes. Remove from the heat and discard the vanilla pod. Fluff quinoa with a fork and set aside.

In a medium bowl, whisk together the milk, butter, sugar, egg, baking powder and salt. Add the cooked quinoa and stir well. Pour the mixture into an 8-inch (2 L) square baking dish. Bake for 25 to 30 minutes, until the center is firm to the touch. Serve warm, scooped into individual serving dishes. Serve with fresh fruit and cream if desired.

PER SERVING: Energy 210 calories; Protein 6 g; Carbohydrates 28 g; Dietary Fiber 1 g; Fat 9 g; Sugar 14 g; Cholesterol 65 mg; Sodium 380 mg

If you don't have a vanilla bean, use 2 tsp (10 mL) pure vanilla extract.

SPICED CARROT & RAISIN CEREAL

Nothing satisfies like a hot home-cooked breakfast. This will become one of your favorite breakfast recipes with its ever-popular combination of carrots, raisins and cinnamon.

Combine the water, apple juice and quinoa in a medium saucepan. Bring to a boil, reduce to a simmer, cover and cook for 15 minutes. Stir in the carrots, raisins and cinnamon. Continue to simmer, covered, for another 7 minutes. Remove from the heat and stir in the vanilla and the walnuts and maple syrup (if using). Serve hot.

PER SERVING: Energy 210 calories; Protein 7 g; Carbohydrates 41 g; Dietary Fiber 4 g; Fat 2.5 g; Sugar 10 g; Cholesterol 0 mg; Sodium 25 mg

SERVES 2

¾ cup (175 mL) water

¼ cup (60 mL) unsweetened apple juice

½ cup (125 mL) quinoa

½ cup (125 mL) grated carrots

2 Tbsp (30 mL) seedless raisins

¼ tsp (1 mL) cinnamon

¾ tsp (4 mL) pure vanilla extract

1 Tbsp (15 mL) chopped walnuts (optional)

1 Tbsp (15 mL) pure maple syrup or honey (optional)

COCONUT OMEGA-3 CEREAL

Rich in omega-3 fatty acids and fiber, this quinoa cereal is a super dose of superfoods. We don't need to tell you why fiber is great, and omega-3 oil supports healthy brain development and functioning. Literally, it's great food for thought.

Combine the coconut milk, water, quinoa and raisins in a medium saucepan. Bring to a boil, reduce to a simmer, cover and cook for 17 minutes. Remove from the heat and stir in the chia and flax-seeds. Serve.

PER SERVING: Energy 390 calories; Protein 11 g; Carbohydrates 51 g; Dietary Fiber 9 g; Fat 16 g; Sugar 5 g; Cholesterol 0 mg; Sodium 30 mg

SERVES 2

1 cup (250 mL) light coconut milk

⅔ cup (150 mL) water

⅔ cup (150 mL) quinoa

2 Tbsp (30 mL) seedless raisins or chopped pitted prunes or dates

2 Tbsp (30 mL) chia seeds

1 Tbsp (15 mL) ground flaxseeds

CREAMY CHOCOLATE BREAKFAST CEREAL

SERVES 2

1½ cups (375 mL) 1% milk

½ cup (125 mL) quinoa

1 Tbsp (15 mL) unsweetened
    cocoa powder

2 large egg whites

½ tsp (2 mL) pure vanilla extract

1 Tbsp (15 mL) pure maple syrup

Who says you can't have chocolate for breakfast? Sprinkle some toasted nuts on top for added crunch, if you like.

Combine the milk, quinoa and cocoa in a medium saucepan. Bring to a boil on medium heat, then reduce to a simmer. Cover and cook for 18 minutes.

Whisk together the egg whites and vanilla in a small bowl. Temper the egg whites by whisking in a spoonful of the hot quinoa mixture. Repeat, whisking in spoonfuls of quinoa mixture 4 more times. Stir the egg mixture into the hot quinoa mixture and cook for another 2 to 3 minutes, until thickened. Stir in the maple syrup. Serve.

PER SERVING: Energy 300 calories; Protein 16 g; Carbohydrates 45 g; Dietary Fiber 4 g; Fat 5 g; Sugar 15 g; Cholesterol 10 mg; Sodium 140 mg

GRAB & GO BREAKFAST CEREAL

SERVES 1

¼ cup (60 mL) quinoa flakes

1 Tbsp (15 mL) dried blueberries
    (or fruit of your choice)

1 Tbsp (15 mL) chopped walnuts
    (or nut of your choice)

1 tsp (5 mL) chia seeds

Pinch of cinnamon

½ cup (125 mL) boiling water

This is a great cereal for when you are on the go and need to take a hot, nutritious breakfast with you. Multiply this recipe and premeasure the dry mix into resealable plastic bags ahead of time, then simply grab one on your way out the door. Add your choice of sweetener and milk, if you like. Don't forget to take along a bowl and cover (such as foil), if needed.

Put the quinoa flakes, fruit, nuts, chia seeds and cinnamon into a resealable plastic bag or other container.

When ready to prepare, pour the contents into a bowl and add the boiling water. Give it one quick stir. Cover with a plate or foil and let sit for 9 to 10 minutes. Make sure all the water has been absorbed before eating. Serve with a sweetener, such as honey, syrup or sugar, as well as milk, if desired.

PER SERVING: Energy 210 calories; Protein 6 g; Carbohydrates 30 g; Dietary Fiber 5 g; Fat 8 g; Sugar 3 g; Cholesterol 0 mg; Sodium 260 mg

CREAMY BANANA BREAKFAST CEREAL

This breakfast cereal is creamy and smooth, and naturally sweetened with banana. It makes a delicious morning meal for both adults and children and is a cereal babies are sure to gobble up. (If using as a baby food, purée the banana together with the quinoa mixture.)

Bring the water and quinoa to a boil in a medium saucepan. Reduce to a simmer, cover and cook for 16 to 17 minutes. The quinoa should be overcooked and extra-plump. Fluff with a fork and set aside to cool slightly.

While still warm (but not hot), process the cooked quinoa in a food processor or blender until completely smooth and creamy. It should be the consistency of thick pudding. Add the milk, cinnamon and nutmeg. Blend well. Remove from the food processor and fold in the banana. Serve warm.

PER SERVING: Energy 250 calories; Protein 9 g; Carbohydrates 45 g; Dietary Fiber 5 g; Fat 5 g; Sugar 10 g; Cholesterol 5 mg; Sodium 35 mg

SERVES 2

1 cup (250 mL) water

½ cup (125 mL) quinoa

½ cup (125 mL) whole milk

1 tsp (5 mL) cinnamon

½ tsp (2 mL) nutmeg

½ cup (125 mL) chopped
   ripe banana

- Need a quick breakfast ready to go every day during the work week? Cook and purée the quinoa and store it in the refrigerator in an airtight container. Every morning, place a serving of the puréed quinoa in a small saucepan on low to medium heat. Add milk, cinnamon, nutmeg and mashed banana. Heat and stir until the mixture is smooth. This same method can be used daily for baby food.

- If you want to switch up the flavors, replace the banana with 4 or 5 stewed and chopped (or mashed for baby food) pitted prunes or apricots.

HOT PISTACHIO CEREAL WITH GREEK YOGURT & HONEY

Something a bit different. Quinoa and the buttery taste of pistachios are more than enough to provide a great-tasting, wholesome breakfast.

Combine the water and quinoa in a medium saucepan and bring to a boil. Reduce to a simmer, cover and cook for 17 minutes. Remove from the heat and stir in the pistachios and vanilla. Divide between 2 dishes and top each with ¼ cup (60 mL) yogurt and 1 tsp (5 mL) honey. Serve.

PER SERVING: Energy 260 calories; Protein 11 g; Carbohydrates 39 g; Dietary Fiber 4 g; Fat 7 g; Sugar 10 g; Cholesterol 5 mg; Sodium 50 mg

SERVES 2

1 cup (250 mL) water

½ cup (125 mL) quinoa

2 Tbsp (30 mL) chopped unsalted pistachios

¼ tsp (1 mL) pure vanilla extract

½ cup (125 mL) low-fat plain thick Greek yogurt

2 tsp (10 mL) liquid honey

Cooked quinoa already on hand? Reheat or use cold 1½ cups (375 mL) cooked quinoa instead of cooking the quinoa in this recipe.

HOT CINNAMON ZUCCHINI BREAKFAST

SERVES 2

1½ cups (375 mL) water

½ cup (125 mL) quinoa

1 cup (250 mL) grated zucchini

1 Tbsp (15 mL) pure maple
   syrup or honey

½ tsp (2 mL) cinnamon

½ tsp (2 mL) pure vanilla extract

1 Tbsp (15 mL) chopped pecans

Zucchini is a versatile vegetable, having a plain flavor that works as a blank slate in many different applications. This tasty hot breakfast gives you yet another way to use all that zucchini you have in your garden.

Combine the water and quinoa in a medium saucepan. Bring to a boil, reduce to a simmer, cover and cook for 12 minutes. Stir in the zucchini. Return to a boil, cover, reduce to a simmer and cook for another 8 minutes or until the quinoa is cooked and fluffy. Remove from the heat and stir in the maple syrup, cinnamon and vanilla. Divide the cereal between 2 bowls and sprinkle with pecans. Serve.

PER SERVING: Energy 220 calories; Protein 7 g; Carbohydrates 37 g; Dietary Fiber 4 g; Fat 5 g; Sugar 8 g; Cholesterol 0 mg; Sodium 15 mg

- Young zucchini are best as they have not developed large seeds in the center.
- Measure easy-to-use portions of grated zucchini in sealed freezer bags and store in the freezer for up to 2 months.

ORANGE GINGER QUINOA BREAKFAST CEREAL

The mixture of orange, ginger, apricots, dates and toasted almonds is sure to perk up your morning—and you just might want to have it again for lunch! Combine all the ingredients in one saucepan and serve warm or cold. If you're feeling indulgent, serve with cream.

Bring the water and quinoa to a boil in a medium saucepan. Reduce to a simmer, cover and cook for 15 minutes. Fluff with a fork. Add the dates, apricots, ginger and cinnamon; stir well to combine. Add the orange juice and zest and mix well. Sprinkle with the almonds and serve.

PER SERVING: Energy 170 calories; Protein 5 g; Carbohydrates 32 g; Dietary Fiber 4 g; Fat 4 g; Sugar 13 g; Cholesterol 0 mg; Sodium 10 mg

SERVES 4

1 cup (250 mL) water

½ cup (125 mL) quinoa

⅓ cup (75 mL) chopped pitted dates

¼ cup (60 mL) chopped dried apricots

1 tsp (5 mL) grated fresh ginger

½ tsp (2 mL) cinnamon

¼ cup (60 mL) freshly squeezed orange juice

½ tsp (2 mL) grated orange zest

¼ cup (60 mL) toasted sliced almonds

> To toast nuts, preheat the oven to 350°F (180°C). Spread the nuts on a baking sheet and toast in the oven, stirring once if necessary, for 5 to 7 minutes, until fragrant and lightly toasted.

STRAWBERRY RHUBARB BREAKFAST

1⅓ cups (325 mL) water

⅔ cup (150 mL) quinoa

½ tsp (2 mL) cinnamon

1 cup (250 mL) fresh or frozen chopped rhubarb

1 cup (250 mL) quartered strawberries

1 Tbsp (15 mL) honey or pure maple syrup (optional)

2 Tbsp (30 mL) toasted sliced almonds (optional)

Why not bring a delicious dessert combination to the breakfast table? A hot and healthy breakfast made with comfort foods is a great way to positively kick-start your day.

Bring the water, quinoa and cinnamon to a boil in a medium saucepan. Reduce to a simmer, cover and cook for 10 minutes. Stir in the rhubarb and strawberries. Again bring to a boil. Cover, reduce to a simmer and cook for another 10 minutes. Remove from the heat when the rhubarb is tender. Stir in the honey (if using). Serve topped with toasted almonds (if using) and milk or vanilla yogurt, if desired.

PER SERVING: Energy 250 calories; Protein 9 g; Carbohydrates 45 g; Dietary Fiber 7 g; Fat 4 g; Sugar 4 g; Cholesterol 0 mg; Sodium 5 mg

> To toast nuts, preheat the oven to 350°F (180°C). Spread the nuts on a baking sheet and toast in the oven, stirring once if necessary, for 5 to 7 minutes, until fragrant and lightly toasted.

BLUEBERRY SPROUT SMOOTHIE

This is a favorite smoothie of ours—and breakfast is the perfect time for veggies! The taste of spinach is completely unnoticeable in this recipe. A fabulously refreshing breakfast (or even lunch) that is great any morning, especially in hot weather.

Combine all the ingredients in a blender and purée. Serve immediately.

PER SERVING: Energy 120 calories; Protein 7 g; Carbohydrates 22 g; Dietary Fiber 2 g; Fat 1 g; Sugar 15 g; Cholesterol 0 mg; Sodium 80 mg

SERVES 2

1 cup (250 mL) fresh or
    frozen blueberries

¼ cup (60 mL) quinoa sprouts
    (pages 10 and 11)

½ cup (125 mL) fresh spinach

½ cup (125 mL) low-fat plain yogurt

½ cup (125 mL) skim milk

SUNSHINE SPROUT SMOOTHIE

A sprout smoothie is a great thing to wake up to, or if you need some extra energy before or after a tough workout. The sprouts and orange juice blend delightfully together for a fresh and healthful breakfast.

Combine all the ingredients in a blender and blend until smooth. Serve immediately.

PER SERVING: Energy 160 calories; Protein 6 g; Carbohydrates 29 g; Dietary Fiber 2 g; Fat 2 g; Sugar 16 g; Cholesterol 5 mg; Sodium 45 mg

SERVES 2

1 cup (250 mL) unsweetened
    orange juice

⅓ cup (75 mL) quinoa sprouts
    (pages 10 and 11)

½ cup (125 mL) low-fat
    vanilla yogurt

½ medium banana

Make your own vanilla yogurt by combining ½ cup (125 mL) plain yogurt, 1 tsp (5 mL) honey and ¼ tsp (1 mL) pure vanilla extract.

GREEN VEGGIE SUPER SHAKE

SERVES 2

½ cup (125 mL) unsweetened
  apple juice

½ cup (125 mL) water

½ to ⅔ cup (125 to 150 mL)
  quinoa sprouts (pages 10 and 11)

⅔ cup (150 mL) peeled and sliced
  English cucumber

⅔ cup (150 mL) baby spinach

Getting all the vegetables you need can be difficult in a busy day. Consuming vegetables in the morning will get you off on the right foot, give you energy and help you feel fantastic. These flavors complement each other well and go down smooth. It is up to you how much sprouts you use.

Place the apple juice, water and quinoa sprouts in a blender. Blend until sprouts are puréed or are very small pieces. Add the cucumber and spinach. Blend again until the shake is as smooth as possible. Serve immediately.

PER SERVING: Energy 110 calories; Protein 4 g; Carbohydrates 22 g; Dietary Fiber 2 g; Fat 1.5 g; Sugar 7 g; Cholesterol 0 mg; Sodium 15 mg

Don't have apple juice on hand? Use ½ cup (125 mL) of diced apple or applesauce.

ANYTIME BREAKFAST BARS

CHOCOLATE HAZELNUT BARS
MAKES 10 BARS

1½ cups (375 mL) quinoa flakes

1½ cups (375 mL) quick-cooking rolled oats (gluten-free if required)

1 cup (250 mL) mashed ripe bananas

¾ cup (175 mL) hazelnuts, coarsely chopped

½ cup (125 mL) unsweetened applesauce

⅓ cup (75 mL) unsweetened cocoa powder

2 Tbsp (30 mL) chia seeds (optional)

2 Tbsp (30 mL) liquid honey

1½ tsp (7 mL) pure vanilla extract

CRANBERRY COCONUT BARS
MAKES 12 BARS

1½ cups (375 mL) quinoa flakes

1½ cups (375 mL) quick-cooking rolled oats (gluten-free if required)

1 cup (250 mL) mashed ripe bananas

⅔ cup (150 mL) sweetened dried cranberries

½ cup (125 mL) unsweetened applesauce

½ cup (125 mL) unsweetened shredded coconut

2 Tbsp (30 mL) chia seeds (optional)

2 Tbsp (30 mL) liquid honey

2 tsp (10 mL) cinnamon

1½ tsp (7 mL) pure vanilla extract

When you are short on time and need to get out the door, these yummy, filling bars are great to grab on the run or to tuck into your pocket for later. And they're great pre- or post-workout fuel! Choose your favorite lightly sweetened combination! You can freeze these bars for up to 1 month.

Preheat the oven to 350°F (180°C). Lightly grease a baking sheet or line with parchment.

Mix together all the ingredients in a medium bowl. (The dough will be sticky.) Using a ¼-cup (60 mL) measure, place scoops of dough on the baking sheet. Dampen your hands with water and use the palm of your hand to flatten each scoop until ¾ inch (2 cm) thick. Form dough into circles or rectangles, arranging them 1½ inches (4 cm) apart.

Bake for 12 minutes. These bars do not brown much, so be careful not to overbake. Let cool on the baking sheet before storing in an airtight container.

CHOCOLATE HAZELNUT BARS

PER SERVING: Energy 180 calories; Protein 5 g; Carbohydrates 29 g; Dietary Fiber 4 g; Fat 6 g; Sugar 7 g; Cholesterol 0 mg; Sodium 125 mg

CRANBERRY COCONUT BARS

PER SERVING: Energy 170 calories; Protein 4 g; Carbohydrates 33 g; Dietary Fiber 4 g; Fat 4 g; Sugar 12 g; Cholesterol 0 mg; Sodium 130 mg

MORE ANYTIME BREAKFAST BARS

A busy schedule requires quality fuel at hand. These two types of naturally sweet, naturally nourishing bars will power you through your day. You can freeze these bars for up to 1 month.

Preheat the oven to 350°F (180°C). Lightly grease a baking sheet or line with parchment.

Mix together all the ingredients in a medium bowl. (The dough will be sticky.) Using a ¼-cup (60 mL) measure, place scoops of dough on the baking sheet. Dampen your hands with water and use the palm of your hand to flatten each scoop until ¾ inch (2 cm) thick. Form dough into circles or rectangles, arranging them 1½ inches (4 cm) apart.

Bake for 12 minutes. These bars do not brown much, so be careful not to overbake. Let cool on the baking sheet before storing in an airtight container.

DARK CHOCOLATE CHERRY BARS

PER SERVING: Energy 170 calories; Protein 4 g; Carbohydrates 33 g; Dietary Fiber 5 g; Fat 3 g; Sugar 10 g; Cholesterol 0 mg; Sodium 125 mg

DATE AND WALNUT BARS

PER SERVING: Energy 180 calories; Protein 5 g; Carbohydrates 32 g; Dietary Fiber 4 g; Fat 5 g; Sugar 11 g; Cholesterol 0 mg; Sodium 125 mg

DARK CHOCOLATE CHERRY BARS
MAKES 12 BARS

1½ cups (375 mL) quinoa flakes

1½ cups (375 mL) quick-cooking rolled oats (gluten-free if required)

1 cup (250 mL) mashed ripe bananas

¾ cup (175 mL) coarsely chopped dried sour cherries

½ cup (125 mL) unsweetened applesauce

⅓ cup (75 mL) semisweet mini chocolate chips or carob chips

2 Tbsp (30 mL) chia seeds (optional)

2 Tbsp (30 mL) liquid honey (optional)

2 tsp (10 mL) cinnamon

2 tsp (10 mL) pure vanilla extract

DATE AND WALNUT BARS
MAKES 12 BARS

1½ cups (375 mL) quinoa flakes

1½ cups (375 mL) quick-cooking rolled oats (gluten-free if required)

1 cup (250 mL) mashed ripe bananas

¾ cup (175 mL) coarsely chopped pitted dates

½ cup (125 mL) unsweetened applesauce

½ cup (125 mL) chopped walnuts

2 Tbsp (30 mL) chia seeds (optional)

1 Tbsp (15 mL) liquid honey (optional)

2 tsp (10 mL) cinnamon

1½ tsp (7 mL) pure vanilla extract

Pinch of nutmeg

MAPLE PECAN GRANOLA

SERVES 6

¼ cup (60 mL) quinoa

2 cups (500 mL) large-flake rolled
  oats (gluten-free if required)

½ cup (125 mL) chopped pecans

2 Tbsp (30 mL) unsweetened
  flaked coconut

¼ cup (60 mL) pure maple syrup

1 Tbsp (15 mL) liquid honey

1 tsp (5 mL) cinnamon

½ tsp (2 mL) pure vanilla extract

¼ cup (60 mL) seedless raisins

Avoid the high fat and calories often found in store-bought granola by making it yourself. This granola is highly portable and a terrific complement to plain yogurt, so take a serving of each along with you and mix them together when you need a snack.

Preheat the oven to 350°F (180°C). Lightly spray or grease a baking sheet or line with parchment.

Place the quinoa in a small resealable plastic bag. Roll over it with gentle pressure a few times with a rolling pin to crack the seeds. (Why crack the seeds? See page 11.) Pour the quinoa into a medium bowl and stir in the oats, pecans and coconut.

Whisk together the maple syrup, honey, cinnamon and vanilla; pour over the quinoa mixture. Stir until completely coated. Pour onto the baking sheet, spread it out in an even layer and bake for 10 minutes. Stir, then bake for another 5 minutes. Stir again and bake for 3 to 5 minutes. Granola can quickly burn, so watch it closely. It should be golden brown. Remove from the oven, stir in the raisins and let cool. Store in an airtight container for up to 2 months.

PER SERVING: Energy 270 calories; Protein 7 g; Carbohydrates 41 g; Dietary Fiber 5 g; Fat 10 g; Sugar 15 g; Cholesterol 0 mg; Sodium 0 mg

PEANUT BUTTER & TOMATO SPROUT TOAST

Sweet vine-ripened tomatoes paired with the creamy saltiness of peanut butter is a surprisingly delicious combination. Sprinkle on some sprouts and you have a quick, nutritious breakfast. This recipe is perfect if you have leftover sprouts from another recipe.

Toast the bread and spread with peanut butter. Sprinkle with quinoa sprouts and top with slices of tomato. Serve.

PER SERVING (whole-grain bread): Energy 190 calories; Protein 7 g; Carbohydrates 20 g; Dietary Fiber 3 g; Fat 9 g; Sugar 3 g; Cholesterol 0 mg; Sodium 210 mg

SERVES 1

1 slice sprouted whole grain or gluten-free bread

1 Tbsp (15 mL) smooth or chunky natural peanut butter

1 Tbsp (15 mL) quinoa sprouts (pages 10 and 11)

2 to 3 slices ripe tomato

Hit a local farmers' market for fresh produce. Not only do these markets support the local economy, but the food will taste even better than store bought.

QUINOA MUSHROOM OMELET

SERVES 4

½ cup (125 mL) water

¼ cup (60 mL) quinoa

1 tsp (5 mL) grapeseed or vegetable oil

½ cup (125 mL) sliced brown or white mushrooms

1 large egg

4 large egg whites

2 Tbsp (30 mL) shredded reduced-fat aged Cheddar cheese

2 tsp (10 mL) sliced green onions

Fluffy quinoa, eggs and sautéed mushrooms make a delicious high-protein breakfast.

Bring the water and quinoa to a boil in a small saucepan. Reduce to a simmer, cover and cook for 15 minutes. Fluff with a fork and set aside.

Heat the oil in a skillet on medium heat. Add the mushrooms. Cook until tender, 5 to 7 minutes. In a small bowl, whisk together the egg, egg whites and cooked quinoa. Pour the egg mixture over the mushrooms. Cook, covered, for 2 minutes. Using a spatula, fold omelet in half. Cook, covered, for another 2 to 4 minutes, until egg is set. Turn off the heat and sprinkle omelet with cheese and green onions. Cover for another minute or two, until the cheese is melted. Cut into quarters and serve.

PER SERVING: Energy 140 calories; Protein 10 g; Carbohydrates 15 g; Dietary Fiber 2 g; Fat 4 g; Sugar 1 g; Cholesterol 50 mg; Sodium 115 mg

Cooked quinoa already on hand? Add ¾ cup (175 mL) to the eggs in this recipe.

SMOKED GOUDA & ONION OMELET

Reconnect with your better half over breakfast, lunch or supper by sharing a delicious omelet for two. Add as much or as little mustard as you prefer. Colored quinoa looks best in this recipe, but white will work. Increase the nutrition even more by using ½ cup (125 mL) of sprouted quinoa instead of regular cooked quinoa.

Combine the water and quinoa in a small saucepan and bring to a boil. Reduce to a simmer, cover and cook for 15 minutes. Remove from the heat, fluff with a fork and set aside.

Heat a 10-inch (25 cm) nonstick skillet on medium-low heat. Add 1 tsp (5 mL) of the oil. Add the onions and a spoonful of water. Cover and cook, stirring occasionally, for 10 minutes or until the onions are soft and transparent. Transfer to a bowl and stir in the mustard. Set aside.

Rinse out the skillet and wipe dry. Heat the skillet again on medium-low. Add the remaining 1 tsp (5 mL) oil. Whisk together the egg, egg whites and milk. Pour the egg mixture into the pan and cook until firm enough to flip, 3 to 4 minutes. Flip the omelet over. Cook until set. Sprinkle the cooked quinoa and onions on one half of the omelet. Fold in half, cut in half and place on plates. Sprinkle with cheese and serve.

PER SERVING: Energy 210 calories; Protein 14 g; Carbohydrates 18 g; Dietary Fiber 2 g; Fat 8 g; Sugar 4 g; Cholesterol 95 mg; Sodium 220 mg

SERVES 2

⅓ cup (75 mL) water

2 Tbsp + 2 tsp (40 mL) quinoa

2 tsp (10 mL) grapeseed or vegetable oil

1 cup (250 mL) onions sliced ½ inch (1 cm) thick

1 to 2 tsp (5 to 10 mL) of your favorite Dijon or grainy mustard

1 large egg

4 large egg whites

2 tsp (10 mL) 1% or 2% milk

3 Tbsp (45 mL) shredded smoked Gouda or Cheddar cheese

Cooked quinoa already on hand? Sprinkle ⅓ to ½ cup (75 to 125 mL) over the omelet in this recipe.

SUNDAY BRUNCH CASSEROLE

SERVES 12

1 lb (450 g) ground turkey, chicken or pork

1 tsp (5 mL) minced fresh sage

1 tsp (5 mL) minced fresh parsley (optional)

1 tsp (5 mL) pure maple syrup or honey

¼ tsp (1 mL) minced fresh thyme

¾ tsp (4 mL) salt (optional)

½ tsp (2 mL) black pepper

Pinch of ground cloves

1 cup (250 mL) water

½ cup (125 mL) quinoa

1 Tbsp (15 mL) grapeseed oil or vegetable oil

1 cup (250 mL) chopped red bell pepper

1 cup (250 mL) shredded reduced-fat (or regular) aged Cheddar cheese

½ cup (125 mL) thinly sliced green onion

6 large eggs + 12 large egg whites (or 12 whole, large eggs total)

¼ cup (60 mL) 1% milk

2 tsp (10 mL) minced garlic

2 tsp (10 mL) ground mustard

Prepare the sausage meat and vegetables ahead of time and have them ready in the refrigerator so you can easily make this in the morning.

In a medium bowl, combine the ground turkey, sage, parsley (if using), maple syrup, thyme, ¼ tsp of the salt (if using), ¼ teaspoon of the pepper and the ground cloves. Mix well. Refrigerate until needed.

Bring the water and quinoa to a boil in a medium saucepan. Reduce to a simmer, cover and cook for 15 minutes. Remove from the heat and let sit, covered, for another 5 minutes. Fluff with a fork. Set aside to cool.

Meanwhile, preheat the oven to 375°F (190°C). Lightly grease a 13- × 9-inch (3 L) baking dish.

Heat the oil in a large skillet on medium heat. Add the sausage meat and fry until browned and no pink remains. Spread the sausage mixture evenly in the baking dish. Equally distribute the quinoa and red pepper. Sprinkle with Cheddar and green onions.

In a medium bowl, whisk together the eggs, egg whites, milk, garlic, mustard, remaining salt (if using) and remaining ¼ tsp black pepper. Pour the egg mixture evenly into the casserole dish. Bake for 35 to 45 minutes or until the center is set and the edges have browned. Let sit for 8 minutes, then cut into 12 pieces. Serve.

PER SERVING (including sausage filling): Energy 190 calories; Protein 18 g; Carbohydrates 7 g; Dietary Fiber 1 g; Fat 9 g; Sugar 2 g; Cholesterol 125 mg; Sodium 180 mg

TRADITIONAL BREAKFAST SAUSAGE ROUNDS

Traditional Breakfast Sausage rounds can be used wherever you would normally use regular breakfast sausage. Fry in a small amount of oil or bake for an even lower-fat option. The cooked sausage patties can also be frozen for up to 1 month.

Bring the water and quinoa to a boil in a small saucepan. Reduce to a simmer, cover and cook for 15 minutes. Remove from the heat and keep covered for another 10 minutes. Fluff with a fork. Set aside to cool completely.

In a medium bowl, mix together the cooled quinoa and the ground turkey, sage, parsley (if using), syrup, thyme, salt (if using), pepper and cloves.

PAN-FRY METHOD Heat the oil in a large skillet on medium-low heat. Scoop out ¼-cup (60 mL) servings of sausage mixture and with wet hands shape into rounds 1 inch (2.5 cm) thick. Fry for about 4 minutes on each side, until cooked through and golden brown. Serve.

OVEN METHOD Preheat the oven to 350°F (180°C). Line a baking sheet with parchment. Scoop out ¼-cup (60 mL) servings of sausage mixture and with wet hands shape into rounds 3 inches (8 cm) wide and ½ inch (1 cm) thick. Arrange on the baking sheet about 1½ inches (4 cm) apart. Bake for 10 minutes per side. Serve.

PER SERVING: Energy 200 calories; Protein 19 g; Carbohydrates 8 g; Dietary Fiber 1 g; Fat 9 g; Sugar 1 g; Cholesterol 65 mg; Sodium 55 mg

MAKES 10 ROUNDS, SERVING 5

⅔ cup (150 mL) water

⅓ cup (75 mL) quinoa

1 lb (450 g) ground turkey, chicken or pork

1 tsp (5 mL) minced fresh sage

1 tsp (5 mL) minced fresh parsley (optional)

1 tsp (5 mL) pure maple syrup or honey

¼ tsp (1 mL) minced fresh thyme

¼ tsp (1 mL) salt (optional)

¼ tsp (1 mL) black pepper

Pinch of cloves

2 tsp (10 mL) grapeseed or vegetable oil (pan-fry method only)

REVOLUTIONIZE
SALADS,
SIDES & SNACKS

REVOLUTIONIZE SALADS, SIDES & SNACKS

QUINOA is all about versatility and simplicity, so it is often used in side dishes and salads, yet sometimes it's so good it ends up putting the rest of the meal to shame. These recipes may do just that—but we hope instead that they'll complement the other foods you're serving.

The versatility of quinoa means that many times quinoa side dishes work equally great as a lunch or a snack. Most of the recipes in this chapter serve multiple duty, as they're terrific for any occasion and work well as a side dish, a lunch salad or an after-school snack and for entertaining. Just be warned that your guests may ask you for the recipe! Want something new and interesting? Try Crisp Lemon Snap Pea Salad (page 56) and Basil Watermelon Salad (page 49).

With quinoa you can feel okay about snacking between meals. Actually, eating small snacks throughout the day can keep you alert and keep your metabolism in check. Portability is really the key to eating well with our busy lifestyles. Having something within reach that's healthful and ready to eat when you need it helps you avoid having to opt for nutritionally inferior convenience foods. Salads that can be prepared in advance and are ready to grab from the refrigerator on your way out the door, and sides that are balanced and filling enough all on their own, are ideal solutions. For convenient, simple foods that are fresh and exciting, try Berry Cucumber Salad with White Balsamic Dressing (page 51) and Red Cabbage & Sprout Slaw (page 64). For a stunning and delicious recipe that is great for guests, try the Pear, Walnut & Blue Cheese Salad with Thyme Dressing in Radicchio Cups (page 61).

APPLE CABBAGE SPROUT SALAD

SERVES 6

2 cups (500 mL) quinoa
   sprouts (pages 10 and 11)

1 cup (250 mL) thinly sliced or
   shredded red cabbage

1 cup (250 mL) grated carrots

½ cup (125 mL) sliced green onions

1 cup (250 mL) grated apple

½ cup (125 mL) toasted
   slivered almonds

3 Tbsp (45 mL) olive or
   flaxseed oil

2 Tbsp (30 mL) apple cider vinegar

2 tsp (10 mL) pure maple syrup
   or honey

¼ tsp (1 mL) salt (optional)

High in vitamin A, this salad is versatile enough for any season. This fresh and tasty slaw will be a great addition to any casual lunch or supper. Consider using flaxseed oil in your salads to meet your omega-3 requirements.

Combine the sprouts, cabbage, carrots, green onions, apple and almonds in a medium bowl. In a separate bowl, whisk together the oil, vinegar, maple syrup and salt (if using). Toss veggie mixture with the dressing and serve.

PER SERVING: Energy 220 calories; Protein 5 g; Carbohydrates 23 g; Dietary Fiber 4 g; Fat 13 g; Sugar 5 g; Cholesterol 0 mg; Sodium 20 mg

To toast nuts, preheat the oven to 350°F (180°C). Spread the nuts on a baking sheet and toast in the oven, stirring once if necessary, for 5 to 7 minutes, until fragrant and lightly toasted.

AVOCADO BASIL PESTO SALAD

SERVES 10

3 cups (750 mL) water

1½ cups (375 mL) quinoa

1 avocado, peeled and diced

½ cup (125 mL) fresh basil leaves

⅓ cup (75 mL) grated
   Parmesan cheese

2 Tbsp (30 mL) water

2 Tbsp (30 mL) extra virgin olive oil

1 tsp (5 mL) minced garlic

¼ tsp (1 mL) each salt and freshly
   ground black pepper

¼ tsp (1 mL) cayenne pepper

The robust tastes of basil and garlic are blended with creamy avocado for a smooth, luxurious side dish worthy of taking its place alongside a barbecued chicken or steak and a glass of red wine.

Bring the water and quinoa to a boil in a large saucepan. Reduce to a simmer, cover and cook for 15 minutes. Fluff with a fork and set aside to cool completely.

In a food processor, purée the avocado, basil, Parmesan, water, olive oil, garlic, salt, black pepper and cayenne. Pour mixture over cooked quinoa. Mix well and serve immediately or chilled.

PER SERVING: Energy 160 calories; Protein 5 g; Carbohydrates 18 g; Dietary Fiber 3 g; Fat 8 g; Sugar 0 g; Cholesterol 0 mg; Sodium 100 mg

Cooked quinoa already on hand? Add the avocado mixture to 4 ½ cups (1.125 L) cooked quinoa.

BASIL WATERMELON SALAD

Treat your guests (or yourself!) to something a bit different—sweet watermelon and basil are a delicious match. Watermelon not only always makes eating fun and joyful, but it also has many surprising health benefits. It contains a good dose of antioxidants and is thought to help reduce inflammation in the body.

Bring the water and quinoa to a boil in a medium saucepan. Reduce to a simmer, cover and cook for 15 minutes. Fluff with a fork and set aside to cool completely.

Combine the quinoa, watermelon, feta, olives, basil and red onion in a medium bowl. Add the lime juice and olive oil. Gently toss until well combined. Serve chilled.

PER SERVING: Energy 200 calories; Protein 6 g; Carbohydrates 24 g; Dietary Fiber 2 g; Fat 10 g; Sugar 8 g; Cholesterol 15 mg; Sodium 260 mg

SERVES 4

1 cup (250 mL) water

½ cup (125 mL) quinoa

3 cups (750 mL) diced seedless watermelon

½ cup (125 mL) crumbled feta cheese

3 Tbsp (45 mL) chopped pitted black olives

1 Tbsp (15 mL) chopped fresh basil

1 Tbsp (15 mL) finely chopped red onion

2 Tbsp (30 mL) lime juice

1 Tbsp (15 mL) extra virgin olive oil

> Cooked quinoa already on hand? Add 1 ½ cups (375 mL) cooked quinoa to the other ingredients.

BERRY CUCUMBER SALAD WITH WHITE BALSAMIC DRESSING

Consider this dynamic combination of berries, cucumber, onion and almonds an adventure for your taste buds. This salad is an impressive dish to serve for a brunch or a lunch.

Combine the water and quinoa in a medium saucepan and bring to a boil. Reduce to a simmer, cover and cook for 15 minutes. Transfer to a salad bowl to cool completely.

Whisk together the vinegar, maple syrup and olive oil; stir into the quinoa. Gently toss in the blueberries, strawberries, cucumber and red onion. Just before serving, sprinkle with almonds (if using).

PER SERVING: Energy 170 calories; Protein 5 g; Carbohydrates 30 g; Dietary Fiber 3 g; Fat 4 g; Sugar 8 g; Cholesterol 0 mg; Sodium 10 mg

> To toast nuts, preheat the oven to 350°F (180°C). Spread the nuts on a baking sheet and toast in the oven, stirring once if necessary, for 5 to 7 minutes, until fragrant and lightly toasted.

SERVES 6

2 cups (500 mL) water

1 cup (250 mL) quinoa

¼ cup (60 mL) white balsamic vinegar

1 Tbsp (15 mL) pure maple syrup or honey

1 Tbsp (15 mL) extra virgin olive oil

1 cup (250 mL) fresh blueberries

1 cup (250 mL) quartered fresh strawberries

1 cup (250 mL) diced English cucumber

¼ cup (60 mL) thinly sliced red onion cut into ¾-inch (2 cm) lengths

¼ cup (60 mL) toasted slivered or sliced almonds (optional)

CARROT & RAISIN SPROUT SALAD

SERVES 6

1½ cups (375 mL) grated carrots

1⅓ cups (325 mL) quinoa sprouts
(pages 10 and 11)

½ cup (125 mL) sliced green onions

⅓ cup (75 mL) toasted cashews

⅓ cup (75 mL) seedless raisins

¼ cup (60 mL) lemon juice

3 Tbsp (45 mL) olive oil

1 to 2 Tbsp (15 to 30 mL)
pure maple syrup

¼ tsp (1 mL) curry powder

A lively salad with the fresh, crunchy snap of quinoa sprouts and grated carrot, blended with the natural sweetness of raisins and creamy toasted cashews.

Combine the carrots, sprouts, green onions, cashews and raisins in a medium bowl. Whisk together the lemon juice, olive oil, maple syrup and curry powder. Toss with sprout mixture and serve.

PER SERVING: Energy 220 calories; Protein 4 g; Carbohydrates 27 g; Dietary Fiber 3 g; Fat 12 g; Sugar 9 g; Cholesterol 0 mg; Sodium 25 mg

To toast nuts, preheat the oven to 350°F (180°C). Spread the nuts on a baking sheet and toast in the oven, stirring once if necessary, for 5 to 7 minutes, until fragrant and lightly toasted.

CHERRY, FETA & THYME SALAD

Quinoa tossed with fresh thyme, cherries, feta cheese and honey makes this slightly sweet side dish an instant favorite as part of a quick lunch or as a snack with your favorite cup of tea.

Bring the water and quinoa to a boil in a medium saucepan. Reduce to a simmer, cover and cook for 15 minutes. Fluff with a fork and set aside to cool completely.

Add the cherries, cheese and thyme. Whisk together the olive oil, lemon juice, honey and salt and pepper. Pour over the quinoa mixture and stir until well combined. Chill for at least 1 hour before serving.

PER SERVING: Energy 260 calories; Protein 7 g; Carbohydrates 32 g; Dietary Fiber 3 g; Fat 12 g; Sugar 10 g; Cholesterol 10 mg; Sodium 260 mg

SERVES 2

⅔ cup (150 mL) water

⅓ cup (75 mL) quinoa

½ cup (125 mL) quartered pitted fresh cherries

¼ cup (60 mL) crumbled feta cheese

2 tsp (10 mL) minced fresh thyme

1 Tbsp (15 mL) extra virgin olive oil

1 Tbsp (15 mL) lemon juice

1 Tbsp (15 mL) liquid honey

Pinch each of salt and freshly ground black pepper

Cooked quinoa already on hand? Combine 1 cup (250 mL) cooked quinoa with the cherries, cheese and thyme.

CHIPOTLE BLACK BEAN SALAD

SERVES 6

2 cups (500 mL) water

1 cup (250 mL) quinoa

1 can (14 oz/398 mL) black beans, drained and rinsed (or 1½ cups/ 375 mL cooked black beans)

1 cup (250 mL) thawed frozen corn

¼ cup (60 mL) finely chopped red onion

¼ cup (60 mL) chopped fresh cilantro

¼ cup (60 mL) extra virgin olive oil or flaxseed oil

¼ cup (60 mL) lime juice (from about 1½ limes)

2 tsp (10 mL) finely chopped chipotle pepper in adobo sauce, with seeds

½ tsp (2 mL) minced garlic

A chipotle pepper is a smoked jalapeño pepper that is known for its spicy, smoky flavor. It is a superb option when you want to add a lot of flavor to a dish without using ingredients that may add unnecessary fat. Chipotle peppers can be found in small cans in adobo sauce in the Mexican section of most grocery stores. Leftover canned peppers can be frozen.

Bring the water and quinoa to a boil in a medium saucepan. Reduce to a simmer, cover and cook for 15 minutes. Fluff with a fork and set aside to cool completely.

Combine the cooled quinoa, black beans, corn, red onion and cilantro in a medium bowl. Whisk together the oil, lime juice, chipotle pepper and garlic. Toss with the quinoa mixture and serve.

PER SERVING: Energy 280 calories; Protein 9 g; Carbohydrates 36 g; Dietary Fiber 6 g; Fat 11 g; Sugar 1 g; Cholesterol 0 mg; Sodium 25 mg

> Dried beans are lower in sodium than canned beans—and half the cost. Cook up a batch ahead of time, then freeze in pre-measured servings in freezer bags for easy use.

GRAPE & CUCUMBER SALAD WITH CHEDDAR

Herbes de Provence give this cheery salad a delectable earthy flavor. Sharp Cheddar, fresh cucumbers and sweet grapes add to the rich combination.

Bring the water and quinoa to a boil in a medium saucepan. Reduce to a simmer, cover and cook for 15 minutes. Fluff with a fork and set aside to cool completely.

Combine the quinoa, tomatoes, cucumber, yellow pepper, grapes and green onions in a medium bowl. Whisk together the olive oil, vinegar, herbes de Provence and salt (if using). Pour over the quinoa mixture and add the cheese. Gently toss until well combined. Serve chilled.

PER SERVING: Energy 240 calories; Protein 11 g; Carbohydrates 22 g; Dietary Fiber 6 g; Fat 11 g; Sugar 5 g; Cholesterol 20 mg; Sodium 251 mg

Cooked quinoa already on hand? Add 1 ½ cups (375 mL) cooked quinoa to the vegetables in this recipe.

SERVES 4

1 cup (250 mL) water

½ cup (125 mL) quinoa

½ cup (125 mL) halved cherry tomatoes

½ cup (125 mL) diced seeded cucumber

½ cup (125 mL) diced yellow bell pepper

½ cup (125 mL) halved green grapes

2 Tbsp (30 mL) chopped green onions

2 Tbsp (30 mL) extra virgin olive oil

2 Tbsp (30 mL) apple cider vinegar

1 tsp (5 mL) herbes de Provence

Pinch of salt (optional)

½ cup (125 mL) diced reduced-fat aged Cheddar cheese

CRISP LEMON SNAP PEA SALAD

SERVES 6

2 cups (500 mL) water

1 cup (250 mL) quinoa

2 cups (500 mL) fresh sweet snap
   peas cut diagonally into thirds

1½ cups (375 mL) button
   mushrooms, cut into quarters
   or eighths if large

⅓ cup (75 mL) thinly sliced red onion
   cut into 1-inch (2.5 cm) lengths

1 Tbsp (15 mL) chopped fresh dill

⅓ cup (75 mL) white balsamic
   vinegar

¼ cup (60 mL) olive oil or
   flaxseed oil

1 tsp (5 mL) grated lemon zest

1 Tbsp (15 mL) lemon juice

1 tsp (5 mL) pure maple syrup

Crisp, sweet snap peas are blended with the fresh fragrance of lemon. This salad is even better the next day, after the dressing has completely soaked into the mushrooms.

Combine the water and quinoa in a medium saucepan and bring to a boil. Reduce to a simmer, cover and cook for 15 minutes. Fluff with a fork and set aside to cool completely.

Combine the peas, mushrooms, red onion and dill in a medium bowl. Whisk together the vinegar, oil, lemon zest, lemon juice and maple syrup. Pour over the cooled quinoa in the saucepan and stir until evenly dispersed. Add to the vegetable mixture, toss and serve.

PER SERVING: Energy 230 calories; Protein 6 g; Carbohydrates 28 g; Dietary Fiber 3 g; Fat 11 g; Sugar 5 g; Cholesterol 0 mg; Sodium 10 mg

Unable to find fresh sweet snap peas? Use crisp snow peas instead.

GREEK QUINOA SALAD

SERVES 6

1⅓ cups (325 mL) water

⅔ cup (150 mL) quinoa

1 cup (250 mL) diced English cucumber

½ cup (125 mL) diced red bell pepper

½ cup (125 mL) sliced or chopped pitted black olives

½ cup (125 mL) crumbled reduced-fat feta cheese

¼ cup (60 mL) diced red onion (optional)

3 Tbsp (45 mL) olive oil

3 Tbsp (45 mL) red wine vinegar

1 tsp (5 mL) dried oregano

Cracked black pepper to taste

This full-flavored quinoa salad with a light dressing and healthful vegetables will instantly have you feeling like a god or goddess. Plus, it's so quick and easy, you won't even break a sweat!

Bring the water and quinoa to a boil in a medium saucepan. Reduce to a simmer, cover and cook for 15 minutes. Fluff with a fork and set aside to cool completely.

Combine the cucumber, red pepper, olives, feta and red onion (if using) in a medium bowl. Add the cooled quinoa. Whisk together the olive oil, vinegar and oregano. Pour the dressing over the quinoa mixture and gently toss until evenly distributed. Add cracked black pepper to taste.

PER SERVING: Energy 180 calories; Protein 5 g; Carbohydrates 15 g; Dietary Fiber 2 g; Fat 12 g; Sugar 1 g; Cholesterol 5 mg; Sodium 160 mg

> Cooked quinoa already on hand? Add 2 cups (500 mL) cooked quinoa to the vegetables and feta in this recipe.

MINTED CUCUMBER SPROUT SALAD WITH TOASTED PEANUTS

Cucumber, mint, lime and toasted peanuts are a terrific, fresh-tasting blend that will pleasantly surprise you. When you are tired of your other salad recipes, try this one!

Combine the quinoa sprouts, cucumber, red onion, mint and peanuts in a medium bowl. Whisk together the lime juice, oil and salt (if using). Pour over the quinoa mixture and gently toss until coated. Serve immediately.

Salad can be stored in the refrigerator for up to 1 day. (Sprouts deteriorate quickly once they're combined in a salad.)

PER SERVING: Energy 290 calories; Protein 8 g; Carbohydrates 32 g; Dietary Fiber 4 g; Fat 11 g; Sugar 2 g; Cholesterol 0 mg; Sodium 0 mg

SERVES 6

3 cups (750 mL) quinoa sprouts (pages 10 and 11)

1½ cups (375 mL) diced English cucumber

⅓ cup (75 mL) thinly sliced red onion cut into 1-inch (2.5 cm) pieces

¼ cup (60 mL) chopped fresh mint

¼ cup (60 mL) chopped toasted peanuts

¼ cup (60 mL) lime juice (from about 1½ limes)

¼ cup (60 mL) olive oil or flaxseed oil

Pinch of salt (optional)

To toast nuts, preheat the oven to 350°F (180°C). Spread the nuts on a baking sheet and toast in the oven, stirring once if necessary, for 5 to 7 minutes, until fragrant and lightly toasted.

PEAR, WALNUT & BLUE CHEESE SALAD WITH THYME DRESSING IN RADICCHIO CUPS

Even though this stunningly delicious salad is perfect for a late-summer or early-fall dinner party, it can be enjoyed at any time of the year. All white quinoa looks great, but to maximize the dramatic colors in this dish use half black and half white quinoa. Do not separate the radicchio leaves until just before serving to prevent wilting.

Combine the water and quinoa in a medium saucepan and bring to a boil. Reduce to a simmer, cover and cook for 15 minutes. Fluff with a fork and set aside to cool completely.

In a medium bowl, whisk together the apple juice, vinegar, oil, thyme and salt (if using).

Peel the pears if the skin is thick. Core and dice the pears to make 1½ cups (375 mL). Add the pears to the dressing and gently toss to coat completely. Add the cooled quinoa, walnuts, blue cheese and green onions. Toss gently.

Just before serving, separate the radicchio leaves by cutting at the base of the head. Leaves that are 3½ to 4 inches (9 to 10 cm) across are the perfect size. Place one leaf on each plate and divide the salad between the cups. Serve immediately.

PER SERVING: Energy 240 calories; Protein 5 g; Carbohydrates 27 g; Dietary Fiber 4 g; Fat 13 g; Sugar 9 g; Cholesterol 5 mg; Sodium 90 mg

SERVES 4

1⅓ cups (325 mL) water

⅔ cup (150 mL) quinoa

6 Tbsp (90 mL) unsweetened apple juice

¼ cup (60 mL) white wine vinegar

3 Tbsp (45 mL) flaxseed oil or olive oil

1 tsp (5 mL) chopped fresh thyme

Pinch of salt (optional)

2 to 3 ripe pears (Bartlett, Bosc or Anjou)

¼ cup (60 mL) walnuts or pecans, coarsely chopped

¼ cup (60 mL) crumbled blue cheese (gluten-free if required)

¼ cup (60 mL) sliced green onions

1 head radicchio

Always buy pears that are not too soft or bruised. Ripen hard fruit for a few days in a paper bag at room temperature, then store in the refrigerator. Serve at room temperature.

PEACH & CHICKEN QUINOA

SERVES 6

2 cups (500 mL) water

1 cup (250 mL) quinoa

1 Tbsp (15 mL) grapeseed oil

2 boneless, skinless chicken breasts

2 medium peaches,
    coarsely chopped

⅓ cup (75 mL) chopped
    toasted pecans

¼ cup (60 mL) low-fat plain yogurt

¼ tsp (1 mL) each black pepper,
    onion powder and paprika

Pinch each of dried thyme,
    garlic powder, ground cumin
    and cayenne pepper

Delightfully fresh peaches, gently spiced up and tossed with chicken and creamy yogurt, make this delicious dish unusual and refreshing.

Bring the water and quinoa to a boil in a large saucepan. Reduce to a simmer, cover and cook for 15 minutes. Fluff with a fork and set aside.

In a medium skillet on medium heat, heat the oil. Cook the chicken, turning once, for 6 minutes per side, or until it is no longer pink inside. Chop into bite-size pieces and set aside to cool completely.

In a medium bowl, mix together the peaches, toasted pecans and yogurt. Add the pepper, onion powder, paprika, thyme, garlic powder, cumin and cayenne; mix thoroughly. Add the quinoa and chicken pieces. Mix well and serve immediately or chilled.

PER SERVING: Energy 230 calories; Protein 14 g; Carbohydrates 24 g; Dietary Fiber 3 g; Fat 10 g; Sugar 4 g; Cholesterol 25 mg; Sodium 55 mg

- Cooked quinoa already on hand? Add 3 cups (750 mL) cooked quinoa along with the chicken pieces in this recipe.

- To toast nuts, preheat the oven to 350°F (180°C). Spread the nuts on a baking sheet and toast in the oven, stirring once if necessary, for 5 to 7 minutes, until fragrant and lightly toasted.

PINE NUT & ROASTED RED PEPPER SALAD

A no-fuss, throw-together salad that is a little different than many of the salads you've had before. This looks great with any color of quinoa. You may replace the roasted red pepper with fresh bell pepper, if desired.

Bring the water and quinoa to a boil in a medium saucepan. Reduce to a simmer, cover and cook for 15 minutes. Fluff with a fork and set aside to cool completely.

In a medium bowl, combine the cooled quinoa, roasted peppers, feta, green onions and pine nuts. Whisk together the lemon juice, oil and black pepper. Fold dressing into the quinoa mixture. Serve.

PER SERVING: Energy 210 calories; Protein 7 g; Carbohydrates 23 g; Dietary Fiber 4 g; Fat 10 g; Sugar 2 g; Cholesterol 5 mg; Sodium 80 mg

SERVES 6

2 cups (500 mL) water

1 cup (250 mL) quinoa

1¼ cups (300 mL) chopped roasted red peppers (homemade or store-bought)

½ cup (125 mL) crumbled reduced-fat feta cheese

⅓ cup (75 mL) thinly sliced green onions

¼ cup (60 mL) pine nuts

2 Tbsp (30 mL) lemon juice

2 Tbsp (30 mL) olive oil or flaxseed oil

Pinch of freshly ground black pepper

ROASTED RED PEPPERS
It's easy to make your own roasted red peppers. Once you roast them yourself, you'll experience a flavor that cannot be beat. They can be used wherever you like, including on sandwiches and burgers and in salads, omelets and quiches. For this recipe, broil 2 red bell peppers in the oven on a baking sheet. The skin of the peppers will turn black and char. Turn the peppers gradually until the whole pepper has charred. Place the peppers in a covered bowl or closed paper bag. Allow to sit for 15 to 20 minutes for easy removal of the skin. Slice peppers in half and remove the seeds and skin. Peppers will keep in the refrigerator for up to 5 days.

RED CABBAGE & SPROUT SLAW

SERVES 8

2 cups (500 mL) quinoa sprouts
     (pages 10 and 11)

2 cups (500 mL) shredded red
     cabbage

2 cups (500 mL) grated carrots

½ cup (125 mL) sliced green onions

¾ cup (175 mL) reduced-fat or
     regular sour cream
     (gluten-free if required)

¼ cup (60 mL) liquid honey

3 Tbsp (45 mL) apple cider vinegar

1 Tbsp (15 mL) flaxseed oil or olive oil

¼ tsp (1 mL) salt (optional)

White pepper to taste

Need a healthy, crisp coleslaw that is creamy but without a heavy dressing? Make this one ahead, then mix with the dressing just before serving. This coleslaw is meant to be served alongside the delectable Smoky Chipotle BBQ Pulled Beef on page 146.

Combine the sprouts, cabbage, carrots and green onions in a large serving bowl. Set aside in the refrigerator if not serving immediately.

Whisk together the sour cream, honey, vinegar, oil, salt (if using) and white pepper. Set aside in the refrigerator if not serving immediately.

Just before serving, gently stir dressing into the vegetable mixture. Adjust seasoning if desired and serve.

PER SERVING: Energy 140 calories; Protein 4 g; Carbohydrates 27 g; Dietary Fiber 2 g; Fat 2.5 g; Sugar 10 g; Cholesterol 0 mg; Sodium 60 mg

Red cabbage is full of antioxidants that help the body eliminate toxins, prevent disease and illness and boost immunity.

SUMMER
VEGETABLE SALAD

Summer brings wonderful local produce to our tables. This salad features the classic combination of basil, zucchini and tomatoes.

Bring the water and quinoa to a boil in a medium saucepan. Reduce to a simmer, cover and cook for 15 minutes. Fluff with a fork and set aside to cool completely.

In a large salad bowl, mix the zucchini, tomatoes, bocconcini and cooled quinoa. Whisk together the oil, lemon juice, basil, garlic and salt. Pour dressing over the vegetable mixture and toss. Serve.

PER SERVING: Energy 200 calories; Protein 9 g; Carbohydrates 16 g; Dietary Fiber 2 g; Fat 12 g; Sugar 1 g; Cholesterol 10 mg; Sodium 75 mg

Try something different. Instead of using green zucchini, use young yellow zucchini for a brighter, even more beautiful salad.

SERVES 8

2 cups (500 mL) water

1 cup (250 mL) quinoa

1½ cups (375 mL) diced zucchini

1½ cups (375 mL) halved cherry or grape tomatoes

1 cup (250 mL) halved light small bocconcini cheese (one 200 g container)

¼ cup (60 mL) flaxseed oil or olive oil

¼ cup (60 mL) lemon juice

1 tsp (5 mL) finely chopped fresh basil

1 tsp (5 mL) minced garlic

¼ tsp (1 mL) salt

SWEET POTATO SALAD

SERVES 8

1½ cups (375 mL) water

¾ cup (175 mL) black quinoa

2½ cups (625 mL) peeled sweet
   potatoes cut into 1-inch
   (2.5 cm) chunks

½ cup (125 mL) thinly sliced
   green onions

½ cup (125 mL) chopped
   fresh parsley

⅓ cup (75 mL) toasted pecans

1½ tsp (7 mL) grated lemon zest

¼ cup (60 mL) lemon juice

¼ cup (60 mL) olive oil

¼ tsp (1 mL) ground ginger

¼ tsp (1 mL) salt (optional)

This high-contrast color combination will also delight your taste buds. The flavor combo of sweet potato, toasted pecans, green onions, lemon and quinoa will have you loving every bite. Black quinoa has the most dramatic appearance in this salad, but you can use any color.

Bring the water and quinoa to a boil in a small saucepan. Reduce to a simmer, cover and cook for 15 minutes. Fluff with a fork and set aside to cool.

Meanwhile, place the sweet potatoes in a medium saucepan with just enough water to cover. Bring to a boil, reduce to a simmer, cover and cook until potatoes are just tender (don't overcook). Drain the potatoes and cool completely.

Combine the quinoa and sweet potato with the green onions, parsley and pecans in a medium bowl. Whisk together the lemon zest, lemon juice, olive oil, ginger and salt (if using). Gently toss dressing with potato mixture until evenly distributed. Serve immediately or refrigerate.

PER SERVING: Energy 170 calories; Protein 3 g; Carbohydrates 15 g; Dietary Fiber 2 g; Fat 11 g; Sugar 2 g; Cholesterol 0 mg; Sodium 10 mg

To toast nuts, preheat the oven to 350°F (180°C). Spread the nuts on a baking sheet and toast in the oven, stirring once if necessary, for 5 to 7 minutes, until fragrant and lightly toasted.

TAHINI TOMATO SALAD

Tahini, a toasted sesame paste, makes a creamy, nutty addition to dressings, salads and even granola bars. Here it adds aromatic flair to a fresh tomato salad. Tahini can be found in the ethnic section of grocery or health-food stores.

Bring 1 cup (250 mL) water and the quinoa to a boil in a medium saucepan. Reduce to a simmer, cover and cook for 15 minutes. Fluff with a fork and set aside to cool.

Whisk together the lukewarm water and tahini in a small bowl. Add the lemon juice, mustard, garlic, pepper and salt (if using). Place the cooled quinoa in a salad bowl and toss with the dressing until evenly coated. Gently stir in the tomatoes, cucumber and red onion. Serve.

PER SERVING: Energy 110 calories; Protein 4 g; Carbohydrates 15 g; Dietary Fiber 2 g; Fat 5 g; Sugar 2 g; Cholesterol 0 mg; Sodium 30 mg

SERVES 6

1 cup (250 mL) water

½ cup (125 mL) quinoa

¼ cup (60 mL) lukewarm water

3 Tbsp (45 mL) tahini

2 Tbsp (30 mL) lemon juice

1 tsp (5 mL) Dijon mustard

½ tsp (2 mL) minced garlic

Pinch of freshly cracked
    black pepper

Pinch of salt (optional)

1½ cups (375 mL) diced
    fresh tomatoes

1½ cups (375 mL) diced
    English cucumber

⅓ cup (75 mL) diced red onion

TANGY LENTIL PEPPER SALAD

SERVES 6

2 cups (500 mL) water

⅔ cup (150 mL) quinoa

⅓ cup (75 mL) dried
    red lentils, rinsed

1 cup (250 mL) cooked chickpeas

1 cup (250 mL) chopped
    red bell pepper

½ cup (125 mL) sliced green onions

⅓ cup (75 mL) chopped
    fresh cilantro

3 Tbsp (45 mL) olive oil

2 Tbsp (30 mL) lemon juice

2 Tbsp (30 mL) apple cider vinegar

1 Tbsp (15 mL) liquid honey

Pinch each of curry powder and
    ground cardamom

¼ tsp (1 mL) salt (optional)

Red lentils cook quickly and make for an easy and different ingredient in this fresh salad along with red pepper, cilantro and green onions.

Combine the water and quinoa in a medium saucepan and bring to a boil. Reduce to a simmer, cover and cook for 10 minutes. Stir in the lentils and bring to a boil again. Reduce to a simmer, cover and cook for 8 more minutes or until the lentils are tender. Fluff with a fork and set aside to cool completely.

In a large bowl, combine the cooled quinoa mixture, chickpeas, red pepper, green onions and cilantro; mix well. Whisk together the olive oil, lemon juice, vinegar, honey, curry powder, cardamom and salt (if using). Pour dressing over the quinoa mixture and toss to coat thoroughly. Serve.

PER SERVING: Energy 230 calories; Protein 8 g; Carbohydrates 30 g; Dietary Fiber 5 g; Fat 9 g; Sugar 5 g; Cholesterol 0 mg; Sodium 100 mg

TUNA & WHITE KIDNEY BEAN SALAD

A fresh and high-protein salad for a wholesome lunch or a light dinner. White kidney beans are sometimes labeled cannellini beans.

Bring the water and quinoa to a boil in a medium saucepan. Reduce to a simmer, cover and cook for 15 minutes. Fluff with a fork and set aside to cool completely.

Combine the beans, celery, red pepper, green onions, tuna and quinoa in a medium bowl. Whisk together the olive oil, vinegar, mustard, basil, black pepper and salt (if using). Pour dressing over the bean mixture and stir until well combined.

Place romaine lettuce in a salad bowl or on a plate and scoop the tuna salad on top. Sprinkle with feta cheese (if using). Serve.

PER SERVING: Energy 260 calories; Protein 21 g; Carbohydrates 25 g; Dietary Fiber 6 g; Fat 8 g; Sugar 3 g; Cholesterol 25 mg; Sodium 135 mg

Cooked quinoa already on hand? Add 1½ cups (375 mL) cooked quinoa to the bean mixture in this salad.

SERVES 6

1 cup (250 mL) water

½ cup (125 mL) quinoa

1 can (19 oz/540 mL) white kidney
beans, drained and rinsed

½ cup (125 mL) chopped
celery hearts

½ cup (125 mL) chopped
red bell pepper

3 Tbsp (45 mL) chopped
green onions

2 cans (6 oz/170 g each)
sodium-reduced white
albacore tuna, drained

2 Tbsp (30 mL) olive oil

2 Tbsp (30 mL) balsamic vinegar

2 Tbsp (30 mL) Dijon mustard

1 Tbsp (15 mL) chopped fresh basil

¼ tsp (1 mL) black pepper

¼ tsp (1 mL) salt (optional)

4 cups (1 L) romaine lettuce
(or other salad greens)

½ cup (125 mL) crumbled feta
cheese (optional)

WALDORF SALAD

SERVES 8

2 cups (500 mL) water

1 cup (250 mL) quinoa

¾ cup (175 mL) halved red grapes

⅔ cup (150 mL) thinly sliced celery

½ cup (125 mL) thinly sliced
    green onions

½ cup (125 mL) halved fresh or
    thawed frozen cranberries

½ cup (125 mL) toasted
    walnut pieces

½ cup (125 mL) freshly
    squeezed orange juice

2 Tbsp (30 mL) flaxseed oil

¼ tsp (1 mL) salt (optional)

Pinch of cinnamon

¾ cup (175 mL) cored
    and diced apple

This flavorful recipe is a modern take on the classic Waldorf salad. It can be an everyday salad or it can be served at Christmas, Thanksgiving dinner or brunch. This recipe tastes great and looks even better if you use half white and half black quinoa.

Bring the water and quinoa to a boil in a medium saucepan. Reduce to a simmer, cover and cook for 15 minutes. Fluff with a fork and set aside to cool.

In a medium bowl, combine the cooled quinoa with the grapes, celery, green onions, cranberries and walnut pieces. In a small bowl, whisk together the orange juice, oil, salt (if using) and cinnamon. Toss diced apple in dressing, then toss dressing and apples together with the quinoa mixture. This salad is best served after resting for about 2 hours in the refrigerator but can be served right away.

PER SERVING: Energy 190 calories; Protein 5 g; Carbohydrates 22 g; Dietary Fiber 3 g; Fat 10 g; Sugar 6 g; Cholesterol 0 mg; Sodium 10 mg

- Cooked quinoa already on hand? Add 3 cups (750 mL) to the salad ingredients in this recipe.

- To toast nuts, preheat the oven to 350°F (180°C). Spread the nuts on a baking sheet and toast in the oven, stirring once if necessary, for 5 to 7 minutes, until fragrant and lightly toasted.

BAKED ROASTED
RED PEPPER DIP

Fluffy cooked quinoa puréed with meaty roasted peppers and creamy feta adds plenty of hidden nutrition to this favorite dip. Serve with yummy dippers like cucumber and other vegetables, fresh pita or tortilla chips.

Preheat the oven to 350°F (180°C). Spray or grease an 8-inch (20 cm) square baking dish.

Bring the water and quinoa to a boil in a medium saucepan. Reduce to a simmer, cover and cook for 15 minutes. The quinoa must be extra-fluffy. Fluff with a fork and let cool slightly.

In a food processor or using a hand blender, purée the quinoa with ¾ cup (175 mL) of the feta. Add the red peppers and garlic; process until smooth. Pour mixture into the baking dish and top with the remaining feta.

Bake for 20 to 22 minutes, until the top and edges are beginning to brown. Serve warm with your favorite dipping treats.

PER SERVING: Energy 80 calories; Protein 4 g; Carbohydrates 6 g; Dietary Fiber 1 g; Fat 4 g; Sugar 1 g; Cholesterol 15 mg; Sodium 220 mg

SERVES 8

⅔ cup (150 mL) water

⅓ cup (75 mL) quinoa

1 cup (250 mL) crumbled feta cheese

1¼ cups (300 mL) roasted red peppers (page 63 or store-bought)

1 tsp (5 mL) minced garlic

> Extra-fluffy cooked quinoa already on hand? Purée 1 cup (250 mL) extra-fluffy cooked quinoa with the feta.

BAKED SPINACH PARMESAN ARANCINI

MAKES 2 DOZEN ARANCINI

1 ⅓ cups (325 mL) water

⅔ cup (150 mL) white quinoa

½ cup (125 mL) dry white wine

1 cup (250 mL) chopped
    fresh spinach

1 tsp (5 mL) minced garlic

1 cup (250 mL) grated
    Parmesan cheese

2 Tbsp (30 mL) basil pesto

3 oz (85 g) fresh mozzarella cheese

2 eggs

¾ cup (175 mL) fine rice flour or
    whole wheat flour

¾ cup (175 mL) fine dry bread
    crumbs (gluten-free if required)

Warm marinara sauce for dipping
    (optional)

The arancini balls will not change much in color while cooking. Keep an eye on the balls and take them out of the oven if you see any cheese bubbling out. You don't want to overcook them.

Traditional arancini are fried rice balls that originate from Italy. Enjoy this baked version. Serve warm dipped in marinara sauce for an appetizer that doesn't stay around long! Prepare them the day before for an oven-ready appetizer.

Bring the water and quinoa to a boil in a medium saucepan. Reduce to a simmer, cover and cook for 15 minutes. Turn off the burner and let quinoa sit, covered, for another 10 minutes (quinoa should be light and fluffy). Fluff with a fork and set aside.

In a medium skillet, bring the wine to a boil. Reduce heat to medium-low and add the quinoa, spinach and garlic, stirring until the wine has evaporated or been absorbed (the quinoa-spinach mixture should be more dry than wet). Remove from the heat and add the Parmesan and pesto; stir until the cheese is melted. Pour the mixture onto a baking sheet and cool completely.

Cut the mozzarella into twenty-four ½-inch (1 cm) cubes. Take 1 Tbsp (15 mL) of the quinoa mixture and shape it into a ball in the palm of your hand. Press a piece of mozzarella cheese into the center and firmly press the quinoa around it to seal. Repeat and then refrigerate the balls for at least 1 hour.

Preheat the oven to 400°F (200°C). Line a baking sheet with parchment.

In a shallow dish, whisk the eggs. Place the flour and bread crumbs in two separate shallow dishes. Using one hand for wet ingredients and one for dry, roll each ball in the flour, then the egg (letting excess drip off) and finally the bread crumbs, coating thoroughly. Place 1 inch (2.5 cm) apart on the baking sheet.

Bake for 7 to 10 minutes. Serve immediately with warm marinara sauce.

PER SERVING: Energy 80 calories; Protein 4 g; Carbohydrates 8 g; Dietary Fiber 1 g; Fat 3 g; Sugar 0 g; Cholesterol 20 mg; Sodium 85 mg

APPLE CHEDDAR MUFFINS

Fresh thyme adds a surprising flavor to these apple and Cheddar muffins. They're a great portable food to take for lunch or anywhere on the run. Serve as an anytime snack, for brunch or as a breakfast muffin.

Preheat the oven to 400°F (200°C). Lightly grease a 12-cup muffin pan or line with paper liners.

In a medium bowl, whisk together the quinoa flour, baking powder, baking soda and salt. Add the apples and shredded cheese; stir until well combined. In a large bowl, beat the eggs. Stir in the applesauce, sugar, butter, buttermilk and thyme. Add the applesauce mixture to the flour mixture; gently stir just until blended. Use a large spoon or ice-cream scoop to divide the batter evenly among the muffin cups.

Bake for 18 minutes or until a toothpick inserted into the center of a muffin comes out with only one or two crumbs. Cool in the pan.

PER SERVING: Energy 180 calories; Protein 6 g; Carbohydrates 19 g; Dietary Fiber 2 g; Fat 8 g; Sugar 7 g; Cholesterol 50 mg; Sodium 190 mg

MAKES 12 MUFFINS

1½ cups (375 mL) quinoa flour

1½ tsp (7 mL) baking powder

½ tsp (2 mL) baking soda

¼ tsp (1 mL) salt

1 cup (250 mL) chopped peeled apples

1 cup (250 mL) shredded reduced-fat aged Cheddar cheese

2 large eggs

1 cup (250 mL) unsweetened applesauce

¼ cup (60 mL) organic cane sugar or white sugar

¼ cup (60 mL) unsalted butter, softened

¼ cup (60 mL) buttermilk

1 tsp (5 mL) chopped fresh thyme

We highly recommend using fresh thyme, but if you don't have fresh you can always use ½ tsp (2 mL) dried thyme.

BELL PEPPER MUFFINS
WITH CURRANTS

MAKES 12 MUFFINS

1 tsp (5 mL) grapeseed oil
or vegetable oil

⅓ cup (75 mL) chopped
red bell pepper

⅓ cup (75 mL) chopped
yellow bell pepper

¼ cup (60 mL) chopped
green onions

½ tsp (2 mL) minced garlic

1½ cups (375 mL) quinoa flour

2 Tbsp (30 mL) organic
cane sugar or white sugar

1½ tsp (7 mL) baking powder

¼ tsp (1 mL) baking soda

¼ tsp (1 mL) salt

¼ cup (60 mL) cold unsalted
butter, cut into small pieces

⅓ cup (75 mL) dried currants

½ tsp (2 mL) dried basil

2 large eggs

⅔ cup (150 mL) low-fat plain yogurt

¼ cup (60 mL) unsweetened
applesauce

These savory quinoa muffins are filled with sautéed bell peppers and onions and accented with sweet currants. Warm or cold, they make a great take-out breakfast or mid-morning snack.

Preheat the oven to 350°F (180°C). Lightly grease or spray a 12-cup muffin pan or line with paper liners.

In a medium saucepan on medium heat, heat the oil. Cook the red and yellow peppers, green onions and garlic until the peppers and onions have softened, about 5 minutes. Set aside to cool slightly.

In a large bowl, combine the quinoa flour, sugar, baking powder, baking soda and salt. Using your fingers or a pastry blender, cut in the cold butter until the mixture resembles bread crumbs. Stir in the currants and basil.

In a medium bowl, beat the eggs. Whisk in the yogurt and applesauce. Stir in the pepper mixture. Add the egg mixture to the flour mixture and stir until batter is just moistened.

Use a large spoon or ice-cream scoop to divide the batter evenly among the muffin cups. Bake for 20 minutes or until a toothpick inserted into the center of a muffin comes out clean. Cool in the pan.

PER SERVING: Energy 140 calories; Protein 4 g; Carbohydrates 18 g; Dietary Fiber 2 g; Fat 6 g; Sugar 7 g; Cholesterol 40 mg; Sodium 160 mg

OREGANO, OLIVE & FETA STUFFED TOMATOES

Healthy appetizers needed for a healthy crowd? This recipe doubles easily if required. It is possible to use cherry tomatoes, but because they are slightly smaller, they are more challenging to prepare.

Bring the water and quinoa to a boil in a small saucepan. Reduce to a simmer, cover and cook for 15 minutes. Fluff with a fork and set aside to cool completely.

Slice the tomatoes in half. Using a small spoon, scoop out the insides (see Tip).

In a medium bowl, combine the quinoa, green pepper, feta, olives and red onion. Stir in the oil, vinegar and oregano until evenly mixed. Scoop ½ teaspoon (2 mL) of filling into each tomato half and arrange on a tray. Serve.

PER SERVING (5 pieces): Energy 60 calories; Protein 2 g; Carbohydrates 6 g; Dietary Fiber 1 g; Fat 3 g; Sugar 2 g; Cholesterol 5 mg; Sodium 70 mg

MAKES 42 TOMATOES

⅔ cup (150 mL) water

⅓ cup (75 mL) quinoa

1 lb (450 g) cocktail tomatoes

¼ cup (60 mL) finely diced green bell pepper

¼ cup (60 mL) crumbled feta cheese

¼ cup (60 mL) finely chopped pitted black olives

2 Tbsp (30 mL) finely diced red onion

4 tsp (20 mL) olive oil or flaxseed oil

4 tsp (20 mL) red wine vinegar

1½ tsp (7 mL) finely chopped fresh oregano (or ½ tsp/2 mL dried)

Freeze the tomato insides to use in chili or tomato sauce.

SMOKED WILD PACIFIC SALMON, CUCUMBER & QUINOA SPROUT BITES

MAKES 54 BITES

4 oz (115 g) light or regular
   cream cheese

2 Tbsp (30 mL) reduced-fat
   or regular sour cream
   (gluten-free if required)

1 English cucumber, cut into 54 slices
   each ¼ inch (5 mm) thick

½ cup (125 mL) black quinoa
   sprouts (pages 10 and 11)

4 ½ oz (125 g) smoked wild
   Pacific salmon, torn or
   cut into 54 squares each
   1 inch (2.5 cm) wide

Freshly cracked black pepper
   (optional)

54 small sprigs fresh dill

An entertaining favorite, this combination of cucumber, cream cheese and smoked salmon is always a hit. Sprouted black quinoa makes a dramatic appearance and tastes fantastic on these stunning appetizers.

Whip together the cream cheese and sour cream. Place mixture in a piping bag fitted with a small star tip or in a resealable plastic bag. If using a plastic bag, cut ¼ inch (5 mm) off one corner.

Spread out the cucumber slices on a tray and place ½ tsp (2 mL) of sprouts on each. Place a piece of salmon on top of the quinoa sprouts. Pipe ½ tsp (2 mL) swirl of cream cheese mixture on each and grind some pepper (if using) over the tops. Garnish with a small sprig of dill. Keep refrigerated, and serve in small quantities to keep them cool.

PER SERVING: Energy 15 calories; Protein 1 g; Carbohydrates 1 g; Dietary Fiber 0 g; Fat 1 g; Sugar 0 g; Cholesterol 5 mg; Sodium 25 mg

THAI CHICKEN FINGERS

¾ cup (175 mL) low-fat plain yogurt

1 tsp (5 mL) minced garlic

¾ tsp (4 mL) curry powder

½ tsp (2 mL) salt (optional)

¾ cup (175 mL) quinoa flakes

⅓ cup (75 mL) unsweetened
    shredded coconut

¼ cup (60 mL) chopped
    fresh cilantro

1½ lb (675 g) boneless, skinless
    chicken breasts

These tasty chicken fingers are baked, not fried. They can be eaten as a main dish or as an appetizer. Delicious served with a sweet chili dipping sauce.

Preheat the oven to 450°F (230°C). Line the baking sheet with parchment paper.

Stir together the yogurt, garlic, curry powder and salt (if using) in a shallow dish. In another shallow dish, stir together the quinoa flakes, coconut and cilantro.

Cut chicken breasts crosswise into ½-inch (1 cm) slices. Using one hand for dipping (yogurt mixture) and the other for coating (flake mixture), dip one piece of chicken in the yogurt, coating all sides, then repeat with the flakes. Place on a baking sheet 1½ inches (4 cm) apart. Repeat with the remaining chicken.

Bake for 15 minutes or until the center is no longer pink. Serve immediately with a sweet chili dipping sauce.

PER SERVING: Energy 220 calories; Protein 27 g; Carbohydrates 11 g; Dietary Fiber 1 g; Fat 7 g; Sugar 2 g; Cholesterol 75 mg; Sodium 250 mg

APRICOT, PINE NUT & ROSEMARY DRESSING

Try this stuffing-style dressing with your next chicken dinner. Make the quinoa-onion mixture an hour before and toss with the remaining ingredients just before serving.

Heat the oil in a large saucepan on medium-low heat. Add the onions and cook for 7 minutes or until tender and opaque. Add the stock and quinoa. Bring it to a boil. Reduce to a simmer, cover and cook for 15 minutes or until the quinoa is tender.

If not serving immediately, transfer quinoa to a small baking dish, cover and keep warm in a 200°F (100°C) oven for up to 1 hour.

Just before serving, stir in the apricots, pine nuts, butter, parsley, rosemary, lemon zest, salt (if using) and pepper.

PER SERVING: Energy 170 calories; Protein 5 g; Carbohydrates 26 g; Dietary Fiber 3 g; Fat 6 g; Sugar 4 g; Cholesterol 5 mg; Sodium 55 mg

SERVES 6

1 tsp (5 mL) grapeseed oil or vegetable oil

½ cup (125 mL) chopped onions

2 cups (500 mL) vegetable or chicken stock

1 cup (250 mL) quinoa

⅓ cup (75 mL) diced dried apricots

3 Tbsp (45 mL) pine nuts

2 tsp (10 mL) unsalted butter

2 Tbsp (30 mL) chopped fresh parsley (or 2 tsp/10 mL dried)

¾ tsp (4 mL) minced fresh rosemary (or ¼ tsp/1 mL dried)

¼ tsp (1 mL) grated lemon zest

¼ tsp (1 mL) salt (if desired)

Pinch of black pepper

CRANBERRY, HAZELNUT & SAUSAGE DRESSING

Tangy cranberries, apple pieces, hazelnuts and Italian sausage blended with seasoned quinoa make a wonderful gluten-free alternative to any traditional turkey stuffing.

SERVES 8

1 Tbsp (15 mL) grapeseed oil or vegetable oil

½ lb (225 g) Homemade Italian Ground Sausage (recipe follows)

1 cup (250 mL) chopped celery

1 leek (white part only), halved lengthwise and sliced

2 cups (500 mL) sodium-reduced chicken or turkey stock

1 cup (250 mL) quinoa

1 Granny Smith apple, cored and diced

⅓ cup (75 mL) water

¼ cup (60 mL) sweetened dried cranberries

½ cup (125 mL) coarsely chopped hazelnuts

2 Tbsp (30 mL) chopped fresh parsley (or 1½ tsp/7 mL dried)

1 tsp (5 mL) minced fresh thyme (or ¼ tsp/1 mL dried)

1 tsp (5 mL) minced fresh sage (or ¼ tsp/1 mL ground sage)

¼ tsp (1 mL) salt (optional)

Pinch of pepper

Heat the oil in a large saucepan on medium heat. Add the sausage meat and cook until browned and no pink remains. Reduce heat to medium-low and stir in the celery and leek. Cover and cook for another 7 minutes or until the celery is tender (add a spoonful of water if pan is dry). Add the stock, quinoa, apple and ⅓ cup (75 mL) water. Bring to a boil. Reduce to a simmer, cover and cook for 20 minutes. Remove from the heat and let sit, covered, for another 5 minutes. Just before serving, stir in the cranberries, hazelnuts, parsley, thyme, sage, salt (if using) and pepper.

HOMEMADE ITALIAN GROUND SAUSAGE

Freeze any unused portion of this recipe for up to 3 months.

Makes 1 lb (450 g)

¼ tsp (1 mL) fennel seeds

1 lb (450 g) ground turkey, chicken or pork

¼ cup (60 mL) finely chopped onions

1 Tbsp (15 mL) chopped fresh oregano (or 1 tsp/5 mL dried)

1 Tbsp (15 mL) chopped fresh parsley (or 1 tsp /5 mL dried)

1 tsp (5 mL) minced garlic

½ tsp (2 mL) salt (optional)

¼ tsp (1 mL) ground coriander

¼ tsp (1 mL) black pepper

Pinch of cayenne pepper

Break up the fennel seeds with a mortar and pestle or crush with a rolling pin in a resealable plastic bag. Combine all the ingredients and mix well.

PER SERVING (including sausage filling): Energy 130 calories; Protein 4 g; Carbohydrates 19 g; Dietary Fiber 3 g; Fat 4.5 g; Sugar 3 g; Cholesterol 19 mg; Sodium 45 mg

ITALIAN SAUSAGE ROUNDS

Italian sausage rounds can be used wherever you would normally use regular Italian sausage. Fry in a small amount of oil or bake for an even lower-fat option. The cooked sausage patties can also be frozen for up to 1 month.

Bring the water and quinoa to a boil in a small saucepan. Reduce to a simmer, cover and cook for 15 minutes. Remove from the heat and keep covered for another 10 minutes. Fluff with a fork. Set aside to cool completely.

In a medium bowl, mix together the cooled quinoa and the sausage mixture.

PAN-FRY METHOD Heat the oil in a large skillet on medium-low heat. Scoop out ¼ cup (60 mL) servings of sausage mixture and with wet hands shape into rounds 1 inch (2.5 cm) thick. Fry for about 4 minutes on each side, until cooked through and golden brown. Serve.

OVEN METHOD Preheat the oven to 350°F (180°C). Line a baking sheet with parchment. Scoop out ¼ cup (60 mL) servings of sausage mixture and with wet hands shape into rounds 3 inches (8 cm) wide and ½ inch (1 cm) thick. Arrange on the baking sheet about 1½ inches (4 cm) apart. Bake for 10 minutes per side. Serve.

PER SERVING: Energy 200 calories; Protein 20 g; Carbohydrates 9 g; Dietary Fiber 1 g; Fat 10 g; Sugar 0 g; Cholesterol 65 mg; Sodium 55 mg

MAKES 10 ROUNDS, SERVING 5

⅔ cup (150 mL) water

⅓ cup (75 mL) quinoa

1 lb (450 g) Homemade Italian Ground Sausage (page 80)

2 tsp (10 mL) grapeseed oil

JALAPEÑO CORNBREAD

MAKES 24 PIECES

1½ cups (375 mL) quinoa flour

1½ cups (375 mL) yellow cornmeal

¼ cup (60 mL) organic
    cane sugar or white sugar

4 tsp (20 mL) baking powder

½ tsp (2 mL) baking soda

1 tsp (5 mL) salt

2½ cups (625 mL) buttermilk

3 large eggs

6 Tbsp (90 mL) unsalted
    butter, melted

3 Tbsp (45 mL) finely chopped
    pickled jalapeño peppers

Enhance any feast with this moist cornbread. Serve it warm, either plain or with butter. If you don't like jalapeño peppers, this cornbread is still tasty without them.

Preheat the oven to 400°F (200°C). Grease a 13- × 9-inch (3 L) baking pan.

In a large bowl, combine the flour, cornmeal, sugar, baking powder, baking soda and salt. In a medium bowl, whisk together the buttermilk and eggs until well blended. Add the melted butter and jalapeños to buttermilk mixture. Mix well. Add buttermilk mixture to flour mixture and stir just until mixed.

Pour batter into pan. Bake for 20 to 22 minutes or until edges are golden brown and a toothpick inserted into the center comes out clean. Cut lengthwise into 4 strips and cut each strip into 6 pieces. Serve warm.

PER SERVING: Energy 120 calories; Protein 3 g; Carbohydrates 15 g; Dietary Fiber 2 g; Fat 5 g; Sugar 3 g; Cholesterol 35 mg; Sodium 170 mg

No buttermilk on hand? Add 1 Tbsp (15 mL) of lemon juice or white vinegar to every 1 cup (250 mL) of milk, stir and let stand for 5 minutes. Use as directed.

INDIAN-INFUSED QUINOA

Cardamom and cinnamon flavors make this side a great accompaniment to any Indian main dish. It is paired fabulously with Chicken Masala on page 124.

Melt the butter in a medium saucepan on medium heat. Stir in the cardamom pods and bay leaf; heat for 30 seconds. Add the quinoa and stir to coat all the seeds with the butter. Add the water, carrots, cinnamon and salt. Bring to a boil on high heat, then reduce to a simmer, cover and cook for 15 minutes. Turn the heat off and let sit, covered, for another 10 minutes. Discard the cardamom pods and bay leaf and serve.

PER SERVING: Energy 170 calories; Protein 5 g; Carbohydrates 21 g; Dietary Fiber 3 g; Fat 8 g; Sugar 0 g; Cholesterol 15 mg; Sodium 105 mg

SERVES 4

2 Tbsp (30 mL) butter

4 cardamom pods, cracked but not completely broken (or ¼ tsp/1 mL ground cardamom)

½ bay leaf

¾ cup (175 mL) quinoa

1½ cups (375 mL) water

¼ cup (60 mL) finely diced carrots

Pinch of cinnamon

Pinch of salt

JALAPEÑO & CHILI QUINOA PILAF

SERVES 6

1 Tbsp (15 mL) vegetable oil

¼ cup (60 mL) diced onions

¾ cup (175 mL) quinoa

2 cups (500 mL) sodium-reduced chicken or vegetable stock

1 small jalapeño pepper, seeded and diced

1 clove garlic, minced

¼ cup (60 mL) chopped canned green chili peppers

¼ tsp (1 mL) ground cumin

⅓ cup (75 mL) shredded aged white Cheddar or mozzarella cheese

½ cup (125 mL) chopped fresh cilantro

This pilaf packs serious flavor with only a bit of heat, making it perfect alongside any meat dish, any southwestern-style dish or even all by itself for lunch.

Heat the oil in a large saucepan on medium-low heat. Add the onions and cook until translucent and lightly browned. Add the quinoa and cook for 2 to 3 minutes, until the quinoa is slightly toasted. Pour the stock into the pan, then gently stir in the jalapeño, garlic, chilies and cumin. Bring to a boil. Reduce to a simmer, cover and cook for 15 minutes. Turn the heat off and let sit, covered, for another 5 minutes. Mix in the cheese, stirring slowly until melted and well combined. Stir in the cilantro. Serve immediately. Pilaf keeps, covered and refrigerated, for up to 2 days.

PER SERVING: Energy 130 calories; Protein 6 g; Carbohydrates 16 g; Dietary Fiber 2 g; Fat 4.5 g; Sugar 1 g; Cholesterol 0 mg; Sodium 95 mg

Reduce the amount of cheese you use by using an older, sharper cheese. Aged cheese has more flavor, so you need less.

LEMON QUINOA

The light, buttery lemon taste of this side dish makes it a great partner alongside almost any main course. Subtle flavor, and wonderfully simple to prepare.

Bring the stock and quinoa to a boil in a large saucepan. Add the butter, lemon zest, lemon juice and salt. Reduce to a simmer, cover and cook for 15 minutes. Fluff with a fork. Add the parsley and stir well. Serve immediately.

PER SERVING: Energy 190 calories; Protein 6 g; Carbohydrates 30 g; Dietary Fiber 4 g; Fat 5 g; Sugar 1 g; Cholesterol 10 mg; Sodium 220 mg

SERVES 4

2 cups (500 mL) sodium-reduced vegetable stock

1 cup (250 mL) quinoa

1 Tbsp (15 mL) unsalted butter

2 tsp (10 mL) grated lemon zest

2 Tbsp (30 mL) lemon juice

¼ tsp (1 mL) salt

1 Tbsp (15 mL) chopped fresh parsley

Try Meyer lemons! Increasingly available, this cross between a lemon and mandarin or tangerine results in a less acidic, sweeter version that is such a treat!

REVOLUTIONIZE
SOUPS & STEWS

REVOLUTIONIZE SOUPS & STEWS

Quinoa makes an excellent soup ingredient. The whimsy of curly cooked quinoa seeds adds a fanciful touch to any broth soup. Try Chili, Lime & Kale Soup with Aged White Cheddar (page 95). Puréed quinoa mimics a thick and indulgent consistency you'd mistake for a heavy cream soup. Try Butternut Squash & Pear Soup (page 94) or Lemongrass, Sweet Potato & Coconut Stew (page 106).

One quick trip to the farmer's market or the grocery store and you can make warm and wholesome soups that deliver tremendous nutritional benefit with maximum flavor any time of the year. Prepared in advance and refrigerated or frozen, quinoa soups can be quickly reheated on busy weeknights or lazy weekend afternoons.

ARTICHOKE SOUP

SERVES 6

1 cup (250 mL) quinoa

1 Tbsp (15 mL) grapeseed oil or
    unsalted butter

½ cup (125 mL) chopped onions

1 tsp (5 mL) minced garlic

2 Tbsp (30 mL) lemon juice

4 cups (1 L) sodium-reduced
    chicken or vegetable stock

1 can (14 oz/398 mL) artichoke
    hearts, drained

1 bay leaf

½ cup (125 mL) 1% or 2% milk
    or cream

1 tsp (5 mL) organic cane sugar
    or white sugar

¼ tsp (1 mL) salt (optional)

½ tsp (2 mL) black pepper

The smoky flavor of artichoke hearts and the sweet scent of bay leaf make this soup a warm comfort food that engages all your senses. To add even more flavor, top with fresh bacon bits or browned sausage chunks. Serve with crostini or chewy whole-grain baguette.

Place the quinoa in a large dry saucepan on medium heat. Toast the quinoa, stirring frequently, until fragrant, about 5 minutes. Transfer the quinoa to a bowl and set aside.

Heat the oil in the same saucepan and cook the onions and garlic until the onions are opaque and tender, 7 to 8 minutes. Add the toasted quinoa, lemon juice and stock. Bring to a boil, reduce to a simmer, cover and cook until the quinoa is tender, about 15 minutes.

Add the artichoke hearts and bay leaf; simmer for another 5 minutes. Discard the bay leaf. Purée the soup with a hand blender or cool slightly and purée in two batches in a blender or food processor. Return soup to the saucepan. Add the milk and sugar, stirring thoroughly. Season with salt (if using) and pepper. Serve.

PER SERVING: Energy 190 calories; Protein 10 g; Carbohydrates 27 g; Dietary Fiber 2 g; Fat 5 g; Sugar 3 g; Cholesterol 0 mg; Sodium 200 mg

ASPARAGUS QUINOA SOUP

This vibrant soup's asparagus flavor is complemented by fresh lemon, parsley and creamy Parmesan cheese. Puréed quinoa makes this such a luxuriously thick soup, you can even skip the milk if you choose.

Place the quinoa in a large dry saucepan on medium heat. Toast the quinoa, stirring frequently, until fragrant, about 5 minutes. Transfer the quinoa to a bowl and set aside.

Melt the butter in the same saucepan. Cook the onions and celery until the onions are opaque and tender, 7 to 8 minutes. Add the toasted quinoa, asparagus, stock, parsley, lemon zest and lemon juice. Bring to a boil, reduce to a simmer, cover and cook until the quinoa is tender, 15 to 18 minutes.

Remove 6 to 8 of the cooked asparagus tips and set aside. Purée the soup with a hand blender or cool slightly and purée in two batches in a blender or food processor. Return soup to the saucepan. Stir in the milk, Parmesan and mustard. Season with salt (if using), black pepper and cayenne. Add the reserved asparagus tips and reheat gently before serving.

PER SERVING: Energy 220 calories; Protein 9 g; Carbohydrates 29 g; Dietary Fiber 8 g; Fat 8 g; Sugar 8 g; Cholesterol 20 mg; Sodium 200 mg

SERVES 4

½ cup (125 mL) quinoa

2 Tbsp (30 mL) unsalted butter

½ cup (125 mL) chopped onions

¼ cup (60 mL) diced celery

2 lb (900 g) fresh asparagus, trimmed and cut into 1-inch (2.5 cm) pieces

4 cups (1 L) reduced-sodium vegetable or chicken stock

1 Tbsp (15 mL) chopped fresh parsley

2 tsp (10 mL) grated lemon zest

1 Tbsp (15 mL) lemon juice

⅓ cup (75 mL) 2% milk, whole milk or cream

1 Tbsp (15 mL) grated Parmesan cheese

½ tsp (2 mL) Dijon mustard

¼ tsp (1 mL) salt (optional)

Pinch of black pepper

Pinch of cayenne pepper

BUTTERNUT SQUASH & PEAR SOUP

Not at all shy, this thick, golden soup of blended butternut squash, pear and quinoa is accented with the sharp gusto of crumbled blue cheese—a splendid flavor combination.

SERVES 6

1 Tbsp (15 mL) unsalted butter

½ cup (125 mL) chopped onions

1 tsp (5 mL) minced garlic

¼ tsp (1 mL) salt

½ cup (125 mL) quinoa

3 cups (750 mL) diced
butternut squash

3½ cups (875 mL) sodium-reduced
chicken stock

2 cups (500 mL) chopped
fresh pears

½ cup (125 mL) whole milk or
whipping cream

½ tsp (2 mL) ground sage

2 Tbsp (30 mL) crumbled blue
cheese, such as Stilton
(gluten-free if required)

Melt the butter in a large saucepan on medium heat. Add the onions, garlic and salt. Cook until the onions are opaque and tender, 7 to 8 minutes. Add the quinoa, butternut squash and stock. Bring to a boil, reduce to a simmer, cover and cook until the quinoa is tender and the squash is cooked, 15 to 18 minutes. Add the pears.

Purée the soup with a hand blender or cool slightly and purée in two batches in a blender or food processor. Return soup to the saucepan. Stir in the milk and sage. Garnish each bowl of soup with 1 tsp (5 mL) of blue cheese. Serve.

PER SERVING: Energy 180 calories; Protein 7 g; Carbohydrates 30 g; Dietary Fiber 4 g; Fat 5 g; Sugar 9 g; Cholesterol 10 mg; Sodium 190 mg

CHILI, LIME & KALE SOUP
WITH AGED WHITE CHEDDAR

The powerhouse superfood kale is full of vitamin A, vitamin C, calcium and iron and tastes fabulous with lime and aged Cheddar. This quick and easy soup looks dramatic and bold when made with black quinoa.

Heat the oil in a large saucepan on medium-low heat. Stir in the onions and cook, covered, for 7 to 10 minutes, until the onions start to soften. (If the pan gets dry, add a few spoonfuls of water.) Add the garlic and chilies. Cook for another minute. Add the kale, stock, water and quinoa. Bring to a boil, reduce to a simmer, cover and cook for 15 to 20 minutes, until the quinoa is tender. Stir in the lime zest and salt (if using). Serve hot topped with a sprinkle of Cheddar cheese.

PER SERVING: Energy 190 calories; Protein 8 g; Carbohydrates 28 g; Dietary Fiber 5 g; Fat 6 g; Sugar 4 g; Cholesterol 0 mg; Sodium 230 mg

SERVES 4

1 Tbsp (15 mL) grapeseed oil or vegetable oil

1 cup (250 mL) chopped onions

1½ tsp (7 mL) minced garlic

1 to 4 tsp (5 to 20 mL) minced seeded serrano chili or jalapeño pepper

4 cups (1 L) chopped kale, center ribs and stems removed (1 large bunch)

4 cups (1 L) sodium-reduced vegetable or chicken stock

1 cup (250 mL) water

½ cup (125 mL) quinoa

2 tsp (10 mL) grated lime zest

¼ tsp (1 mL) salt (optional)

⅓ cup (75 mL) shredded aged white Cheddar cheese

CHIPOTLE CORN CHOWDER

1 Tbsp (15 mL) grapeseed oil
   or vegetable oil

1 cup (250 mL) chopped onions

¾ cup (175 mL) chopped celery

2 cups (500 mL) fresh or
   thawed frozen corn

1¼ cups (300 mL) peeled
   and diced potatoes

½ cup (125 mL) chopped
   green bell pepper

¾ cup (175 mL) chopped
   red bell pepper

¼ cup (60 mL) tomato paste

¾ tsp (4 mL) minced garlic

½ tsp (2 mL) Worcestershire sauce
   (gluten-free if required)

½ tsp (2 mL) paprika

¼ tsp (1 mL) white pepper

¼ tsp (1 mL) ground chipotle pepper

4 cups (1 L) sodium-reduced
   vegetable or chicken stock

½ cup (125 mL) whole milk or
   10% cream

⅓ cup (75 mL) quinoa flour

Salt (optional) and black
   pepper to taste

With more than just corn, this medley of vegetable flavors comes together perfectly with the subtle heat and smokiness of chipotle pepper. This recipe requires only a small amount of chipotle, but a little goes a long way. Look for ground chipotle pepper in the spice section of the grocery store.

Heat a large saucepan on medium-high heat. Add the oil and reduce the heat to medium-low. Add the onions and celery. Cook for 7 minutes or until the onions are opaque and the celery is tender. Add the corn, potatoes, green pepper, red pepper, tomato paste, garlic, Worcestershire sauce, paprika, white pepper, chipotle pepper and stock. Increase the heat to a boil, then reduce to a simmer, cover and cook for 15 minutes or until the potatoes are tender.

Whisk together the milk and flour in a small bowl. Slowly stir the mixture into the hot chowder. Allow about 3 to 5 minutes to thicken. Season with salt (if using) and pepper if necessary. Serve.

PER SERVING: Energy 170 calories; Protein 5 g; Carbohydrates 32 g; Dietary Fiber 5 g; Fat 4 g; Sugar 8 g; Cholesterol 0 mg; Sodium 135 mg

FENNEL CREAM SOUP

SERVES 6

2 cups (500 mL) sodium-reduced
vegetable stock

1 cup (250 mL) whole milk

½ cup (125 mL) quinoa

2 cups (500 mL) chopped fennel
(about 1 medium bulb)

1 Tbsp (15 mL) chopped
fennel fronds

2 tsp (10 mL) minced garlic

½ tsp (5 mL) salt (optional)

Pinch of black pepper

⅓ cup (75 mL) toasted pine nuts

Enjoy the sweet, subtle taste of anise in a creamy soup, thickened with quinoa and topped with toasted pine nuts. If you use vegetable stock that contains sodium, skip the salt in the recipe.

In a large saucepan on high heat, bring the stock, milk, quinoa, fennel, fennel fronds and garlic to a boil. Reduce to a simmer and cook for 15 minutes. Remove from the heat and let cool for 5 to 10 minutes. Purée the soup with a hand blender or in a blender or food processor. Return soup to the saucepan. Season with salt (if using) and pepper. Reheat before serving. Top each bowl with a sprinkle of toasted pine nuts and serve.

PER SERVING: Energy 130 calories; Protein 5 g; Carbohydrates 15 g; Dietary Fiber 3 g; Fat 5 g; Sugar 3 g; Cholesterol 5 mg; Sodium 85 mg

To toast nuts, preheat the oven to 350°F (180°C). Spread the nuts on a baking sheet and toast in the oven, stirring once if necessary, for 5 to 7 minutes, until fragrant and lightly toasted.

GINGERED CITRUS CARROT SOUP

Carrots shine in this inexpensive but extraordinary soup that is one of our favorites. Ginger, garlic and citrus zest dress it up, and you can make it even more delicious with cream and a final sprinkle of chives. Use a slow cooker if desired.

Heat a large saucepan on medium-low heat. Add the oil and onions. Cover and cook for 7 minutes or until the onions start to soften. (Add a spoonful of water if the pan gets dry.) Stir in the garlic and cook for another minute. Add the carrots, stock, water and quinoa. Cover and simmer for 25 minutes or until the carrots are very tender. Remove from the heat and let cool slightly. Purée in a blender, one half at a time, until smooth or use a hand blender. Return soup to the saucepan and return to a simmer. Add the ginger, zest, salt (if using) and cayenne. Simmer the soup for 2 or 3 minutes. Stir in the cream (if using) or garnish with a drizzle just before serving. Garnish with chives (if using) and serve.

PER SERVING: Energy 130 calories; Protein 3 g; Carbohydrates 22 g; Dietary Fiber 5 g; Fat 3.5 g; Sugar 7 g; Cholesterol 0 mg; Sodium 150 mg

SERVES 6

1 Tbsp (15 mL) grapeseed oil or vegetable oil

1 cup (250 mL) chopped onions

1 tsp (5 mL) minced garlic

4 cups (1 L) sliced carrots

4 cups (1 L) sodium-reduced vegetable or chicken stock

1 cup (250 mL) water

½ cup (125 mL) quinoa

2 tsp (10 mL) grated fresh ginger

1½ tsp (7 mL) grated lemon or lime zest

½ tsp (2 mL) salt (optional)

¼ tsp (1 mL) cayenne pepper or to taste

½ cup (125 mL) 10% cream (optional)

1 Tbsp (15 mL) sliced chives (optional)

If using the slow cooker, add the onions, garlic, carrots, stock, water and quinoa. Cook all ingredients on high for 3 to 3½ hours or on low for 6 to 8 hours. Follow the same instructions to purée and serve the soup.

LEMON GINGER TURKEY SOUP

SERVES 6

1 Tbsp (15 mL) vegetable oil
　　or grapeseed oil

1 cup (250 mL) diced onions

1 cup (250 mL) chopped celery

1 cup (250 mL) chopped carrots

½ tsp (2 mL) minced garlic

4 cups (1 L) chicken or
　　vegetable stock

1 cup (250 mL) water

⅓ cup (75 mL) quinoa

½ tsp (2 mL) dried oregano

½ tsp (2 mL) grated fresh ginger

1½ cups (375 mL) diced
　　cooked turkey or chicken

1 tsp (5 mL) grated lemon zest

Wanting to use up some holiday turkey? Or feeling guilty after indulging during the holiday season? This fresh take on an old favorite will quickly become your family's favored pick-me-up. For a vegetarian option, replace the chicken stock with vegetable stock and the chicken with one can (14 oz/398 mL) drained and rinsed navy or soybeans.

Heat the oil in a large saucepan on medium-low heat. Add the onions, celery and carrots and cook for about 7 minutes, until the onions and celery are tender. (If you find the pan is dry, add a spoonful or two of water and cover with the lid.) Stir in the garlic and cook for another minute. Add the stock, water, quinoa, oregano and ginger. Bring to a boil, reduce to a simmer, cover and cook for 15 minutes or until the quinoa is cooked. Stir in the chicken and lemon zest. Continue to cook until heated through, 3 to 5 minutes.

PER SERVING: Energy 190 calories; Protein 25 g; Carbohydrates 13 g; Dietary Fiber 3 g; Fat 3.5 g; Sugar 4 g; Cholesterol 65 mg; Sodium 170 mg

Want to add another dimension to this soup? Add a thinly sliced stalk of lemongrass to the saucepan at the same time you add the vegetables.

QUINOA CHICKEN SOUP

A favorite standard, chicken soup is not only easy but a go-to meal if you're feeling under the weather. Using sodium-reduced stock means you can salt the soup to your own personal taste.

In a large saucepan on medium-high heat, bring the stock and quinoa to a boil. Reduce to a simmer, cover and cook until the quinoa is tender, 15 to 18 minutes. Add the chicken, carrots, onions, celery, garlic, sage and bay leaf. Continue to simmer for another 20 minutes. Season with salt and pepper. Serve.

PER SERVING: Energy 130 calories; Protein 13 g; Carbohydrates 14 g; Dietary Fiber 2 g; Fat 3 g; Sugar 2 g; Cholesterol 20 mg; Sodium 200 mg

Cayenne pepper contains capsaicin, which naturally warms the body, increases circulation and helps to ease congestion and sore throats.

SERVES 4

4 cups (1 L) sodium-reduced chicken or vegetable stock

¼ cup (60 mL) quinoa

1 cup (250 mL) diced cooked chicken breast

½ cup (125 mL) chopped carrots

½ cup (125 mL) chopped onions

½ cup (125 mL) diced celery

2 tsp (10 mL) minced garlic

¼ tsp (1 mL) ground sage

1 bay leaf

Salt and black pepper to taste

Cayenne pepper to taste

ROASTED GARLIC & MUSHROOM SOUP

Roast the garlic in advance and you can whip up this mushroom soup for a lunch or light supper. Experiment with different types of mushrooms and different stock.

Heat the oil in a large saucepan on medium-low heat. Add the onions and cook, covered, for 8 minutes or until the onions are soft and opaque. (If the pan looks dry, add a few spoonfuls of water.) Add the mushrooms and cook, covered, for another 7 minutes or until they soften. Remove 1½ cups (375 mL) of the mushroom mixture and set aside.

Add the stock, water, quinoa, roasted garlic, thyme, salt (if using) and pepper. Bring to a boil, reduce to a simmer, cover and cook for 15 minutes or until the quinoa is tender. Purée soup with a hand blender or in a blender. Return soup to the saucepan. Stir in the spinach and reserved mushrooms. Cook gently until heated through. Adjust seasoning and serve sprinkled with Parmesan (if using).

PER SERVING: Energy 110 calories; Protein 4 g; Carbohydrates 18 g; Dietary Fiber 3 g; Fat 2.5 g; Sugar 4 g; Cholesterol 0 mg; Sodium 105 mg

SERVES 6

2 tsp (10 mL) grapeseed oil
or vegetable oil

1 cup (250 mL) chopped onions

1 lb (450 g) cremini
mushrooms, sliced

4 cups (1 L) sodium-reduced
vegetable, chicken or beef stock

2 cups (500 mL) water

½ cup (125 mL) quinoa

1 Tbsp (15 mL) roasted garlic
(see Tip)

2 tsp (10 mL) chopped fresh thyme

¾ tsp (4 mL) salt (optional)

¼ tsp (1 mL) black pepper

1 cup (250 mL) chopped
fresh spinach

Freshly grated Parmesan
cheese (optional)

HOW TO ROAST GARLIC
Preheat the oven to 400°F (200°C). Take as many heads of garlic as you like, and slice off the top ½ inch (1 cm) to expose the cloves. Tear off pieces of foil large enough to entirely wrap each head of garlic. Place each head of garlic in the center of a piece of foil and pour about 2 tsp (10 mL) of grapeseed oil (or whichever oil you would like) over the top. Sprinkle with fresh herbs, if desired. Wrap snugly and place on a baking sheet. Bake for 30 to 35 minutes or until the garlic cloves can easily be squeezed from the skins. Add roasted garlic to soups, stews, roasts, spreads and dips. Keep refrigerated in an airtight container for a couple of weeks. Or freeze roasted garlic so you can flavor all your fabulous meals in a snap. First freeze it in ice cube trays, and then transfer the cubes to small freezer bags.

SLOW COOKER VEGETABLE BEAN SOUP

SERVES 6

¾ cup (175 mL) dried navy beans, soaked in water overnight

1 can (28 oz/796 mL) unsalted diced tomatoes with juice

1 cup (250 mL) cubed zucchini or red potatoes

1 cup (250 mL) chopped onions

1 cup (250 mL) chopped celery

1 cup (250 mL) sliced carrots

½ cup (125 mL) quinoa

¾ tsp (4 mL) dried oregano

½ tsp (2 mL) minced garlic

¼ tsp (1 mL) dried marjoram

1 bay leaf

3 cups (750 mL) boiling water

2 cups (500 mL) vegetable, chicken or beef stock

Salt and black pepper (optional)

Croutons (optional)

Easy! Soak the beans and cut up the veggies the night before. In the morning, throw all the ingredients into the slow cooker and turn it on. A hot and delicious meal will be waiting for you when you get home.

Drain the navy beans and rinse under running water. Add the beans and all the other ingredients (except the salt, pepper and croutons) to the slow cooker. Cover and cook on high for 3 ½ to 4 hours or on low for 6 to 8 hours, until the vegetables and beans are tender. Season to taste with salt and pepper (if using) and serve topped with croutons (if using).

PER SERVING (vegetable stock, zucchini): Energy 200 calories; Protein 10 g; Carbohydrates 38 g; Dietary Fiber 10 g; Fat 1.5 g; Sugar 9 g; Cholesterol 0 mg; Sodium 95 mg

---

LIGHT HERB AND GARLIC CROUTONS

4 cups (1 L) of your favorite bread, cut in ¾-inch (2 cm) cubes

2 Tbsp (30 mL) melted salted butter or grapeseed oil

1 tsp (5 mL) minced or pureed garlic

1 tsp (5 mL) each of dried thyme, basil and oregano

¼ tsp (1 mL) salt

Preheat the oven to 400°F (200°C). Heat a small saucepan on medium heat and add the butter and garlic. Cook for 30 seconds and remove from the heat. Toss all ingredients together in a medium bowl until bread cubes are evenly coated. Pour onto an ungreased baking sheet and bake for 7 minutes. Stir and continue to bake for another 7 minutes or until the croutons are lightly golden and dry. Store cooled and dried croutons in a resealable container for up to 1 month.

WEEKNIGHT MEXICAN SOUP

Quick suppers are perfect during the week, and this Mexican-inspired soup is so full of veggies, it's close to being a stew. Customize the heat of this soup with as many jalapeños as you like.

Heat the oil in a large saucepan on medium-low heat. Add the onions and cook for 7 minutes or until they begin to soften. Add the beans, tomatoes, green peppers, corn, quinoa, tomato paste, chili powder, cumin, stock and water. Bring to a boil, reduce to a simmer, cover and cook for 15 minutes or until the quinoa is tender. Stir in the cilantro and lime zest. Season with salt and pepper to taste, if desired. Serve with a tablespoon or two of sour cream. Garnish with crumbled corn tortillas, if desired.

PER SERVING: Energy 240 calories; Protein 10 g; Carbohydrates 39 g; Dietary Fiber 9 g; Fat 6 g; Sugar 6 g; Cholesterol 5 mg; Sodium 220 mg

Increase the vegetables even more by adding ½ to ¾ cup (125 to 175 mL) of chopped fresh yellow or green zucchini.

SERVES 6

1 Tbsp (15 mL) grapeseed oil or vegetable oil

⅔ cup (150 mL) chopped onions

2 cups (500 mL) unsalted cooked black beans (or one 19 oz/540 mL can, drained and rinsed)

1½ cups (375 mL) diced fresh tomatoes (or one 19 oz/540 mL can with juice)

1 cup (250 mL) chopped green bell peppers

¾ cup (175 mL) fresh or frozen corn

⅔ cup (150 mL) quinoa

¼ cup (60 mL) tomato paste

2 tsp (10 mL) chili powder

½ tsp (2 mL) ground cumin

4 cups (1 L) sodium-reduced vegetable or chicken stock

1 cup (250 mL) water

2 Tbsp (30 mL) chopped fresh cilantro

½ tsp (2 mL) grated lime zest

Salt and black pepper (optional)

½ cup (125 mL) reduced-fat sour cream (gluten-free if required)

Corn tortillas (optional)

WINTER BISON SOUP

1 Tbsp (15 mL) grapeseed oil
    or vegetable oil

1 lb (450 g) lean ground bison
    or beef

1½ cups (375 mL) chopped onions

1½ cups (375 mL) diced carrots

1½ cups (375 mL) diced celery

2 tsp (10 mL) minced garlic

3 cups (750 mL) diced fresh
    tomatoes (or one 28 oz/
    796 mL can with juice)

½ cup (125 mL) quinoa

4 cups (1 L) sodium-reduced
    beef stock

1 cup (250 mL) water

2 Tbsp (30 mL) Worcestershire
    sauce (gluten-free if required)

Inspired by traditional hamburger soup, this healthier version is sure to become one of your favorites. This is a great recipe during the fall and winter and can be frozen for a quick meal later on.

Heat the oil in a large saucepan on medium-high heat. Add the bison and cook, stirring frequently, until browned and cooked through. Stir in the onions, carrots and celery. Reduce the heat to medium-low and cook until the onions and celery start to soften. Add the garlic and cook for another minute. Add the tomatoes, quinoa, stock, water and Worcestershire sauce. Bring to a boil, reduce to a simmer, cover and cook for 15 minutes. Serve.

PER SERVING: Energy 230 calories; Protein 22 g; Carbohydrates 25 g; Dietary Fiber 4 g; Fat 5 g; Sugar 9 g; Cholesterol 40 mg; Sodium 210 mg

WONTON SOUP
AU NATUREL

Take the great flavors of wonton soup, remove the wrappers, add quinoa and a generous amount of vegetables and you have a filling and nutritious soup, plain and simple. As a bonus, it's wheat- and gluten-free!

In a medium bowl, mix together the ground meat, green onions, egg yolk, ¼ tsp (1 mL) of the ginger, sesame oil, salt (if using) and pepper. Gently roll tablespoons of the meat mixture into balls and place on a plate. Set aside.

In a large saucepan, combine the stock, water, quinoa, remaining 1 tsp (5 mL) of ginger and garlic. Bring to a boil on medium-high heat. Reduce to a simmer, cover and cook for 8 minutes. Add the bok choy and carrots. Bring to a boil on medium-high heat and drop the meatballs into the hot stock. Reduce to a simmer, cover and cook for another 8 minutes or until the quinoa is tender and the meatballs are cooked. Serve.

PER SERVING: Energy 160 calories; Protein 14 g; Carbohydrates 14 g; Dietary Fiber 2 g; Fat 6 g; Sugar 2 g; Cholesterol 65 mg; Sodium 125 mg

Enjoy shrimp? Add ½ lb (225 g) peeled and deveined raw shrimp 2 to 3 minutes before finishing the soup.

SERVES 6

½ lb (225 g) ground chicken
    or turkey

3 Tbsp (45 mL) thinly sliced
    green onions

1 large egg yolk

1¼ tsp (6 mL) grated fresh ginger

¾ tsp (4 mL) sesame oil

¼ tsp (1 mL) salt (optional)

Pinch of black pepper

4 cups (1 L) sodium-reduced or
    regular chicken stock

1 cup (250 mL) water

½ cup (125 mL) quinoa

¼ tsp (1 mL) minced garlic

2 cups (500 mL) bok choy halved
    down spine and thinly sliced
    (or broccoli florets)

1 cup (250 mL) carrots thinly
    sliced on the diagonal

LEMONGRASS, SWEET POTATO & COCONUT STEW

SERVES 8

2 stalks lemongrass

1 Tbsp (15 mL) grapeseed oil
or vegetable oil

1 medium red onion, halved
lengthwise and cut into ½-inch
(1 cm) thick slices (about
1 cup/250 mL)

2 Tbsp (30 mL) Thai green curry
paste (gluten-free if required)

1½ tsp (7 mL) minced garlic

4 cups (1 L) sodium-reduced
chicken or vegetable stock

1⅔ cups (400 mL) light or regular
coconut milk

1 to 3 tsp (5 to 15 mL) minced fresh
Thai red or green chili or jalapeño
pepper (optional)

2 boneless, skinless chicken breasts
(or 5 or 6 boneless, skinless
thighs), cut crosswise into strips
½ inch (1 cm) thick

1¼ lb (565 g) sweet potatoes, cut
into 1-inch (2.5 cm) cubes (about
3 cups/750 mL)

1 cup (250 mL) fresh or thawed
frozen green beans cut into
1-inch (2.5 cm) pieces

½ cup (125 mL) quinoa

1 cup (250 mL) zucchini cut into
1-inch (2.5 cm) cubes

2 tsp (10 mL) chopped fresh
basil or cilantro

The flavors of Thai green curry (or *gaeng keow wan*) inspired this colorful stew. The complementing flavors of sweet potato, coconut and lemongrass make for a scrumptious home-cooked meal-in-a-bowl. If you want to heat things up, add as many chilies as you like. Thai green curry paste is available in the Asian section of the supermarket. You can make this meal vegetarian by leaving out the chicken and adding 1½ cups (375 mL) of cooked white kidney beans with the zucchini.

Cut off the bottom third of the lemongrass stalks. Peel off the dry outer layers. Slice stalks into paper-thin pieces. Set aside.

Heat the oil in a large saucepan on medium-low heat. Add the red onion, cover and cook, stirring occasionally, for 7 minutes or until the onion starts to soften. (If the pan gets dry, add a spoonful of water.) Add the curry paste and garlic; stir for 1 minute. Add the stock, coconut milk, lemongrass and hot chilies (if using). Bring to a boil.

Add the chicken. Return to a boil. Add the sweet potatoes, green beans and quinoa. Reduce to a simmer, cover and cook for 15 minutes. Stir in the zucchini, cover and simmer for another 10 minutes. Remove the lid and simmer for another 5 minutes, until slightly thickened. Stir in the basil or cilantro and serve.

PER SERVING: Energy 190 calories; Protein 9 g; Carbohydrates 26 g; Dietary Fiber 4 g; Fat 5 g; Sugar 5 g; Cholesterol 20 mg; Sodium 300 mg

LENTIL & KALE STEW

1 Tbsp (15 mL) grapeseed oil
or vegetable oil

1 cup (250 mL) chopped onions

1 cup (250 mL) chopped celery

1 cup (250 mL) sliced carrots

2 tsp (10 mL) chopped garlic

1 Tbsp (15 mL) dried oregano

1 tsp (5 mL) dried marjoram

6 cups (1.5 L) water

1 can (19 oz/540 mL) unsalted
diced tomatoes with juice

1½ cups (375 mL) green lentils

½ cup (125 mL) quinoa

3 cups (575 mL) chopped kale,
center ribs and stems removed
(1 large bunch)

½ tsp (2 tsp) grated lemon zest

¼ tsp (1 mL) salt (optional)

¼ tsp (1 mL) black pepper

With a small bunch of kale and a few pantry staples, you can make this healthy and hearty stew with ease.

Heat the oil in a large saucepan on medium-low heat. Add the onions, celery and carrots. Cook, covered, for 7 to 10 minutes, until the onions and celery start to soften. (Add a few spoonfuls of water if the pan is dry.) Stir in the garlic, oregano and marjoram. Cook for another minute. Pour in the water and tomatoes. Stir in the lentils and quinoa. Bring to a boil, reduce to a simmer, cover and cook for 45 minutes or until the lentils are almost tender. Stir in the kale and cook for another 10 minutes. Add the lemon zest, salt (if using) and pepper. Serve.

PER SERVING: Energy 290 calories; Protein 15 g; Carbohydrates 49 g; Dietary Fiber 12 g; Fat 4.5 g; Sugar 7 g; Cholesterol 0 mg; Sodium 60 mg

Kale is a power-packed superfood! Nutritionally dense, it aids digestion and is detoxifying, strengthens immune and cardio-vascular support, is anti-imflammatory, has cell-building properties and more. Try it! Need we say more?

SIMPLE CHICKEN
POT PIE STEW

We took a time-consuming, calorie-loaded old favorite and made it easy and healthful—keeping all the tasty elements, of course! You can simplify this recipe even more by using leftover holiday turkey or rotisserie chicken.

Heat the oil in a large saucepan on low heat. Add the onions, carrots, celery, salt (if using) and black pepper. Cook for 8 to 9 minutes, until the onions start to become opaque and the celery starts to soften. Stir in the mushrooms and cook for another 5 minutes. Add the potatoes, red peppers, stock and poultry seasoning. Bring to a boil, reduce to a simmer, cover and cook for 10 minutes or until the potatoes are tender. Stir in the chicken.

In a small bowl, whisk together the milk and flour. Slowly stir this mixture into the hot stew. Cook for another 5 minutes or until the stew thickens. Adjust seasoning if desired and serve.

PER SERVING: Energy 210 calories; Protein 21 g; Carbohydrates 20 g; Dietary Fiber 3 g; Fat 6 g; Sugar 5 g; Cholesterol 40 mg; Sodium 125 mg

SERVES 6

1 Tbsp (15 mL) grapeseed oil
   or vegetable oil

1 cup (250 mL) chopped onions

1 cup (250 mL) sliced carrots

1 cup (250 mL) chopped celery

½ tsp (2 mL) salt (optional)

¼ tsp (1 mL) black pepper

8 oz (225 g) button
   mushrooms, sliced

1 cup (250 mL) diced potatoes

½ cup (125 mL) red bell pepper cut
   into 1½-inch (4 cm) lengths

4 cups (1 L) sodium-reduced
   chicken stock

1 tsp (5 mL) dried poultry seasoning

2 cups (500 mL) shredded cooked
   chicken or turkey breast

½ cup (125 mL) 1% milk

⅓ cup (75 mL) quinoa flour

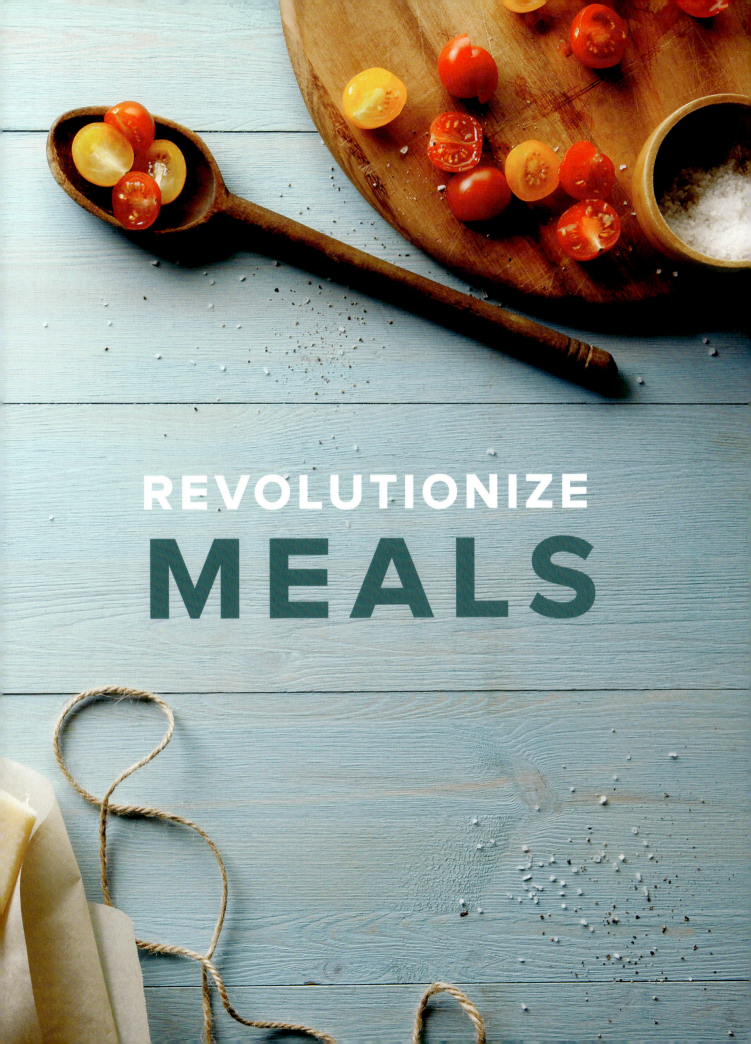

REVOLUTIONIZE
MEALS

REVOLUTIONIZE MEALS

STARVING at the end of a busy day, you want to eat something satisfying but quick. Coming up with creative dinner ideas for yourself or an entire family can be agonizing at times. Quinoa makes dinner easy to plan ahead for. Prepare your quinoa in advance so you can simply cook and serve these recipes or slip them in the oven the minute you walk in the door. If you're really pressed for time, try Kale, Red Pepper & Quinoa Toss (page 141) or Cabbage Crockpot Casserole (page 120). Is it possible that quick, nutritious meals will have your family asking for seconds? Yes, you can have it all with quinoa. These uncomplicated, no-fuss dinners will soon become your go-to recipes. If you're looking for something extra-impressive for guests, try Savory Mushroom Spinach Crêpes (page 142), Grilled Tarragon Vegetable Quinoa (page 122) or Kung Pao Chicken Quinoa (page 115). For a recipe bursting with flavor, freshness and a bit of sweet and spicy, try the Spicy Salmon Burgers (page 147).

BABY BOK CHOY, SNOW PEA & RED PEPPER STIR-FRY

2 cups (500 mL) +
    2 Tbsp (30 mL) water

1 cup (250 mL) quinoa

2 Tbsp (30 mL) sesame oil

2 cups (500 mL) broccoli florets

6 baby bok choy, bases trimmed

1 medium red bell pepper,
    cut into strips

8 oz (225 g) white button or
    cremini mushrooms, quartered

6 oz (170 g) snow peas

1 stalk lemongrass, trimmed,
    sliced in half lengthwise and
    cut paper thin (optional)

1½ tsp (7 mL) minced garlic

1 tsp (5 mL) grated fresh ginger

½ tsp (2 mL) cinnamon

3 Tbsp (45 mL) sodium-reduced
    soy sauce or tamari
    (gluten-free if required)

2 tsp (10 mL) cornstarch

2 cups (500 mL) diced cooked
    chicken, beef or pork
    (or 1½ cups/375 mL diced
    fried extra-firm tofu)

½ cup (125 mL) sliced green onions

1 lime, cut into 6 wedges

Whereas a typical stir-fry is fried in hot oil in a wok and stirred continuously, this dish is cooked in a covered pot to allow the flavorful juices to blend and thicken. The result is a tasty sauce that the quinoa soaks up. Use your choice of cooked meat or choose tofu to make it vegetarian. Most of the ingredients are added all at once, to make it super-easy—perfect for a weeknight.

Bring 2 cups (500 mL) water and the quinoa to boil in a medium saucepan. Reduce to a simmer, cover and cook for 15 minutes. Remove from the heat but keep covered.

Meanwhile, heat the oil in a large saucepan on medium-high heat. Add the broccoli, bok choy, red pepper, mushrooms, snow peas, lemongrass (if using), garlic, ginger, cinnamon and 2 Tbsp (30 mL) water. Stir well. Reduce the heat to medium-low, cover and cook for 10 minutes.

Whisk together the soy sauce and cornstarch in a small bowl. Stir into the vegetable mixture. Add the meat or tofu and ¼ cup (60 mL) of the green onions. Cook, covered, for another 4 to 5 minutes, until the sauce has thickened slightly and the meat or tofu is heated through.

Fluff quinoa with a fork. Serve stir-fry over hot quinoa with a squeeze of lime and sprinkled with the remaining ¼ cup (60 mL) of green onions.

PER SERVING: Energy 240 calories; Protein 16 g; Carbohydrates 29 g; Dietary Fiber 4 g; Fat 8 g; Sugar 3 g; Cholesterol 25 mg; Sodium 350 mg

> Tamari is similar to soy sauce but is frequently made without wheat. It is still important to read labels if you follow a gluten-free diet. Tamari is a deeper brown and slightly thicker than soy sauce, and is also deeper in flavor. Use it where you would normally use soy sauce. Tamari can be found in health-food stores and larger supermarkets.

KUNG PAO
CHICKEN QUINOA

Quinoa along with buttery peanuts, a hint of spice, sweet pineapple and the crunch of broccoli equals a recipe with a big wow factor. Increase the heat by adding as many red hot chili peppers as you like—or can handle.

Stir together the soy sauce, hot chili sauce, ginger, garlic, chili peppers and black pepper in a bowl; pour into a large, resealable plastic bag. Add the chicken. Place in the refrigerator to marinate for at least 1 hour (and up to 24 hours).

Bring 2 cups (500 mL) water and the quinoa to a boil in a medium saucepan. Reduce to a simmer, cover and cook for 15 minutes. Fluff with a fork and set aside.

Place 1 Tbsp (15 mL) of the vegetable oil in a large, wide saucepan on medium heat. When the oil is hot, add the broccoli and 2 Tbsp (30 mL) water and cover the pan. Cook, stirring frequently, until the broccoli is tender, 8 to 10 minutes. If the pan looks dry, add more water. Transfer to a bowl and set aside, keeping warm.

Remove the chicken from the marinade, reserving the marinade. Heat the remaining 1 Tbsp (15 mL) vegetable oil in the same saucepan, then add the chicken. Increase the heat to medium-high and cook the chicken until it is no longer pink, 7 to 8 minutes. Reduce the heat to medium and add the marinade, pineapple, peanuts, peanut butter, green onions and ¾ cup (175 mL) water. Cook for 3 minutes. Remove 2 Tbsp (30 mL) of the sauce; in a small bowl, whisk in the cornstarch until smooth. Stir cornstarch mixture into the chicken mixture and stir until the mixture thickens slightly, 1 to 2 minutes. Divide the quinoa among serving plates and top with the broccoli. Pour chicken mixture on top. Garnish with green onions.

PER SERVING: Energy 430 calories; Protein 28 g; Carbohydrates 37 g; Dietary Fiber 11 g; Fat 19 g; Sugar 10 g; Cholesterol 50 mg; Sodium 400 mg

SERVES 6

3 Tbsp (45 mL) sodium-reduced soy sauce or tamari (gluten-free if required)

2 Tbsp (30 mL) sriracha hot chili sauce

2 tsp (10 mL) minced fresh ginger

1 tsp (5 mL) minced garlic

1 to 2 small red hot chili peppers, sliced lengthwise

Pinch of black pepper

4 boneless, skinless chicken breasts, diced

2 cups (500 mL) + 2 Tbsp (30 mL) + ¾ cup (175 mL) water

1 cup (250 mL) quinoa

2 Tbsp (30 mL) vegetable oil or grapeseed oil

4 cups (1 L) broccoli florets

1 can (14 oz/398 mL) pineapple tidbits, with juice

½ cup (125 mL) chopped roasted unsalted peanuts

3 Tbsp (45 mL) peanut butter

2 green onions, white and green parts chopped separately, some greens reserved for garnish

2 tsp (10 mL) cornstarch

- Cooked quinoa already on hand? Reheat 3 cups (750 mL) cooked quinoa to serve with the chicken.
- Hot peppers contain capsaicin, which has enzymes that help to detoxify the liver. The hotter the peppers, the more capsaicin.

MIDDLE EASTERN STUFFED ACORN SQUASH

SERVES 4

2 acorn squash (1¼ to 1½ lb/
565 to 675 g each)

2 Tbsp (30 mL) salted butter

1 Tbsp (15 mL) olive oil

¼ tsp (1 mL) cinnamon

Pinch of ground cardamom

1⅓ cups (325 mL) water

⅔ cup (150 mL) red quinoa

3 Tbsp (45 mL) toasted
salted cashew pieces

2 Tbsp (30 mL) diced dried apricots

4 tsp (20 mL) chopped fresh mint

This warm, enticing blend of spices and mint will take you away, and this recipe may just become your new household favorite.

Preheat the oven to 400°F (200°C). Cut the acorn squash in half lengthwise and remove the seeds and strings. Place squash cut side down in a shallow baking dish and fill with ¼ inch (5 mm) of water. Bake for 30 to 35 minutes, until the flesh is easily pierced with a fork.

Meanwhile, melt the butter in a small saucepan on medium heat, whisking constantly. Watch closely as brown flecks begin to appear. As soon as the butter turns a caramel brown color and has a nutty fragrance (this should take between 4 to 6 minutes; do not allow the butter to turn black), remove from the heat and transfer to a medium bowl. Stir in the olive oil, cinnamon and cardamom.

Add the water and quinoa to the same saucepan. Bring to a boil, reduce to a simmer, cover and cook for 17 minutes. Remove from the heat and fluff with a fork. Toss 2 cups (500 mL) of the quinoa with the seasoned brown butter, cashews, apricots and mint. Cover the quinoa mixture to keep it warm if the squash needs more time to finish baking.

Equally divide the quinoa filling among the four squash halves. Serve immediately.

PER SERVING: Energy 340 calories; Protein 7 g; Carbohydrates 50 g; Dietary Fiber 6 g; Fat 14 g; Sugar 3 g; Cholesterol 15 mg; Sodium 100 mg

- No mint? For this recipe, replace it with 2 Tbsp (30 mL) thinly sliced green onions. The onions give a different flavor to the dish and are a great option.

- To toast nuts, preheat the oven to 350°F (180°C). Spread the nuts on a baking sheet and toast in the oven, stirring once if necessary, for 5 to 7 minutes, until fragrant and lightly toasted.

BAKED TOMATO & QUINOA–STUFFED ZUCCHINI WITH MOZZARELLA

Bubbly and golden baked mozzarella tops quinoa-stuffed zucchini. If using dried herbs, add them with the chopped garlic.

Combine the water and quinoa in a medium saucepan. Bring to a boil, reduce to a simmer, cover and cook for 15 minutes. Remove from the heat but leave covered for another 10 minutes. Fluff with a fork and set aside to cool slightly.

Preheat the oven to 375°F (190°C). Lightly spray with cooking oil, grease or line with parchment an 11- × 7-inch (2 L) baking dish.

Use a small spoon to scoop out half the insides of each zucchini half. (Reserve zucchini flesh for another use.) Brush zucchini shells with 1 tsp (5 mL) of the oil and place cut side up in baking dish.

Heat the remaining 1 Tbsp (15 mL) oil in a large skillet on medium-low heat. Add the onions; cook, covered, for 5 minutes, stirring occasionally. Stir in the mushrooms and garlic. Cover and cook for another 7 minutes, until the mushrooms are soft. Turn the heat off and stir in 1 cup (250 mL) of the cooked quinoa, the tomato sauce, Parmesan, oregano, basil and salt (if using).

Scoop ¼ cup (60 mL) to ⅓ cup (75 mL) of the quinoa mixture into each of the zucchini halves. Top each with 1 to 2 Tbsp (15 to 30 mL) of mozzarella cheese. Bake for 30 minutes or until the cheese is golden and bubbling. Serve.

PER SERVING: Energy 320 calories; Protein 19 g; Carbohydrates 33 g; Dietary Fiber 6 g; Fat 13 g; Sugar 15 g; Cholesterol 20 mg; Sodium 150 mg

SERVES 4 (OR 8 AS AN APPETIZER OR SIDE DISH)

⅔ cup (150 mL) water

⅓ cup (75 mL) quinoa

4 zucchini (about 7 oz/200 g each), trimmed and halved lengthwise

1 Tbsp (15 mL) grapeseed oil or vegetable oil + 1 tsp (5 mL) for brushing zucchini

⅓ cup (75 mL) finely chopped onions

8 oz (225 g) mushrooms, sliced

½ tsp (2 mL) chopped garlic

1⅔ cups (400 mL) tomato sauce

⅓ cup (75 mL) freshly grated Parmesan cheese

4½ tsp (22 mL) chopped fresh oregano (or 1½ tsp/7 mL dried)

2 tsp (10 mL) chopped fresh basil (or ½ tsp/2 mL dried)

½ tsp (2 mL) salt (optional)

1 cup (250 mL) shredded reduced-fat mozzarella cheese

CABBAGE CROCKPOT CASSEROLE

SERVES 6

1 lb (450 g) lean ground beef

1½ cups (375 mL) chopped onions

4 slices bacon, cooked and chopped (optional)

¾ cup (75 mL) quinoa

1 cup (250 mL) chopped green bell peppers

1 tsp (5 mL) minced garlic

¼ tsp (1 mL) black pepper

4 cups (1 L) green cabbage chopped into 1-inch (2.5 cm) pieces

1 can (28 oz/796 mL) diced tomatoes with juice

3 cups (750 mL) sodium-reduced tomato juice

Salt (optional)

Want supper already waiting the moment you get home? This is an easy slow cooker recipe inspired by the Ukrainian cabbage roll dish called holubtsi. Prepare the ingredients the night before and quickly throw them together before you leave for work.

Heat a large skillet on medium-high heat. Add the ground beef and cook until browned. Stir in the onions and reduce the heat to low. Continue to cook until the onions are starting to soften. Remove from the heat.

Transfer the ground beef mixture to a 6-quart (6 L) slow cooker. Place the bacon (if using) and quinoa on top of the beef. Add the green peppers in one layer. Sprinkle with the garlic and black pepper. Add the cabbage in one layer. Top with the diced tomatoes and the tomato juice. Cook on low for 8 to 9 hours or on high for 4 to 4½ hours. The casserole is done when the quinoa is cooked and the cabbage is tender. Add salt to taste (if using). Serve.

Refrigerate leftovers or freeze in a sealed container for up to 2 months.

PER SERVING: Energy 260 calories; Protein 21 g; Carbohydrates 34 g; Dietary Fiber 6 g; Fat 5 g; Sugar 13 g; Cholesterol 40 mg; Sodium 85 mg

CHAMPIONSHIP CHILI

Here's our take on a white chili with quinoa. It's a simple throw-together recipe full of flavor. Some like it hot, so make it as bold as you want with your choice of salsa. To make this chili vegetarian, replace the chicken with 2 cups (500 mL) cooked navy beans or chickpeas (or one 19 oz/ 540 mL can).

In a large saucepan on medium heat, combine the mushrooms and water. Reduce the heat to medium-low, cover and cook until the mushrooms soften, 5 to 7 minutes.

In a shallow bowl, mash half a can of kidney beans. Add the mashed beans, remaining whole beans, chicken, salsa, quinoa, oregano, cumin and stock to the mushrooms. Combine well and bring to a boil. Reduce to a simmer, cover and cook for 20 minutes. Remove the lid and simmer for another 5 to 7 minutes, until the chili thickens slightly. Stir cheese (if using) into the chili until melted. Serve hot, topped with fresh cilantro (if using).

PER SERVING: Energy 200 calories; Protein 15 g; Carbohydrates 29 g; Dietary Fiber 7 g; Fat 2.5 g; Sugar 4 g; Cholesterol 20 mg; Sodium 380 mg

SERVES 8

8 oz (225 g) white mushrooms, sliced

2 Tbsp (30 mL) water

2 cups (500 mL) cooked white kidney beans (or two 19 oz/ 540 mL cans, drained and rinsed)

2 cups (500 mL) cubed chicken

1½ cups (375 mL) chunky salsa (medium or hot)

½ cup (125 mL) quinoa

2 tsp (10 mL) dried oregano

1¼ tsp (6 mL) ground cumin

4 cups (1 L) sodium-reduced chicken or vegetable stock

1 cup (250 mL) shredded jalapeño havarti cheese (optional)

⅓ cup (75 mL) chopped fresh cilantro (optional)

GRILLED TARRAGON VEGETABLE QUINOA

SERVES 4

8 oz (225 g) white or
 cremini mushrooms

1 cup (250 mL) cherry or
 grape tomatoes

1 cup (250 mL) Spanish onion cut
 into ½-inch (1 cm) rings

8 oz (225 g) asparagus, trimmed

1 Tbsp (15 mL) + 2 tsp (10 mL)
 grapeseed oil or vegetable oil

1⅓ cups (325 mL) water

⅔ cup (150 mL) black or red quinoa

2 Tbsp (30 mL) salted butter

1 tsp (5 mL) fresh tarragon leaves
 cut into thirds

1 tsp (5 mL) minced garlic

½ tsp (2 mL) salt (optional)

⅓ cup (75 mL) soft goat cheese

> There are two ways you
> can remove the woody
> ends of asparagus. Simply
> bend the woody end and it
> will break off naturally, or
> use a vegetable peeler to
> remove the bottom
> 2 inches (5 cm) of the
> tough outer layer.

The delicious flavor of this barbecue recipe will have you looking forward to grilling weather.

If using bamboo skewers, soak in water for 1 hour. Place all the mushrooms on skewers. On separate skewers, place the tomatoes. On separate skewers, skewer each section of onion horizontally through the rings so they will lie flat on the grill. Place all skewered vegetables and the asparagus on a baking sheet. Brush lightly with 2 tsp (10 mL) oil. Set aside.

Bring the water and quinoa to a boil in a medium saucepan. Reduce to a simmer, cover and cook for 15 minutes. Fluff with a fork and set aside.

Melt the butter in a large saucepan on medium heat. Stir in the remaining 1 Tbsp (15 mL) oil, the tarragon, garlic and salt (if using). Heat for 30 seconds. Remove from the heat and set aside.

Preheat the barbecue to medium. Lightly grease the grill. Grill the onions first, for 3 minutes. Flip the onions, then add the mushrooms. Grill for 3 minutes. Flip the onions and mushrooms, then add the asparagus. Grill for another 3 minutes. Turn the vegetables once again and add the tomatoes for the last 3 minutes. Remove all the vegetables from the grill. Remove the tomatoes and mushrooms from the skewers and place in the saucepan with the seasoned butter. Cut the asparagus into thirds, then cut the onion into large dice. Add to the other vegetables. Toss gently to coat vegetables in the seasoned butter and vegetable juices.

Preheat the broiler with the oven rack in the middle. Spread the quinoa evenly in a casserole dish and spoon the grilled vegetables on top. Crumble the goat cheese over the vegetables. Broil for 3 to 5 minutes, until the goat cheese is slightly melted. Serve.

PER SERVING: Energy 290 calories; Protein 10 g; Carbohydrates 28 g; Dietary Fiber 4 g; Fat 17 g; Sugar 4 g; Cholesterol 25 mg; Sodium 120 mg

CHICKEN MASALA

SERVES 4

3 Tbsp (45 mL) grapeseed oil
    or vegetable oil

1½ lb (675 g) skinless, boneless
    chicken breasts, cut into
    1-inch (2.5 cm) pieces

1 cup (250 mL) onions cut into
    1-inch (2.5 cm) pieces

1 cup (250 mL) sliced carrots

2 tsp (10 mL) minced garlic

1 tsp (5 mL) ground coriander

½ tsp (2 mL) salt (optional)

½ tsp (2 mL) turmeric

¼ tsp (1 mL) cayenne pepper

1 can (28 oz/796 mL) diced
    tomatoes with juice

½ cup (125 mL) water

1 cup (250 mL) 2-inch (5 cm)
    cauliflower florets

1 cup (250 mL) green beans cut
    into 2-inch (5 cm) lengths

¾ tsp (4 mL) garam masala

This masala recipe is modeled after an authentically flavored curry. It tastes fantastic paired with the Indian-Infused Quinoa on page 83. See our tip below for the vegetarian version.

Heat 1½ Tbsp (20 mL) of the oil in a large saucepan on medium-high heat. Add the chicken and brown on all sides. Remove from the pan and set aside.

Reduce the heat to medium-low and add the remaining oil. Add the onions and carrots; cook until the onions become soft and opaque. Stir in the garlic, coriander, salt (if using), turmeric and cayenne. Heat for 3 minutes, stirring frequently. Add the chicken, tomatoes and water. Bring to a boil, reduce to a simmer and cook for 10 minutes. Stir in the cauliflower and green beans; cover and simmer for another 8 to 10 minutes, until the vegetables are tender and the chicken is no longer pink. Stir in the garam masala and season with more cayenne if desired. Serve over warm Indian-Infused Quinoa (page 83) or plain cooked quinoa.

PER SERVING: Energy 370 calories; Protein 38 g; Carbohydrates 20 g; Dietary Fiber 4 g; Fat 14 g; Sugar 11 g; Cholesterol 95 mg; Sodium 140 mg

For a vegetarian version, leave out the chicken. Use only 1½ Tbsp (20 mL) oil to cook the onions and carrots, and add 1 can (19 oz/540 mL) chickpeas, drained and rinsed, along with the tomatoes.

QUINOA BEEF STROGANOFF

An alternative to pasta, quinoa makes a delicious stroganoff with beef or low-fat bison. And it uses only one saucepan!

In a large saucepan on medium-high heat, cook beef strips until they are completely cooked through and are slightly browned. If the pan is a little dry, add a spoonful or two of water. Transfer beef to a plate and cover with foil to keep warm.

Heat the olive oil in the same saucepan on medium heat. Add the mushrooms and onions; cook until they are tender and opaque. Add the garlic. Increase the heat to high. Add the stock, water and quinoa. Bring to a boil, reduce to simmer, cover and cook for 12 minutes, until the mixture is thick, the quinoa is fluffy and almost no liquid remains. Stir in the yogurt and beef strips. Simmer for 5 minutes to reheat stroganoff. Serve immediately.

PER SERVING: Energy 440 calories; Protein 44 g; Carbohydrates 33 g; Dietary Fiber 3 g; Fat 13 g; Sugar 4 g; Cholesterol 90 mg; Sodium 120 mg

SERVES 4

1 lb (450 g) beef or bison steaks, cut into strips

1 Tbsp (15 mL) extra virgin olive oil

1½ cups (375 mL) sliced white or brown mushrooms

½ cup (125 mL) chopped onions

1 tsp (5 mL) minced garlic

1¼ cups (300 mL) sodium-reduced beef stock

1 cup (250 mL) water

1 cup (250 mL) quinoa

½ cup (125 mL) plain yogurt

NOUVEAU BOEUF BOURGUIGNON

SERVES 6

2 cups (500 mL) water

1 cup (250 mL) quinoa

1 Tbsp (15 mL) grapeseed oil
   or vegetable oil

1 top sirloin steak (1 to 1¼ lb/
   450 to 565 g), cubed

½ tsp (2 mL) salt (optional)

½ tsp (2 mL) black pepper

1 cup (250 mL) chopped onions

2 cups (500 mL) thickly
   sliced carrots

1 lb (450 g) cremini mushrooms,
   quartered

1½ tsp (7 mL) minced garlic

4 cups (1 L) sodium-reduced
   beef stock

2 Tbsp (30 mL) unsalted
   tomato paste

1 Tbsp (15 mL) chopped
   fresh thyme

1 Tbsp (15 mL) brown sugar

½ cup (125 mL) dry red wine

3 Tbsp (45 mL) cornstarch

Boeuf bourguignon reinvented! Have the length of time and the amount of wine needed to make this dish been holding you back? Here is our version over quinoa that you can enjoy any day of the week, it's that easy! To save even more time, prep your meat and vegetables the night before. Delicious and uncomplicated. If you don't have a large pan, brown the beef in batches.

Bring the water and quinoa to a boil in a medium saucepan. Reduce to a simmer, cover and cook for 15 minutes. Fluff with a fork and set aside.

Meanwhile, heat a large Dutch oven or 12-inch (30 cm) saucepan on medium-high heat. Add the oil to the hot pan, place the beef pieces about 1 inch (2.5 cm) apart and sprinkle with salt (if using) and pepper. Brown the beef on all sides but don't cook the meat all the way through. Remove the beef from the pan and set aside.

Reduce the heat to medium-low and add the onions and carrots. Cook for 5 minutes. (If the pan is a little dry, add a spoonful of water.) Add the mushrooms and cook for another 7 minutes or until the onions are opaque and the mushrooms are starting to soften. Stir in the garlic and cook for 1 minute.

Stir in the beef and any juices, stock, tomato paste, thyme and brown sugar. Reduce the heat to low and simmer for 15 minutes or until the carrots are tender and the beef is cooked through.

Whisk together the red wine and cornstarch. Stir into the beef mixture. Simmer until thickened enough to coat the back of a spoon, about 3 minutes. Adjust seasoning if necessary. Serve over hot quinoa.

PER SERVING: Energy 370 calories; Protein 32 g; Carbohydrates 36 g; Dietary Fiber 4 g; Fat 10 g; Sugar 7 g; Cholesterol 60 mg; Sodium 140 mg

MEDITERRANEAN CHICKEN QUINOA

Quinoa comes to life in this easy-to-prepare Mediterranean dish full of flavor with artichoke hearts, tomatoes, lemon and oregano.

Bring the water and quinoa to a boil in a small saucepan. Reduce to a simmer, cover and cook for 15 minutes. Fluff with a fork and set aside.

Heat the oil in a large skillet on medium-low heat. Add the shallots; cook until transparent and the edges are starting to brown. Add the chicken; cook until the chicken is no longer pink, 6 to 7 minutes. Reduce the heat to low and stir in the quinoa and the garlic, artichoke hearts, tomatoes, feta, parsley, lemon juice and oregano. Gently reheat and serve.

PER SERVING: Energy 210 calories; Protein 20 g; Carbohydrates 22 g; Dietary Fiber 2 g; Fat 4.5 g; Sugar 3 g; Cholesterol 45 mg; Sodium 360 mg

> Cooked quinoa already on hand? Add ¾ cup (175 mL) cooked quinoa to the chicken in this recipe.

SERVES 4

½ cup (125 mL) water

¼ cup (60 mL) quinoa

1 tsp (5 mL) grapeseed oil
or vegetable oil

1 cup (250 mL) chopped shallots

2 chicken breasts, diced

1 tsp (5 mL) minced garlic

1 can (14 oz/398 mL) artichoke
hearts, drained and chopped

1 cup (250 mL) chopped tomatoes

⅓ cup (75 mL) crumbled
feta cheese

2 Tbsp (30 mL) chopped
fresh parsley

1 Tbsp (15 mL) lemon juice

1 tsp (5 mL) dried oregano

QUINOA LASAGNA

Use your favorite tomato sauce in this layered dish of vegetables, quinoa, cheese and herbs. This lasagna is packed full of flavor that is reminiscent of comfort food without being too heavy. You'll still have plenty of room for dessert.

Preheat the oven to 350°F (180°C). Lightly grease a 13- × 9-inch (3 L) casserole dish or spray with cooking oil.

Bring the water and quinoa to a boil in a medium saucepan. Reduce to a simmer, cover and cook for 15 minutes. Fluff with a fork. Evenly spread the cooked quinoa in the casserole dish. Set aside.

Wipe clean the saucepan, then heat the oil in it on medium heat. Add the onions; cook until transparent and starting to brown. Add the mushrooms; cook until mushrooms are softened and very little moisture remains in the pan. Add the garlic and tomato sauce. Stir until hot. Set aside.

In a medium bowl, combine the cottage cheese with the egg; mix well. Stir in the Parmesan, basil and oregano.

Spread one-third of the tomato sauce over the quinoa. Make a layer of all the zucchini, then all the cottage cheese mixture, then one-third of the tomato sauce, then all the spinach, ending with the remainder of the tomato sauce. Spread the mozzarella cheese evenly on top.

Bake for about 35 minutes, until the lasagna is hot and the cheese is melted, bubbling and slightly browned around the edges. Serve.

PER SERVING: Energy 260 calories; Protein 16 g; Carbohydrates 25 g; Dietary Fiber 3 g; Fat 10 g; Sugar 6 g; Cholesterol 40 mg; Sodium 190 mg

SERVES 8

2 cups (500 mL) water

1 cup (250 mL) quinoa

2 Tbsp (30 mL) vegetable oil
    or olive oil

1 cup (250 mL) chopped onions

1 cup (250 mL) sliced brown or
    white mushrooms

2 cloves garlic, minced

2 cups (500 mL) tomato sauce
    or your favorite prepared
    pasta sauce

2 cups (500 mL) sodium-reduced
    pressed (dry curd) cottage
    cheese

1 large egg, beaten

¼ cup (60 mL) grated
    Parmesan cheese

2 Tbsp (30 mL) minced fresh basil
    (or ½ tsp/2 mL dried)

1 Tbsp (15 mL) dried oregano

2 cups (500 mL) sliced zucchini
    (2 small or 1 medium zucchini)

2 cups (500 mL) packed
    fresh spinach

1½ cups (375 mL) shredded
    reduced-fat mozzarella cheese

Cooked quinoa already on hand? Use 3 cups (750 mL) cooked quinoa as the base for this lasagna.

ROASTED VEGETABLE QUINOA WITH DILL

SERVES 8

1 cup (250 mL) vegetable stock

½ cup (125 mL) quinoa

1 Tbsp (15 mL) grapeseed oil
or vegetable oil

4 shallots, finely chopped

3 cloves garlic, minced

2 cups (500 mL) coarsely chopped
mushrooms (any kind)

2 cups (500 mL) coarsely
chopped zucchini

2 cups (500 mL) coarsely chopped
yellow or orange bell peppers

1 cup (250 mL) quartered
grape tomatoes

½ cup (125 mL) chopped fresh dill

1 Tbsp (15 mL) dried oregano

½ tsp (2 mL) paprika

Pinch each of salt and
black pepper

Zucchini, mushrooms, yellow peppers and tomatoes make this colorful quinoa dish an exquisite side. Oregano, dill and the smoky hint of paprika help bring it to life. This dish makes a fantastic lunch salad.

Preheat the oven to 350°F (180°C). Lightly grease a deep 9-inch (23 cm) round baking dish or spray with cooking oil.

Bring the stock and quinoa to a boil in a medium saucepan. Reduce to a simmer, cover and cook for 15 minutes. Fluff with a fork and set aside.

Heat the oil in a large skillet on medium heat. Add the shallots; cook until transparent and the edges are brown. Add the garlic and mushrooms; cook for 7 to 8 more minutes, until the mushrooms sweat. Add the zucchini and yellow peppers; cook until tender, 3 to 5 more minutes. Turn off the heat and toss in the cooked quinoa and the tomatoes, dill, oregano, paprika, salt and black pepper. Stir well. Pour the mixture into the baking dish and bake for 20 minutes or until hot. Serve.

PER SERVING: Energy 100 calories; Protein 3 g; Carbohydrates 15 g; Dietary Fiber 3 g; Fat 3 g; Sugar 4 g; Cholesterol 0 mg; Sodium 65 mg

Cooked quinoa already on hand? Add 1½ cups (375 mL) cooked quinoa to the cooked vegetables in this recipe.

ROASTED TOMATO & OLIVE BRUSCHETTA OVER BAKED HALIBUT & QUINOA

Tomatoes, black olives, basil and cilantro, with a squeeze of fresh orange juice, taste divine over baked halibut, with all the flavors soaking into a warm bed of quinoa. This is a great dish for using tri-color quinoa.

Preheat the oven to 450°F (230°C).

Bring the water and quinoa to a boil in a medium saucepan. Reduce to a simmer, cover and cook for 15 minutes. Remove from the heat and fluff with a fork. Set aside and keep warm.

Meanwhile, gently stir together the tomatoes, olives, oil, garlic, 1½ tsp (7 mL) basil, salt (if using) and pepper in a medium bowl. Pour the mixture into a 13- × 9-inch (3 L) baking dish. Bake for 10 minutes. Place the halibut, skin side up, on top of the tomato mixture. Bake for another 10 to 14 minutes or until the fish is just cooked through (check the fish after 10 minutes to prevent overcooking).

Spoon the quinoa onto plates and top with the halibut. Stir the cilantro, remaining basil and orange juice to taste into the tomato bruschetta. Spoon the bruschetta over the halibut. Serve.

PER SERVING: Energy 250 calories; Protein 11 g; Carbohydrates 29 g; Dietary Fiber 5 g; Fat 11 g; Sugar 6 g; Cholesterol 15 mg; Sodium 140 mg

SERVES 6

2 cups (500 mL) water

1 cup (250 mL) quinoa

3 lb (1.35 kg) Roma tomatoes, chopped

⅔ cup (150 mL) sliced pitted black olives in brine (not vinegar)

3 Tbsp (45 mL) grapeseed oil or vegetable oil

2 tsp (10 mL) minced garlic

1 Tbsp (15 mL) chopped fresh basil

½ tsp (2 mL) salt (optional)

¼ tsp (1 mL) black pepper

6 halibut fillets (each 8 oz/225 g and about 1 inch/2.5 cm thick)

4 tsp (20 mL) chopped fresh cilantro

1 to 2 Tbsp (15 to 30 mL) freshly squeezed orange juice

Know where your fish is coming from! These days, getting any fish in your diet can be difficult with so many questions about which fish are endangered, caught ethically, and healthy to eat. To help you choose fish from healthy, sustainable sources, visit Monterey Bay Aquarium's Seafood Watch at www.montereybayaquarium.org/cr/seafoodwatch.aspx.

ITALIAN SAUSAGE, FETA & TOMATO OVEN-BAKED FRITTATA

SERVES 6

½ cup (125 mL) water

¼ cup (60 mL) quinoa

1 tsp (5 mL) grapeseed oil
or vegetable oil

½ lb (225 g) Homemade Italian
Ground Sausage (page 80)

1 cup (250 mL) halved cherry
tomatoes

1½ cups (375 mL) baby spinach,
coarsely chopped

3 Tbsp (45 mL) sliced green onions

3 Tbsp (45 mL) coarsely chopped
pitted black olives

½ cup (125 mL) crumbled
reduced-fat or regular
feta cheese

2 large eggs + 8 large egg whites
(or 6 whole, large eggs total)

¼ cup (60 mL) 1% milk

Making the Homemade Italian Ground Sausage filling ahead makes for an easy and satisfying weeknight dish that is great served with a simple salad. Save even more time by cooking the sausage, tomatoes and quinoa in advance. For a vegetarian alternative, add 1 cup (250 mL) drained, rinsed cannellini beans along with the spinach.

Bring the water and quinoa to a boil in a small saucepan. Reduce to a simmer, cover and cook for 15 minutes. Fluff with a fork and set aside to cool.

Preheat the oven to 350°F (180°C). Lightly grease a 9-inch (2.5 L) square baking dish or a 9-inch (23 cm) pie plate.

Heat the oil in a medium skillet on medium-low heat. Add the sausage mixture and fry until browned completely. Stir in the tomatoes; cook for another 5 minutes, until the tomatoes have softened and released their juices. Remove from the heat and let cool slightly. Stir in the cooled quinoa, spinach, green onions and olives. Pour the mixture into the baking dish and sprinkle with the feta cheese. Whisk together the eggs and milk and pour over the vegetable mixture. (The egg mixture may not cover all the vegetable mixture but it will cook together perfectly.)

Bake for 40 to 50 minutes, until the top is golden and the center of the frittata has set. Let cool for 5 to 10 minutes. Cut into 6 pieces and serve hot or at room temperature.

PER SERVING: Energy 240 calories; Protein 26 g; Carbohydrates 8 g; Dietary Fiber 2 g; Fat 14 g; Sugar 2 g; Cholesterol 120 mg; Sodium 320 mg

LEEK PARMESAN QUICHE

A delicious quinoa crust is topped with sautéed leeks, fresh tarragon, Parmesan cheese and a hint of nutmeg.

Heat the oil in a medium skillet on medium heat. Add the leeks and cook until softened, 7 to 10 minutes. Add the wine and water; continue to cook for 5 minutes, until the liquid has mostly evaporated but the skillet is not completely dry. When the leeks are almost translucent, transfer them to a bowl and let cool.

Preheat the oven to 400°F (200°C). Lightly grease a 9-inch (23 cm) pie plate or spray with cooking oil. Roll out the pastry and line the pie plate (see page 190).

In a small bowl, beat the eggs and egg whites. Add the milk, Parmesan, tarragon, nutmeg, salt (if using) and pepper. Whisk until well combined. Stir in the cooled leeks. Pour into the pie shell.

Bake for 20 minutes or until the center of the quiche is firm. Let cool for 5 minutes. Run a knife around the outside edge of the quiche to loosen the crust. Slice into wedges and serve hot.

PER SERVING: Energy 300 calories; Protein 7 g; Carbohydrates 29 g; Dietary Fiber 2 g; Fat 17 g; Sugar 3 g; Cholesterol 80 mg; Sodium 200 mg

SERVES 8

1 Tbsp (15 mL) grapeseed oil

2 cups (500 mL) thinly sliced leeks (white part only)

½ cup (125 mL) dry white wine

⅓ cup (75 mL) water

1 unbaked single Flaky Pie Crust (page 190)

2 large eggs

4 large egg whites

½ cup (125 mL) whole milk or whipping cream

¼ cup (60 mL) freshly grated Parmesan cheese

1 Tbsp (15 mL) chopped fresh tarragon

¼ tsp (1 mL) nutmeg

¼ tsp (1 mL) salt (optional)

¼ tsp (1 mL) black pepper

MUSHROOM & SPINACH QUICHE

SERVES 8

⅔ cup (150 mL) water

⅓ cup (75 mL) quinoa

1 tsp (5 mL) vegetable oil
or olive oil

2 shallots, finely chopped

2 cloves garlic, minced

4 cups (1 L) packed fresh spinach,
tough stems removed

2 cups (500 mL) chopped
shiitake mushrooms

1½ tsp (7 mL) herbes de Provence

2 large eggs + 4 large egg whites
(or 4 whole, large eggs total)

¼ cup (60 mL) quinoa flour or
all-purpose flour

⅓ cup (75 mL) shredded, reduced-
fat mozzarella cheese

⅓ cup (75 mL) freshly grated
Parmesan cheese

¼ cup (60 mL) milk or 10% cream

¼ tsp (1 mL) nutmeg

¼ tsp (1 mL) salt

Pinch of black pepper

This simple crustless quiche is full of quinoa, shiitake mushrooms and spinach. Herbs and a hint of nutmeg give this quiche an impressive flavor.

Preheat the oven to 350°F (180°C). Lightly grease a 9-inch (23 cm) round baking dish or spray with cooking oil.

Bring the water and quinoa to a boil in a medium saucepan. Reduce to a simmer, cover and cook for 15 minutes. Fluff with a fork and set aside.

Heat ½ tsp (2 mL) of the oil in a medium saucepan on medium-low heat. Add the shallots and cook until transparent and beginning to brown. (Add a spoonful of water if the pan looks dry.) Add the garlic and spinach; cook for 3 to 4 more minutes, until the spinach is wilted. Transfer the mixture to a bowl. Set aside.

Heat the remaining oil in the same saucepan on medium-low heat. Add the mushrooms and herbes de Provence; cook for 7 to 8 minutes, until the mushrooms begin to sweat. Add to the spinach mixture.

In a medium bowl, whisk together eggs and flour. Stir in the cooked quinoa, mozzarella, Parmesan, milk, nutmeg, salt and pepper. Stir in the spinach mixture.

Pour into the baking dish and bake for 45 to 50 minutes, until the center of the quiche is firm. Remove from the oven and let cool for 10 minutes. Run a knife around the outside edge of the quiche. Slice into wedges and serve hot.

PER SERVING: Energy 180 calories; Protein 13 g; Carbohydrates 20 g; Dietary Fiber 4 g; Fat 6 g; Sugar 3 g; Cholesterol 70 mg; Sodium 260 mg

Cooked quinoa already on hand? Add 1 cup (250 mL) cooked quinoa to the eggs.

SOUTHWEST QUICHE

This quiche is satisfying but not heavy. Quinoa flour gives the crust a nutty flavor, and peppers, spices, cheese and fresh cilantro add taste, dramatic color—and even more nutrition.

Preheat the oven to 375°F (190°C). Lightly grease a 9-inch (23 cm) pie plate or spray with cooking oil. Roll out pastry and line the pie plate (see page 190).

In a medium bowl, whisk together the eggs, milk, green onions, cilantro, chili pepper, chili powder, cumin, salt (if using) and black pepper. Stir in the Cheddar cheese, corn and red pepper. Pour the mixture into the pie shell.

Bake for 40 to 45 minutes or until the center of the quiche is set. Let sit for 8 to 10 minutes before cutting into wedges. Serve immediately.

PER SERVING: Energy 250 calories; Protein 11 g; Carbohydrates 16 g; Dietary Fiber 3 g; Fat 16 g; Sugar 3 g; Cholesterol 80 mg; Sodium 160 mg

> Make it crustless! Instead of using a pastry crust, add ⅓ to ½ cup (75 to 125 mL) cooked quinoa to the egg mixture.

SERVES 8

1 unbaked single Flaky Pie Crust (page 190)

2 large eggs + 4 large egg whites (or 4 whole, large eggs total)

1 cup (250 mL) 2% milk or cream

¼ cup (60 mL) chopped green onions

1 Tbsp (15 mL) minced fresh cilantro

1 Tbsp (15 mL) chopped fresh red hot chili pepper

1 tsp (5 mL) chili powder

½ tsp (2 mL) ground cumin

½ tsp (2 mL) salt (optional)

½ tsp (2 mL) black pepper

1 cup (250 mL) shredded reduced-fat aged Cheddar cheese

½ cup (125 mL) thawed frozen corn

½ cup (125 mL) chopped red bell pepper

BARBECUE BEEF
LETTUCE WRAPS

SERVES 6

½ cup (125 mL) sodium-reduced
   soy sauce or tamari
   (gluten-free if required)

3 Tbsp (45 mL) brown sugar

2 Tbsp (30 mL) sesame oil

1 Tbsp (15 mL) rice vinegar

1 tsp (5 mL) minced garlic

1 tsp (5 mL) minced fresh ginger

½ tsp (2 mL) hot red pepper
   flakes (optional)

1 lb (450 g) sirloin steak

1 cup (250 mL) water

½ cup (125 mL) quinoa (any color)

2 hearts romaine or 1 head butter
   lettuce, leaves separated

½ cup (125 mL) shredded carrots

¼ cup (60 mL) thinly sliced
   green onions

1 Tbsp (15 mL) sesame seeds

1 can (8 oz/230 g) water chestnuts,
   drained and halved (optional)

Beef bulgogi is a traditional Korean favorite. Include the hot pepper flakes if you prefer a little heat. You can either grill the meat or cook it on your stovetop. Either way, it's easy!

BARBECUE METHOD In a large bowl or resealable plastic bag, combine the soy sauce, brown sugar, sesame oil, vinegar, garlic, ginger and hot pepper flakes (if using). Add the steak. Place in the refrigerator to marinate for at least 1 hour and up to 24 hours.

Bring the water and quinoa to a boil in a medium saucepan. Reduce to a simmer, cover and cook for 15 minutes. Remove from the heat and set aside, covered.

Preheat the barbecue to medium-high. Brush the grill lightly with oil. Remove the steak from the bag and drain off the marinade (discard the marinade). Grill the steak for about 4 minutes per side for medium-rare, or cook to your preferred doneness. Transfer the steak to a cutting board and let rest for 8 minutes. Slice thinly across the grain with a sharp knife.

Fluff quinoa with a fork and spoon onto each romaine leaf. Top with a few beef strips, carrots, green onions, a sprinkle of sesame seeds and water chestnuts (if using). Wrap and serve.

STOVETOP METHOD Freeze the steak for about 30 minutes, until semi-firm. Using a sharp knife, slice into strips ⅛ inch (3 mm) to ¼ inch (5 mm) thick. Place the meat in a large resealable plastic bag or a bowl and add the soy sauce, brown sugar, sesame oil, vinegar, garlic, ginger and hot pepper flakes (if using). Refrigerate for at least 1 hour and up to 24 hours. Cook meat, with the marinade, in a large saucepan on medium-high heat until meat is cooked through.

PER SERVING: Energy 220 calories; Protein 26 g; Carbohydrates 14 g; Dietary Fiber 2 g; Fat 6 g; Sugar 2 g; Cholesterol 60 mg; Sodium 350 mg

If desired, cook marinade on medium heat for 2 minutes and serve cooled with the wraps for dipping.

HEALTHY BAKED
QUINOA FALAFELS

MAKES 28 FALAFELS

1 cup (250 mL) water

½ cup (125 mL) quinoa

1½ cups (375 mL) cooked
   chickpeas (or one 14 oz/
   398 mL can chickpeas,
   drained and rinsed)

½ cup (125 mL) chopped
   fresh parsley

2 tsp (10 mL) chopped garlic

1 large egg

3 Tbsp (45 mL) grapeseed oil
   or vegetable oil

1 tsp (5 mL) ground coriander

1 tsp (5 mL) ground cumin

¼ tsp (1 mL) cayenne pepper

¼ tsp (1 mL) salt (optional)

Enjoy these falafels in a pita or on a plate of greens along with yogurt dip, tomato, cucumbers, green peppers and red onion for a light dinner.

Preheat the oven to 400°F (200°C). Lightly grease or spray with cooking oil a baking sheet or line with parchment.

Bring the water and quinoa to a boil in a medium saucepan. Reduce to a simmer, cover and cook for 15 minutes. Remove from the heat and let sit, covered, for another 10 minutes. The quinoa should be extra-fluffy.

In a food processor, combine the quinoa, chickpeas, parsley and garlic. Pulse until the chickpeas are finely chopped but not a paste. Add the egg, oil, coriander, cumin, cayenne and salt (if using). Pulse a few times to combine. Scoop out tablespoons of the mixture and arrange 1 inch (2.5 cm) apart on the baking sheet. With wet hands, press down on the balls to make patties ½ inch (1 cm) thick.

Bake the falafels for 10 minutes on each side. Let cool for 5 minutes before serving. Enjoy in a pita or on a salad.

PER SERVING: Energy 40 calories; Protein 1 g; Carbohydrates 4 g; Dietary Fiber 1 g; Fat 2 g; Sugar 0 g; Cholesterol 5 mg; Sodium 35 mg

> Cooked quinoa already on hand? Make these falafels with 1½ cups (375 mL) extra-fluffy cooked quinoa.

FRESH SPRING ROLLS WITH GINGER LIME PEANUT SAUCE

Full of fresh, lively flavors, this recipe can easily be modified to accommodate your tastes. Be as creative or as colorful as you want. These rolls are terrific in lunches or as appetizers (use smaller wrappers if you prefer).

For the sauce, in a small saucepan whisk together the water, peanut butter, soy sauce and ginger. Bring to a boil on medium heat. Reduce heat and simmer for 2 to 3 minutes, whisking until smooth. If the sauce becomes too thick, add a spoonful of water. Remove from the heat and add lime juice to taste. Set aside.

For the spring rolls, bring the water and quinoa to a boil in a medium saucepan. Reduce to a simmer, cover and cook for 15 minutes. Remove from the heat and let sit, covered, for another 10 minutes. Fluff with a fork and set aside to cool completely.

Fill a large bowl with warm water. Soak 1 rice paper wrapper in the water for 20 seconds, then lay flat on a work surface. In a line at the edge closest to you, sprinkle a small amount of sesame seeds. Top with a few cilantro leaves, a few pieces of cucumber, a strip or two of red pepper, a spoonful or two of shredded carrot and some sliced spinach. Top the vegetables with ¼ cup (60 mL) of cooked quinoa. Fold the sides over the filling and fold the bottom up. Continue to tightly roll the wrapper from the bottom to enclose the filling completely, then press the edges together to seal. (See the instructions on the wrapper packaging for additional clarification.) Repeat with the remaining ingredients. Serve on a platter with the ginger-lime peanut sauce.

PER SERVING: Energy 150 calories; Protein 5 g; Carbohydrates 20 g; Dietary Fiber 2 g; Fat 5 g; Sugar 2 g; Cholesterol 0 mg; Sodium 120 mg

MAKES 8 SPRING ROLLS

SAUCE

⅓ cup (75 mL) water

3 Tbsp (45 mL) smooth or crunchy natural peanut butter

1 Tbsp (30 mL) sodium-reduced soy sauce or tamari (gluten-free if required)

¼ tsp (1 mL) grated fresh ginger

Squeeze of fresh lime juice to taste

SPRING ROLLS

1⅓ cups (325 mL) water

⅔ cup (150 mL) quinoa

8 rice paper wrappers (8 ½ inches/21 cm)

2 Tbsp (30 mL) sesame seeds

¼ cup (60 mL) whole cilantro leaves

1 cup (250 mL) unpeeled English cucumber cut into thin half-moons

¼ cup (60 mL) thinly sliced red bell pepper

1 cup (250 mL) shredded carrot

1 cup (250 mL) thinly sliced baby spinach

Feeling experimental? Try one or more of these ingredients in your spring rolls: green onions, bean sprouts, thin slices of plain omelet, thinly sliced mango, cooked shrimp, thinly sliced pork, avocado slices, chopped peanuts or smoked salmon.

KALE, RED PEPPER & QUINOA TOSS

This recipe can be made in less time than you'd wait for take-out delivery. Satisfy your desire for a super-nutritious hot meal made in 20 minutes.

Combine 1⅓ cups (325 mL) of water and quinoa in a medium saucepan and bring to a boil. Reduce to a simmer, cover and cook for 15 minutes. Remove from the heat and set aside.

Pour ½ cup (125 mL) of water into a large saucepan. Layer the kale, red pepper and cannellini beans in the pan—do not stir. Bring to a boil, reduce to a simmer, cover and cook for 4 to 5 minutes (peek once to ensure the water does not completely cook away) or until the red pepper is tender and the beans are hot. Remove from the heat and drain away any remaining water.

Stir the pesto into the quinoa. Add the quinoa and 2 Tbsp (30 mL) of the Parmesan cheese to the kale mixture; toss well. Spoon the quinoa mixture into a serving bowl and sprinkle with the remaining Parmesan cheese. Sprinkle with lemon juice and serve immediately.

PER SERVING: Energy 230 calories; Protein 11 g; Carbohydrates 32 g; Dietary Fiber 7 g; Fat 7 g; Sugar 2 g; Cholesterol 5 mg; Sodium 170 mg

SERVES 6

1⅓ cups (325 mL) + ½ cup (125 mL) water

⅔ cup (150 mL) quinoa (any color)

4 cups (1 L) chopped kale, center ribs and stems removed

1 cup (250 mL) red bell pepper sliced into 2-inch (5 cm) lengths

1 can (19 oz/540 mL) cannellini or white kidney beans, drained and rinsed

3 Tbsp (45 mL) basil pesto

¼ cup (60 mL) grated Parmesan cheese

2 Tbsp (30 mL) lemon juice

SAVORY MUSHROOM SPINACH CRÊPES

MAKES 12 (6-INCH/15 CM) CRÊPES, SERVING 6

CRÊPES

⅓ cup (75 mL) quinoa flour

¼ cup (60 mL) brown rice flour or whole wheat flour

2 tsp (10 mL) cornstarch

2 large eggs + 2 large egg whites (or 3 whole, large eggs total)

1 cup (250 mL) 1% or 2% milk

FILLING

1 Tbsp (15 mL) salted butter

1 lb (450 g) cremini mushrooms, thinly sliced

¼ tsp (1 mL) salt (optional)

2 tsp (10 mL) minced garlic

1½ tsp (7 mL) minced fresh thyme

¾ tsp (4 mL) minced fresh rosemary

1 bag (10 oz/280 g) fresh baby spinach

¾ cup (175 mL) crumbled soft unripened goat cheese

These delicious and healthful crêpes will not last long! Not only are they great for a light supper with salad, they are wonderful served at brunch. If desired, in place of fresh spinach you can use a 10-oz (284 g) package of frozen spinach, thawed and well drained.

For the crêpes, stir together the quinoa flour, rice flour and cornstarch in a medium bowl. Add the eggs, egg whites and milk. Whisk until smooth.

Heat a lightly oiled 6-inch (15 cm) skillet on medium-high heat. Pour 2 Tbsp (30 mL) of batter into the center of the pan; quickly tilt the pan in a circular motion to spread the batter over the bottom. Flip crêpe when the edges begin to curl, after about 30 to 45 seconds. Cook the other side for another 30 seconds, then remove from the pan. Place the hot crêpe on a plate and cover with foil. Repeat with the remaining batter.

For the filling, melt the butter in a large nonstick skillet on medium heat. Add the mushrooms and salt (if using). Cook, stirring occasionally, for 8 to 10 minutes, until the mushrooms soften. Add the garlic, thyme and rosemary; cook for 30 seconds longer. Stir in the spinach and cook, stirring occasionally, for 4 minutes or until spinach has wilted. Remove from the heat.

Place a crêpe on a plate and spoon 1 Tbsp (15 mL) of crumbled goat cheese and ¼ cup (60 mL) of mushroom mixture in a line down the center. Fold in the edges (like a burrito). Serve immediately.

PER SERVING: Energy 210 calories; Protein 12 g; Carbohydrates 22 g; Dietary Fiber 4 g; Fat 9 g; Sugar 4 g; Cholesterol 80 mg; Sodium 240 mg

INDIVIDUAL MIGHTY MEAT LOAVES

Take the guesswork out of what equals a serving size of meat loaf. This traditional-style meat loaf made with quinoa is baked in individual portions. This recipe makes enough to freeze extra for future meals or to make easy lunch sandwiches the next day.

Preheat the oven to 375°F (190°C). Lightly grease or spray with cooking oil a baking sheet or line with parchment.

Combine the water and quinoa in a medium saucepan and bring to a boil. Reduce to a simmer, cover and cook for 15 minutes. Remove from the heat and leave the lid on for an additional 10 minutes. Fluff with a fork and set aside to cool.

Heat the oil in a small skillet on medium-low heat. Add the onions and cook for about 5 minutes, until the onions are tender. (Add a spoonful of water to the pan if dry.) Add the thyme and garlic; continue to cook for 1 minute. Remove from the heat and let cool slightly.

In a medium bowl, beat the eggs. Add the quinoa, onion mixture, ground beef, parsley, milk, Worcestershire sauce, mustard and salt (if using); mix until combined. Scoop out ½-cup (125 mL) portions of the mixture and shape into 9 oval patties ¾ inch (2 cm) thick. Arrange on the baking sheet about 2 inches (5 cm) apart. Bake for 15 minutes.

Meanwhile, stir together the ketchup, brown sugar and vinegar in a small bowl. Using the back of a spoon, spread an even amount of the topping over each meat loaf. Bake for another 20 minutes or until the loaves have browned and the topping is bubbling. Serve hot.

PER SERVING: Energy 150 calories; Protein 13 g; Carbohydrates 12 g; Dietary Fiber 1 g; Fat 5 g; Sugar 3 g; Cholesterol 70 mg; Sodium 150 mg

MAKES 9 INDIVIDUAL MEAT LOAVES

1 cup (250 mL) water

½ cup (125 mL) quinoa

1 Tbsp (15 mL) grapeseed oil or vegetable oil

1 cup (250 mL) finely chopped onions

2¼ tsp (11 mL) chopped fresh thyme (or ¾ tsp/4 mL dried)

1½ tsp (7 mL) minced garlic

2 large eggs

1 lb (450 g) extra-lean ground beef

⅓ cup (75 mL) chopped fresh parsley (or 2 Tbsp/30 mL dried)

¼ cup (60 mL) skim milk

1 Tbsp (15 mL) Worcestershire sauce (gluten-free if required)

2 tsp (10 mL) mild Dijon mustard

½ tsp (2 mL) salt (optional)

½ cup (125 mL) sugar-reduced ketchup

2 Tbsp (30 mL) packed brown sugar

1 tsp (5 mL) apple cider vinegar

MINI MEXICAN MEAT LOAVES

MAKES 6 INDIVIDUAL
MEAT LOAVES

1 cup (250 mL) water

½ cup (125 mL) quinoa

1 large egg

2 large egg whites

1 lb (450 g) ground chicken

¾ cup (175 mL) salsa

1½ tsp (7 mL) chili powder

1¼ tsp (6 mL) dried oregano

1 tsp (5 mL) minced garlic

⅓ cup (75 mL) shredded
reduced-fat aged
Cheddar cheese

These individual moist meat loaves are full of Mexican flavor, and making them as individual portions reduces the cooking time. By using quinoa in your favorite dishes such as this one, you can reduce the amount of meat you eat and gain nutrition from another protein source. These meat loaves can easily be frozen.

Preheat the oven to 350°F (180°C). Lightly grease a baking sheet or line with parchment.

Combine the water and quinoa in a medium saucepan and bring to a boil. Reduce to a simmer, cover and cook for 15 minutes. Remove from the heat and leave the lid on for an additional 5 minutes. Fluff with a fork and set aside to cool.

In a medium bowl, beat the egg and egg whites. Add 1½ cups (375 mL) cooked quinoa and the ground chicken, salsa, chili powder, oregano and garlic. Stir until well combined. Scoop out ½-cup (125 mL) portions of the mixture and shape into 6 oval patties ¾ inch (2 cm) thick. Arrange on the baking sheet about 2 inches (5 cm) apart.

Bake for 15 minutes. Sprinkle with the Cheddar. Bake for another 15 minutes or until no longer pink and slightly browned. Serve hot.

PER SERVING: Energy 200 calories; Protein 19 g; Carbohydrates 12 g; Dietary Fiber 2 g; Fat 8 g; Sugar 2 g; Cholesterol 95 mg; Sodium 360 mg

SMOKED SALMON SANDWICH WITH AVOCADO & QUINOA SPROUTS

This is a revamped version of the popular lox and cream cheese usually served on a bagel. Add quinoa sprouts and avocado and this open-faced sandwich is nutritious and bursting with flavor. This sandwich is a great way to use up any extra quinoa sprouts.

Toast the bread, if desired. Spread the herbed goat cheese over the bread. Sprinkle with the quinoa sprouts. Top with salmon, avocado and red onion. Serve immediately.

PER SERVING: Energy 240 calories; Protein 13 g; Carbohydrates 24 g; Dietary Fiber 5 g; Fat 11 g; Sugar 1 g; Cholesterol 15 mg; Sodium 420 mg

SERVES 1

1 slice sprouted grain sandwich bread or gluten-free bread

4 tsp (20 mL) herbed goat cheese

2 Tbsp (30 mL) quinoa sprouts (pages 10 and 11)

3 slices smoked wild Alaskan salmon

¼ avocado, peeled and thinly sliced

1 Tbsp (15 mL) thinly sliced red onion

An avocado is ripe when the skin is a dark brown/green color. A ripe avocado will give under gentle pressure.

SMOKY CHIPOTLE BBQ PULLED BEEF WITH RED CABBAGE & SPROUT SLAW

SERVES 8

PULLED BEEF

2 ½ lb (1.125 kg) inside round
   beef roast

¼ tsp (1 mL) salt (optional)

¼ tsp (1 mL) black pepper

1 Tbsp (15 mL) grapeseed oil
   or vegetable oil

2 cups (500 mL) beef stock

8 buns of your choice (optional)

BARBECUE SAUCE

(MAKES ABOUT 2 CUPS/500 ML)

1 cup (250 mL) water or cooking
   liquid from the slow cooker
   (fat removed)

1 can (5 ½ oz/156 mL) tomato paste

⅓ cup (75 mL) dark brown sugar

1 Tbsp (15 mL) Worcestershire sauce
   (gluten-free if required)

1 Tbsp (15 mL) white vinegar

1 Tbsp (15 mL) lemon juice

1 tsp (5 mL) minced garlic

1 tsp (5 mL) fancy molasses

½ tsp (2 mL) salt (optional)

½ tsp (2 mL) minced chipotle
   pepper in adobo sauce

¼ tsp (1 mL) chili powder

This recipe should be served with the Red Cabbage & Sprout Slaw on page 64. The fresh crunch of the salad along with the smoky chipotle is a spectacular combination. For a pork alternative, use an equivalent weight of pork tenderloin instead.

For the pulled beef, pat the roast dry with paper towel and rub with salt (if using) and pepper. Heat the oil in a large skillet on medium-high heat. Add the roast and sear on all sides, using tongs to turn the meat as it browns (each side should take 30 to 60 seconds). Place the roast in a 6-quart (6 L) slow cooker. Add the stock and just enough water to cover the roast. Cook on low for 7 to 8 hours or on high for 5 to 6 hours. Remove the roast when the internal temperature reaches 170°F (75°C). Cool the roast for 10 minutes, then shred the meat using 2 forks. Transfer meat to a medium bowl.

For the barbecue sauce, in a large saucepan, combine the water, tomato paste, brown sugar, Worcestershire sauce, vinegar, lemon juice, garlic, molasses, salt (if using), chipotle pepper and chili powder. Cook on medium-low heat, stirring occasionally, for about 8 minutes, until the sauce is thick enough to coat the back of a spoon. Stir in the shredded meat and cook until heated through. Spoon ⅓ cup (75 mL) pulled beef onto buns (if using). Serve with Red Cabbage & Sprout Slaw.

PER SERVING (without bun): Energy 360 calories; Protein 40 g; Carbohydrates 11 g; Dietary Fiber 1 g; Fat 16 g; Sugar 9 g; Cholesterol 120 mg; Sodium 170 mg

> Cook your meat consistently to perfection by using a digital or dial instant-read meat thermometer.

SPICY SALMON BURGERS

These salmon burgers burst with flavor! Sweet mango, creamy avocado, crisp red onion and a bit of heat are a brilliant match for salmon. Toast the buns for the best flavor and texture. Also delicious with grilled pineapple rings, if you like.

For the burgers, bring the water and quinoa to a boil in a medium saucepan. Reduce to a simmer, cover and cook for 15 minutes. Remove from the heat and let sit, covered, for another 5 minutes. Fluff with a fork and set aside to cool.

Preheat the oven to 400°F (200°C). Lightly grease or spray with cooking oil a baking sheet or line with parchment.

Flake the salmon with a fork in a shallow bowl. Add the cooled quinoa, egg, green onions, cilantro, sriracha sauce, honey, ginger and garlic. Mix until well combined. Form into 6 patties and place on the baking sheet. Bake for 7 minutes on each side, flipping gently.

For the yogurt topping, stir together the yogurt, lime juice and lime zest in a small bowl.

Place a cooked salmon burger on half of a toasted bun and top with a few pieces of sliced mango and avocado (or a pineapple ring, if you prefer). Top with a dollop of yogurt topping, a sprinkle of red onion and a sprig of cilantro. Serve immediately.

PER SERVING (with ½ bun): Energy 310 calories; Protein 23 g; Carbohydrates 32 g; Dietary Fiber 5 g; Fat 12 g; Sugar 12 g; Cholesterol 70 mg; Sodium 190 mg

SERVES 6

SALMON BURGERS

⅔ cup (150 mL) water

⅓ cup (75 mL) quinoa

2 cans (7 ½ oz/213 g each) sodium-reduced wild Pacific salmon, drained, larger bones removed

1 large egg, beaten

½ cup (125 mL) thinly sliced green onions

2 Tbsp (30 mL) chopped fresh cilantro

1 Tbsp (15 mL) sriracha or other hot chili sauce

1 tsp (5 mL) liquid honey

½ tsp (2 mL) grated fresh ginger

½ tsp (2 mL) minced garlic

3 whole wheat or gluten-free buns, halved and toasted

YOGURT TOPPING

¾ cup (175 mL) nonfat plain thick Greek yogurt

¾ tsp (4 mL) lime juice

½ tsp (2 mL) grated lime zest

GARNISHES

1 mango, peeled and thinly sliced

1 avocado, peeled and thinly sliced

6 grilled pineapple rings (optional)

¼ cup (60 mL) minced red onion

6 small sprigs fresh cilantro

THE BETTER BURGER

SERVES 8

1 cup (250 mL) water

½ cup (125 mL) red quinoa

1 Tbsp (15 mL) grapeseed oil
    or vegetable oil

1 cup (250 mL) diced onions

2 cups (500 mL) finely chopped
    cremini or white button
    mushrooms

1 tsp (5 mL) minced garlic

¾ tsp (4 mL) dried marjoram

¼ tsp (1 mL) dried oregano

1 large egg

⅔ cup (150 mL) shredded
    reduced-fat aged
    Cheddar cheese

½ cup (125 mL) toasted pecans,
    finely chopped

⅓ cup (75 mL) quick-cooking rolled
    oats (gluten-free if required)

1 Tbsp (15 mL) sodium-reduced
    soy sauce or tamari
    (gluten-free if required)

This burger is better! A meatless meat-lover's burger, this is a full-flavor burger with the perfect combination of toasted pecans, mushrooms, aged Cheddar, herbs and, of course, red quinoa. These patties hold together well for freezing, making for a quick and easy meal.

Preheat the oven to 350°F (180°C). Lightly grease a baking sheet or line with parchment.

Combine the water and quinoa in a medium saucepan. Bring to a boil, reduce to a simmer, cover and cook for 15 minutes. Remove from the heat and let sit, covered, for another 10 minutes. Fluff with a fork and set aside to cool.

Heat the oil in a large saucepan on medium heat. Add the onions and cook for about 5 minutes or until the onions start to become soft and transparent. Add the mushrooms, garlic, marjoram and oregano; cook for another 5 minutes or until the mushrooms are tender. Set aside to cool.

In a medium bowl, beat the egg. Add the quinoa, mushroom mixture, cheese, toasted pecans, oats and soy sauce. Scoop ½-cup (125 mL) portions of the mixture onto the baking sheet and shape into 8 or 9 patties 1 inch (2.5 cm) thick, leaving 1 inch (2.5 cm) between them. Bake for 27 to 30 minutes, until slightly browned and crispy. Serve with your favorite garnishes.

PER SERVING: Energy 150 calories; Protein 7 g; Carbohydrates 13 g; Dietary Fiber 2 g; Fat 9 g; Sugar 2 g; Cholesterol 25 mg; Sodium 130 mg

- These burgers can also be fried in an oiled skillet or grilled on a barbecue baking sheet.

- To toast nuts, preheat the oven to 350°F (180°C). Spread the nuts on a baking sheet and toast in the oven, stirring once if necessary, for 5 to 7 minutes, until fragrant and lightly toasted.

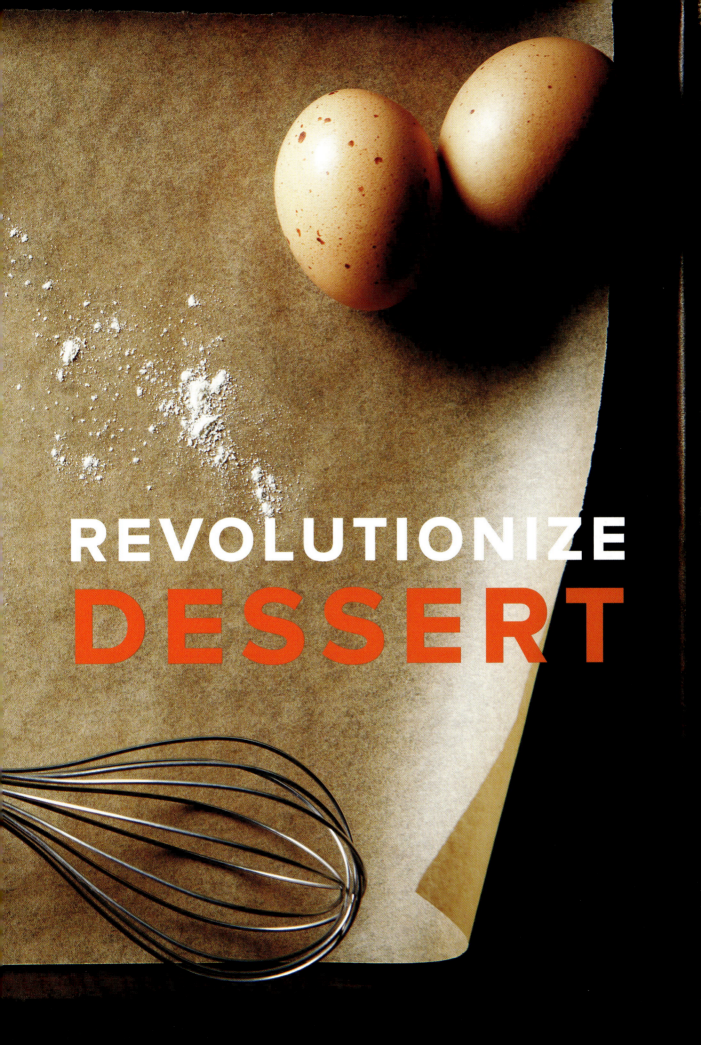

REVOLUTIONIZE
DESSERT

REVOLUTIONIZE DESSERT

NOT just a high-calorie afterthought, a delicious dessert can be healthful and an impressive finale to any meal, whether for guests or even just for yourself. It doesn't have to be full of fat and sugar to taste good, but no one else needs to know that. In this chapter, quinoa seeds, flour and flakes play a star role in desserts. In fact, the flavor of quinoa desserts may pleasantly surprise you.

Many of these satisfying and delectable desserts are a hit for gatherings and entertaining, convenient for weekday family snacks or perfect to take along to the office. For entertaining, try the Lemon Ginger Blueberry Crisp (page 200) or the Country Apple Pecan Pie (page 189). Chocolate Chip Fruit Granola Bars (page 184) make great family snacks that are easy to grab on the run. If you'd like to get the kids involved, try the Banana Mouse Pops (page 170) or Black Forest Goat Cheese Brownies (page 159). Great treats to show off at work include the Almond Butter Blondies (page 154) and the Salted Caramel Pecan Bites (page 160).

For a treat with frosting that has no refined sugar or added fat, try the Chocolate Cream Mini Cupcakes with Avocado Icing (page 179).

ALMOND BUTTER BLONDIES

¼ cup (60 mL) unsalted butter, softened

¾ cup (175 mL) smooth or crunchy natural almond butter

2 large eggs

¾ cup (175 mL) brown sugar

1 tsp (5 mL) pure vanilla extract

¾ cup (175 mL) quinoa flour

1 tsp (5 mL) baking powder

¼ tsp (1 mL) salt

1 cup (250 mL) semisweet chocolate chips

People likely won't even notice that these delightfully nutty blondies have quinoa in them. Chewy with just a hint of chocolate.

Preheat the oven to 350°F (180°C). Lightly grease or spray with cooking oil an 8-inch (2 L) square cake pan and line pan with parchment.

In a medium bowl, cream the butter and almond butter. Beat in the eggs, sugar and vanilla.

In a small bowl, whisk together the flour, baking powder and salt. Mix into the almond butter mixture. Stir in the chocolate chips. Spread the batter evenly in the prepared pan.

Bake for 18 to 20 minutes or until a toothpick inserted into the center comes out with just a few crumbs on it. Do not overbake. Let cool in the pan for 15 minutes before cutting into 24 squares.

Store in a sealed container in the refrigerator for up to 1 week.

PER SERVING: Energy 140 calories; Protein 3 g; Carbohydrates 13 g; Dietary Fiber 2 g; Fat 9 g; Sugar 9 g; Cholesterol 20 mg; Sodium 70 mg

ALMOND BUTTER PUFF SQUARES

These squares are so easy to make—and to eat! Rice syrup has a mild sweetness that doesn't overpower in this recipe. Rice syrup, puffed quinoa and almond butter are all widely available at most health-food stores and well-stocked grocery stores.

Lightly grease an 8-inch (2 L) square cake pan.

Measure the puffed quinoa into a large bowl. In a small saucepan, heat the rice syrup and almond butter on medium heat, whisking constantly. When the mixture is hot but not boiling, remove from the heat and stir in the vanilla. Pour the mixture over the puffed quinoa and stir until all puffs are coated. Stir in the almonds until evenly distributed. Firmly press the mixture into the prepared pan and cover with plastic wrap. Refrigerate for 1 hour before cutting into 16 squares.

Store in a sealed container in the refrigerator for up to 1 week.

PER SERVING: Energy 70 calories; Protein 2 g; Carbohydrates 8 g; Dietary Fiber 1 g; Fat 3.5 g; Sugar 4 g; Cholesterol 0 mg; Sodium 10 mg

MAKES 16 SQUARES

3 cups (750 mL) puffed quinoa

⅓ cup (75 mL) rice syrup

¼ cup (60 mL) almond butter

½ tsp (2 mL) pure vanilla extract

⅓ cup (75 mL) sliced almonds

CHOCOLATE PUFF SQUARES

MAKES 16 SQUARES

1 cup (250 mL) seedless raisins

1 cup (250 mL) hot water

1 cup (250 mL) unsalted natural peanut or almond butter

3 Tbsp (45 mL) unsweetened cocoa powder

1 Tbsp (15 mL) flax meal

1 tsp (5 mL) pure vanilla extract

1 tsp (5 mL) sesame oil

3 cups (750 mL) quinoa puffs

Decadent-tasting treats don't have to be made with highly processed ingredients. This simple, naturally sweet snack is scrumptious, but won't make you feel guilty.

Lightly grease or spray with cooking oil an 8-inch (2 L) cake pan. Set aside.

Place the raisins in a small bowl and add the hot water. Soak raisins, covered, for 10 to 15 minutes or until they are plump and soft. Drain. Combine the raisins and peanut butter in a food processor and blend until combined. Add the cocoa, flax meal, vanilla and sesame oil. Process until fairly smooth and no raisin chunks remain.

In a large bowl, combine the quinoa puffs and raisin mixture. Stir to coat the puffs well. Press the mixture into the prepared pan. Refrigerate, covered, until chilled and set. Cut into 16 squares.

Store in a sealed container in the refrigerator for up to 1 month.

PER SERVING: Energy 170 calories; Protein 5 g; Carbohydrates 18 g; Dietary Fiber 4 g; Fat 10 g; Sugar 6 g; Cholesterol 0 mg; Sodium 0 mg

NORI PEANUT BUTTER PUFF BARS

Nori, an edible seaweed, is best known as a sushi wrap. Less well known is that it partners fantastically with peanut butter for a very tasty (as well as nutritious) snack. Did we say tasty? A must-try!

Lightly grease an 8-inch (2 L) cake pan.

Combine the syrup, peanut butter and sesame oil in a large saucepan on medium-low heat. Stir constantly until blended well and hot but not boiling. Use a rubber spatula to stir in the puffed quinoa and nori pieces, stirring until well coated. Press into the prepared pan and allow to set for 1 hour. Cut into 16 pieces.

Store in a sealed container for up to 1 week.

PER SERVING: Energy 130 calories; Protein 3 g; Carbohydrates 18 g; Dietary Fiber 2 g; Fat 5 g; Sugar 6 g; Cholesterol 0 mg; Sodium 45 mg

MAKES 16 BARS

½ cup (125 mL) brown rice syrup

½ cup (125 mL) chunky
     natural peanut butter

1 tsp (5 mL) sesame oil

3 cups (750 mL) puffed quinoa

2 sheets nori, broken into
     ½-inch (1 cm) pieces

BLACK FOREST GOAT CHEESE BROWNIES

A dense and chewy brownie with a sophisticated sweetness. Buttermilk and goat cheese add a fresh flavor along with the familiar cherry goodness of Black Forest cake.

Preheat the oven to 325°F (160°C). Grease or spray with cooking oil a 9-inch (2.5 L) square cake pan and line pan with parchment.

In a small saucepan on medium-low heat, melt the chocolate chips and butter together, stirring until smooth. Set aside to cool.

Place the cherries in a small bowl, cover with boiling water and let sit for 10 minutes to hydrate. Drain the cherries.

Beat the sugar, eggs and vanilla in a medium bowl until combined. Beat in the melted chocolate mixture. Mix in the flour just until blended, then mix in the buttermilk until well blended.

Pour half of the brownie batter into the prepared pan and spread it evenly. Top with the cherries and goat cheese. Pour the other half of the brownie batter on top, spreading evenly.

Bake for 30 minutes or until the middle of the cake springs back when gently pressed. Do not overbake. Cool in the pan. Chill before cutting into 25 squares.

Store in a sealed container in the refrigerator for up to 1 week.

PER SERVING: Energy 160 calories; Protein 3 g; Carbohydrates 17 g; Dietary Fiber 2 g; Fat 10 g; Sugar 11 g; Cholesterol 30 mg; Sodium 30 mg

MAKES 25 BROWNIES

1½ cups (375 mL) semisweet chocolate chips

¾ cup (175 mL) unsalted butter

¾ cup (175 mL) dried whole cherries

½ cup (125 mL) organic cane sugar or white sugar

2 large eggs

1 tsp (5 mL) pure vanilla extract

1 cup (250 mL) quinoa flour

¼ cup (60 mL) buttermilk

1 cup (250 mL) crumbled goat cheese

SALTED CARAMEL PECAN BITES

CARAMEL BITES

1¼ cups (300 mL) quinoa flour

¼ tsp (1 mL) baking soda

¼ tsp (1 mL) salt

1 large egg

½ cup (125 mL) unsalted butter, melted and cooled

½ cup (125 mL) brown sugar

1 tsp (5 mL) pure vanilla extract

⅓ cup (75 mL) semisweet chocolate chips

⅓ cup (75 mL) chopped pecans

CARAMEL TOPPING

⅓ cup (75 mL) brown sugar

¼ cup (60 mL) 18% cream

2½ Tbsp (37 mL) unsalted butter

½ tsp (2 mL) coarse sea salt

These tasty little morsels are just the right size to satisfy a hankering for sweet and savory, with a bit of chocolate and caramel topped off with the tiniest sprinkle of coarse sea salt.

Preheat the oven to 350°F (180°C). Grease or thoroughly spray with cooking oil two 12-cup muffin pans. (You can use mini muffin pans, if you prefer.)

For the caramel bites, in a medium bowl, whisk together the flour, baking soda and salt. In a small bowl, beat the egg, then stir in the butter, brown sugar and vanilla. Add the butter mixture to the flour mixture and mix well. Stir in the chocolate chips and pecans. Chill the dough for 20 to 30 minutes.

Use a tablespoon to scoop out dough and roll into 1-inch (2.5 cm) balls. Place one ball in each muffin cup. (You will not use all the dough.) Bake for 7 minutes. Do not overbake. Cool in the pan. Repeat with remaining dough.

For the caramel topping, in a medium saucepan, bring the brown sugar, cream and butter to a boil on high heat, stirring. Reduce the heat to medium-low and stir constantly until the mixture is a thick caramel sauce, about 15 minutes. Remove from the heat and let cool for 10 minutes.

Drop a teaspoon of caramel sauce on top of each pecan bite. Top each with a tiny sprinkle of coarse sea salt.

Store in a sealed container in the refrigerator for up to 1 week.

PER SERVING: Energy 100 calories; Protein 1 g; Carbohydrates 10 g; Dietary Fiber 1 g; Fat 7 g; Sugar 5 g; Cholesterol 20 mg; Sodium 75 mg

ALMOND CINNAMON COOKIES

Inspiration for these cookies came from *Fave dei Morti* (or "beans of the dead"), small bean-shaped cakes made by Italians for All Souls' Day. It is the combination of almonds, pine nuts, lemon and cinnamon that makes for such a flavorful combination.

Preheat the oven to 325°F (160°C). Line a baking sheet with parchment.

In a food processor, combine the almonds and pine nuts. Process until the nuts are approximately ¼-inch (5 mm) pieces. Add the flour, honey, egg, egg white, butter, cornstarch, cinnamon and lemon zest. Pulse just until the almonds become the texture of meal but stop before the mixture becomes nut butter. (You will know you have reached this point when there is a small amount of nut butter forming on the edge of the bowl.) Using a teaspoon, drop the dough onto the baking sheet, about 1½ inches (4 cm) apart.

Bake for 12 to 15 minutes, until the edges begin to turn golden. Cool cookies on a rack.

Store in a sealed container for up to 2 weeks.

PER SERVING: Energy 35 calories; Protein 1 g; Carbohydrates 3 g; Dietary Fiber 0 g; Fat 2 g; Sugar 2 g; Cholesterol 5 mg; Sodium 0 mg

MAKES 50 COOKIES

¾ cup (175 mL) whole raw almonds

¼ cup (60 mL) pine nuts

⅓ cup (75 mL) quinoa flour

⅓ cup (75 mL) liquid honey

1 large egg

1 large egg white

2 Tbsp (30 mL) unsalted butter, softened

2 Tbsp (30 mL) cornstarch

1 tsp (5 mL) cinnamon

1½ tsp (7 mL) grated lemon zest

Don't like having to grease baking sheets or use parchment? Try a silicone baking sheet liner, available at most kitchen supply stores. Liners make for easy cleanup and aid even heat distribution.

PEANUT BUTTER CHIA COOKIES

MAKES 30 COOKIES

½ cup (125 mL) natural
    peanut butter

½ cup (125 mL) unsalted
    butter, softened

¾ cup (175 mL) brown sugar

1 large egg

1 tsp (5 mL) pure vanilla extract

1 cup (250 mL) quinoa flour

¾ tsp (4 mL) baking soda

½ tsp (2 mL) baking powder

2 Tbsp (30 mL) chia seeds

½ cup (125 mL) chopped
    unsalted peanuts

These cookies are soft, sweet and simple, with a delicious crisp texture and the added crunch of peanuts. Chia seeds do not need to be ground before eating. They provide additional calcium, fiber and omega-3s.

Preheat the oven to 375°F (190°C). Grease a baking sheet or line with parchment.

In a large bowl, beat the peanut butter, butter, sugar, egg and vanilla until combined well. In a medium bowl, whisk together the flour, baking soda and baking powder. Stir in the chia seeds and peanuts. Add the flour mixture to the peanut butter mixture and mix well. Scoop the dough into 1-inch (2.5 cm) balls and place them 2 inches (5 cm) apart on the baking sheet.

Bake for 10 minutes or until bottoms are lightly golden. Allow the cookies to sit for 4 minutes before transferring to a rack to cool.

Store in a sealed container for up to 1 week or freeze for up to 1 month.

PER SERVING: Energy 100 calories; Protein 2 g; Carbohydrates 8 g; Dietary Fiber 1 g; Fat 7 g; Sugar 4 g; Cholesterol 15 mg; Sodium 60 mg

DOUBLE CHOCOLATE MINT COOKIES

Everyone loves these soft and chewy chocolate cookies with the fresh flavor of mint.

Preheat the oven to 375°F (190°C).

Cream the butter with the sugar in a large bowl until light and fluffy. Beat in the eggs until well combined. Beat in the mint extract until the mixture is smooth. In another large bowl, whisk together the flour, cocoa, baking soda and salt. Add the butter mixture to the flour mixture and blend well. Stir in the chocolate chips. Roll dough into 1¼-inch (3 cm) balls. Place the balls 2 inches (5 cm) apart on a baking sheet and flatten slightly with the palm of your hand.

Bake for 8 to 10 minutes or until the edges are slightly crispy but cookies are still soft and chewy. Allow the cookies to sit on the baking sheet for 5 minutes before transferring them to a rack to cool.

Store in a sealed container for up to 1 week or freeze for up to 1 month.

PER SERVING: Energy 120 calories; Protein 2 g; Carbohydrates 14 g; Dietary Fiber 2 g; Fat 7 g; Sugar 8 g; Cholesterol 25 mg; Sodium 85 mg

MAKES 24 COOKIES

½ cup (125 mL) unsalted butter, softened

¾ cup (175 mL) brown sugar

2 large eggs, beaten

½ tsp (2 mL) pure mint or peppermint extract

1¼ cups (300 mL) quinoa flour

⅓ cup (75 mL) sifted unsweetened cocoa powder

1 tsp (5 mL) baking soda

¼ tsp (1 mL) salt

1 cup (250 mL) semisweet chocolate chips

OATMEAL DATE SANDWICH COOKIES

MAKES 24 COOKIES

2 cups (500 mL) large-flake rolled
    oats (gluten-free if required)

2 cups (500 mL) quinoa flour

½ tsp (2 mL) baking powder

¼ tsp (1 mL) baking soda

½ cup (125 mL) unsalted
    butter, softened

⅔ cup (150 mL) brown sugar

½ cup (125 mL) unsweetened
    applesauce

½ cup (125 mL) buttermilk

1 tsp (5 mL) pure vanilla extract

1¼ cups (300 mL) chopped
    pitted dates

⅔ cup (150 mL) water

⅓ cup (75 mL) organic
    cane sugar or white sugar

1 tsp (5 mL) lemon juice

An old-fashioned favorite transformed. Oats, vanilla and lemony dates complement the nutty fragrance of quinoa flour.

Preheat the oven to 350°F (180°C). Lightly grease a baking sheet or line with parchment.

In a large bowl, whisk together the oats, flour, baking powder and baking soda. In a separate bowl, cream the butter with the sugar until light and fluffy. Stir in the applesauce, buttermilk and vanilla. Pour the butter mixture into the flour mixture and blend until well combined. Place tablespoons of dough 2 inches (5 cm) apart on the baking sheet and gently flatten with the palm of your hand. (If dough is too sticky, place in the refrigerator for 15 to 20 minutes first.)

Bake for 13 to 15 minutes, until the edges are just starting to brown. Allow the cookies to cool for 10 minutes before transferring them to a rack to cool.

In a medium saucepan, combine the dates, water and sugar. Bring to a boil, reduce the heat to medium, and continue to cook, stirring frequently, until the mixture is thick and fairly smooth. Stir in the lemon juice. Set aside to cool for 10 minutes.

Spread ½ tsp (2 mL) of the date mixture on the bottom of one cookie and sandwich it with another cookie. Repeat with remaining cookies.

Store in a sealed container in the refrigerator for up to 1 week.

PER SERVING: Energy 160 calories; Protein 3 g; Carbohydrates 26 g; Dietary Fiber 3 g; Fat 5 g; Sugar 13 g; Cholesterol 10 mg; Sodium 30 mg

PEANUT BUTTER & JELLY SANDWICH COOKIES

These easy-to-make bite-size treats will satisfy your childhood urge for a PB&J sandwich.

Preheat the oven to 350°F (180°C). Lightly grease or spray with cooking oil a baking sheet or line with parchment.

In a large bowl, beat the peanut butter, sugar, quinoa flakes and egg until combined. If texture appears crumbly, add 1 to 2 Tbsp (15 to 30 mL) water and massage into dough until no longer crumbly. Measure out teaspoons of dough and place them ½ inch (1 cm) apart on the baking sheet. Flatten to about 1 inch (2.5 cm) across with the palm of your hand.

Bake for 5 minutes, until the bottoms are slightly golden. Transfer to a rack to cool.

Spread ¼ tsp (1 mL) of jam on the bottom of one cookie and sandwich it with another cookie. Repeat with remaining cookies.

Store in a sealed container in the refrigerator for up to 1 week.

PER SERVING: Energy 90 calories; Protein 3 g; Carbohydrates 8 g; Dietary Fiber 1 g; Fat 6 g; Sugar 4 g; Cholesterol 5 mg; Sodium 60 mg

MAKES 30 COOKIES

1 ¼ cups (300 mL) natural peanut butter

½ cup (125 mL) organic cane sugar or white sugar

½ cup (125 mL) quinoa flakes

1 large egg

3 Tbsp (45 mL) low-sugar raspberry or strawberry jam

PUMPKIN CHOCOLATE PECAN COOKIES

MAKES 40 COOKIES

½ cup (125 mL) unsalted butter, softened

¾ cup (175 mL) brown sugar

1 large egg

1½ cups (375 mL) pumpkin purée

1¾ cups (425 mL) quinoa flour

1 tsp (5 mL) baking soda

¼ tsp (1 mL) salt

1½ tsp (7 mL) cinnamon

1 tsp (5 mL) nutmeg

1 tsp (5 mL) ground ginger

½ tsp (2 mL) ground cloves

½ cup (125 mL) semisweet chocolate chips

⅓ cup (75 mL) chopped pecans

Full of pumpkin spice, these small cookies are soft, moist and nutty. If you prefer a larger cookie, increase size to 2-inch (5 cm) balls and bake for 15 minutes instead.

Preheat the oven to 350°F (180°C). Grease 2 baking sheets or line with parchment.

In a large bowl, cream the butter with the sugar until light and fluffy. Add the egg and pumpkin; stir well. In a medium bowl, whisk together the flour, baking soda, salt, cinnamon, nutmeg, ginger and cloves; stir into the pumpkin mixture until combined. Stir in the chocolate chips and pecans. Roll dough into 1¼-inch (3 cm) balls and place 2 inches (5 cm) apart on the baking sheets.

Bake cookies, 1 sheet at a time, for 12 to 13 minutes, until cookies are golden on the edges. Do not overbake. Allow to cool for 10 minutes before transferring to a rack to cool completely.

Store in a sealed container for up to 1 week.

PER SERVING: Energy 70 calories; Protein 1 g; Carbohydrates 8 g; Dietary Fiber 1 g; Fat 4 g; Sugar 4 g; Cholesterol 10 mg; Sodium 35 mg

RAISIN SPICE COOKIES

This soft cookie is full of chewy raisins and the warm aroma of spices and nuts. If you prefer a smaller cookie, simply make 1-inch (2.5 cm) balls and decrease the cooking time to 10 minutes.

Preheat the oven to 350°F (180°C). Grease or spray with cooking oil 2 baking sheets or line with parchment.

Place the raisins in a small bowl, cover with boiling water and let sit for 10 minutes to hydrate.

Meanwhile, in a medium bowl, beat the butter with the sugar until smooth and fluffy. Beat in the eggs, then beat in the vanilla until well blended. In a large bowl, whisk together the quinoa flour, almond flour, baking soda, salt, cinnamon, nutmeg and cloves. Add the butter mixture to the flour mixture and stir until mixed well. Drain the raisins and fold them and the walnuts into the dough until well mixed.

Scoop the dough into 2-inch (5 cm) balls and place 2 inches (5 cm) apart on the baking sheets.

Bake cookies, 1 sheet at a time, for 12 minutes or until edges are light golden. Allow cookies to cool 10 minutes before transferring to a rack to cool completely.

Store in a sealed container in the refrigerator for up to 1 week or freeze for up to 2 weeks.

PER SERVING: Energy 190 calories; Protein 3 g; Carbohydrates 17 g; Dietary Fiber 2 g; Fat 13 g; Sugar 10 g; Cholesterol 35 mg; Sodium 85 mg

MAKES 24 COOKIES

1 cup (250 mL) seedless raisins

½ cup (125 mL) unsalted butter, softened

¾ cup (175 mL) organic cane sugar or white sugar

2 large eggs, beaten

1 tsp (5 mL) pure vanilla extract

1½ cups (375 mL) quinoa flour

½ cup (125 mL) almond flour

1 tsp (5 mL) baking soda

¼ tsp (1 mL) salt

1½ tsp (7 mL) cinnamon

½ tsp (2 mL) nutmeg

½ tsp (2 mL) ground cloves

1 cup (250 mL) chopped walnuts

APRICOT COCONUT SNOWBALLS

MAKES 70 BALLS

½ cup (125 mL) unsweetened
    shredded coconut

2 cups (500 mL) dried apricots

1½ cups (375 mL) quinoa flakes

1 cup (250 mL) seedless raisins

1 tsp (5 mL) grated orange zest

⅓ cup (75 mL) freshly
    squeezed orange juice

Feeling peckish? These treats are ideal for popping in your mouth when you need that after-dinner sweet fix. Also perfect for giving, these snowballs make great fare for a Christmas or New Year's snack tray.

Preheat the oven to 350°F (180°C). Spread the coconut on a baking sheet and toast until light golden, about 3 minutes. (Watch the coconut closely, as it burns quickly.) Set aside in a shallow bowl to cool.

Place the apricots, quinoa flakes, raisins, orange zest and orange juice in a food processor; process until relatively smooth and no apricot or raisin chunks remain.

Spoon out apricot mixture with a teaspoon and roll into a ball. Roll in toasted coconut.

Store in a sealed container with each layer separated by parchment or waxed paper. Store in the refrigerator for up to 1 month.

PER SERVING: Energy 45 calories; Protein 1 g; Carbohydrates 9 g; Dietary Fiber 1 g; Fat 1 g; Sugar 3 g; Cholesterol 0 mg; Sodium 60 mg

NO-BAKE CHOCOLATE MACAROONS

We've reinvented the chocolate macaroon in this naturally sweetened, deliciously chewy, no-bake recipe.

Line a baking sheet with parchment or waxed paper.

Melt the honey and butter together in a large saucepan on medium heat. Stir until combined. Stir in the cocoa and vanilla until smooth. When mixture is heated through, remove from the heat. Add the quinoa flakes, oats, coconut and flax meal; stir until the dry ingredients are completely coated. Using a tablespoon, scoop the mixture into mounds on the baking sheet. Reshape any mounds that fall apart. Leave macaroons to sit at room temperature or colder for 1 hour or more to set.

Store macaroons in a sealed container, with each layer separated by parchment or waxed paper. Store at room temperature for up to 1 week or refrigerated for up to 1 month.

PER SERVING: Energy 100 calories; Protein 2 g; Carbohydrates 15 g; Dietary Fiber 2 g; Fat 4.5 g; Sugar 7 g; Cholesterol 5 mg; Sodium 60 mg

MAKES 36 MACAROONS

1 cup (250 mL) honey

⅓ cup (75 mL) salted butter

½ cup (125 mL) unsweetened cocoa powder

1½ tsp (7 mL) pure vanilla extract

1½ cups (375 mL) quinoa flakes

1¼ cups (300 mL) quick-cooking rolled oats (gluten-free if required)

1¼ cups (300 mL) unsweetened shredded coconut

⅓ cup (75 mL) flax meal

BANANA MOUSE POPS

SERVES 1

1 small unpeeled banana

1 Tbsp (15 mL) quinoa flakes

1 Tbsp (15 mL) unsweetened
   shredded or flaked coconut

1 Tbsp (15 mL) + 1 tsp (5 mL)
   smooth natural peanut butter

1 large dried apricot, halved
   crosswise

3 dried currants

Scrumptious and fun, these quinoa pops can be made with marshmallow ears and chocolate chip eyes, or apricot ears and currant eyes for a healthier version. Easily multiply the ingredients to make as many pops as you please.

Cut 1 inch (2.5 cm) from the stem end of the banana. Insert a wooden food stick into cut end, pushing it in 2 to 3 inches (5 to 8 cm). (If desired, insert the stick into the underside of the banana, as shown.) Remove banana peel, cover banana with plastic wrap and freeze until firm, 3 to 4 hours.

Meanwhile, preheat the oven to 350°F (180°C). Spread the quinoa flakes and coconut on a baking sheet and bake until fragrant and toasted, about 5 minutes. Set aside to cool.

Remove plastic wrap from the frozen banana and spread 1 Tbsp (15 mL) of the peanut butter over the banana. Place the quinoa-coconut mixture on a plate. Roll the banana in the flakes, making sure to cover the entire banana. Using the remaining 1 tsp (5 mL) peanut butter as glue, attach the apricot halves for ears and currants for eyes and nose. Serve immediately.

PER SERVING: Energy 250 calories; Protein 7 g; Carbohydrates 34 g; Dietary Fiber 5 g; Fat 12 g; Sugar 14 g; Cholesterol 0 mg; Sodium 180 mg

ROSEMARY WALNUT CRISPS WITH CRANBERRIES

MAKES 72 COOKIES

¾ cup (175 mL) quinoa flour

¼ cup (60 mL) brown rice flour

2 Tbsp (30 mL) cornstarch

½ tsp (2 mL) baking powder

½ tsp (2 mL) salt

½ cup (125 mL) sweetened dried cranberries

⅓ cup (75 mL) chopped walnuts

2 tsp (10 mL) chopped fresh rosemary

1 cup (250 mL) reduced-fat or regular sour cream (gluten-free if required)

⅓ cup (75 mL) light brown sugar

1 large egg

2 tsp (10 mL) fancy molasses

Similar to a biscotti, these twice-baked thin, crunchy crisps are delicious eaten as-is or dipped in coffee.

Preheat the oven to 350°F (180°C). Lightly grease a 9- × 5-inch (2 L) loaf pan. Line the bottom with parchment.

In a medium bowl, whisk together the quinoa flour, rice flour, cornstarch, baking powder and salt. Stir in the cranberries, walnuts and rosemary. In a small bowl, whisk together the sour cream, brown sugar, egg and molasses. Pour the wet mixture into the flour mixture and stir just until combined. Pour the batter into the loaf pan, using a spatula to level the top evenly.

Bake for 30 minutes or until the loaf has risen slightly and a toothpick inserted in the center comes out clean. Cool completely in the pan.

Turn the loaf out onto a cutting board. Slice in half lengthwise. Holding the loaf together carefully with one hand and using a sharp knife, cut into thin slices (¼ inch/5 mm). If the loaf crumbles and is difficult to slice, wrap it in plastic wrap and place in the refrigerator for at least 1 hour or overnight.

Place the oven racks one above and one below the center of the oven. Preheat the oven to 300°F (150°C). Line 2 baking sheets with parchment.

Arrange the slices on the baking sheets. Bake for 15 minutes. Turn the crisps over. Place baking sheets in opposite positions and bake for another 15 minutes, keeping an eye on them in the last 5 minutes to make sure they do not get too dark. Let cool and dry out on the baking sheets.

Store in a sealed container for up to 1 month.

PER SERVING: Energy 25 calories; Protein 0 g; Carbohydrates 3 g; Dietary Fiber 0 g; Fat 1 g; Sugar 1 g; Cholesterol 5 mg; Sodium 25 mg

BLUEBERRY ALMOND MUFFINS

Healthy blueberry muffins are here! No white flour necessary. Filled with wholesome almonds, blueberries and quinoa, these aren't just a super dessert but make a terrific snack any time of the day.

Preheat the oven to 400°F (200°C). Lightly grease or spray with cooking oil a 12-cup muffin pan or line with paper liners.

In a small saucepan, bring the water and quinoa to a boil. Reduce to a simmer, cover and cook for 15 minutes. Remove from the heat and leave covered for another 10 minutes. The quinoa must be fluffy.

In a blender, combine the eggs, applesauce, brown sugar, oil, vanilla and ¼ cup (60 mL) of the quinoa. Blend until smooth. Repeat adding ¼ cup (60 mL) quinoa, puréeing after each addition, until you have added 1½ cups (375 mL).

In a large bowl, whisk together the almond flour, oats, cornstarch, baking powder, baking soda and salt. Add the blueberries and stir to coat with flour mixture. Add the quinoa purée, using a spatula to get all the purée out. Stir just until blended. Divide batter among muffin cups.

Bake for 30 minutes or until a toothpick inserted in the center comes out clean. Transfer to a rack to cool.

Store in a sealed container for up to 1 week.

PER SERVING: Energy 160 calories; Protein 4 g; Carbohydrates 17 g; Dietary Fiber 2 g; Fat 9 g; Sugar 6 g; Cholesterol 30 mg; Sodium 160 mg

MAKES 12 MUFFINS

1 cup (250 mL) water

½ cup (125 mL) white quinoa

2 large eggs, beaten

1 cup (250 mL) unsweetened applesauce

¼ cup (60 mL) lightly packed brown sugar

¼ cup (60 mL) grapeseed oil or vegetable oil

1 tsp (5 mL) pure vanilla extract

⅔ cup (150 mL) almond flour

⅓ cup (75 mL) quick-cooking rolled oats (gluten-free if required)

3 Tbsp (45 mL) cornstarch

1 tsp (5 mL) baking powder

½ tsp (2 mL) baking soda

¼ tsp (1 mL) salt

1 cup (250 mL) fresh or frozen blueberries

CHAI CHOCOLATE CHIP MUFFINS

MAKES 12 MUFFINS

1½ cups (375 mL) quinoa flour

1½ tsp (7 mL) baking powder

½ tsp (2 mL) baking soda

¼ tsp (1 mL) salt

½ tsp (2 mL) ground cardamom

¼ tsp (1 mL) cinnamon

¼ tsp (1 mL) ground ginger

¼ tsp (1 mL) ground cloves

¼ tsp (1 mL) black pepper

¼ cup (60 mL) unsalted butter, softened

¼ cup (60 mL) organic cane sugar or white sugar

2 large eggs

¼ cup (60 mL) buttermilk

1 cup (250 mL) unsweetened applesauce

½ cup (125 mL) semisweet chocolate chips

2 Tbsp (30 mL) sliced almonds

The warm, spicy blend of chai seasoning makes these quinoa muffins great with hot tea or coffee—or whenever you need a treat to awaken your senses.

Preheat the oven to 400°F (200°C). Lightly grease a 12-cup muffin pan.

In a large bowl, whisk together the quinoa flour, baking powder, baking soda, salt, cardamom, cinnamon, ginger, cloves and pepper. In a medium bowl, cream the butter and sugar together just until blended. Beat in the eggs, 1 at a time. Beat in the buttermilk and applesauce. Add this mixture to the flour mixture and stir just until blended. Stir in the chocolate chips. Use a large spoon or ice-cream scoop to divide the batter evenly among the muffin cups. Top each muffin with 2 or 3 almond slices.

Bake for 16 to 18 minutes or until a toothpick inserted into the center of a muffin comes out clean. Cool in the pan.

Store in a sealed container for up to 1 week.

PER SERVING: Energy 170 calories; Protein 4 g; Carbohydrates 22 g; Dietary Fiber 3 g; Fat 8 g; Sugar 10 g; Cholesterol 40 mg; Sodium 180 mg

CHOCOLATE BROWNIE
SOUR CREAM MUFFINS

Mmm... are they muffins or cupcakes? Without frosting it is a muffin, and with frosting it's a cupcake. Either way, it's a moist and delicious dessert or snack.

Preheat the oven to 400°F (200°C). Lightly grease or spray with cooking oil a 12-cup muffin pan or line with paper liners.

In a medium bowl, whisk together the flour, cocoa, sugar, baking powder, baking soda and salt. In a small bowl, beat the egg; whisk in the sour cream, milk, oil and vanilla. Add this mixture to the flour mixture and stir just until combined. Stir in the chocolate chips and nuts. Evenly divide the batter among the muffin cups.

Bake for 15 minutes or until a toothpick inserted in the center of a muffin comes out clean. Cool in the pan.

Store in a sealed container in the refrigerator for up to 1 week.

PER SERVING: Energy 220 calories; Protein 5 g; Carbohydrates 24 g; Dietary Fiber 3 g; Fat 13 g; Sugar 11 g; Cholesterol 25 mg; Sodium 280 mg

MAKES 12 MUFFINS

1¼ cups (300 mL) quinoa flour

½ cup (125 mL) sifted unsweetened cocoa powder

½ cup (125 mL) organic cane sugar or white sugar

2½ tsp (12 mL) baking powder

½ tsp (2 mL) baking soda

½ tsp (2 mL) salt

1 large egg

1 cup (250 mL) reduced-fat sour cream (gluten-free if required)

¾ cup (175 mL) 1% milk

⅓ cup (75 mL) grapeseed oil or vegetable oil

1 tsp (5 mL) pure vanilla extract

¼ cup (60 mL) semisweet mini chocolate chips

¼ cup (60 mL) chopped toasted walnuts or pecans

- To toast nuts, preheat the oven to 350°F (180°C). Spread the nuts on a baking sheet and toast in the oven, stirring once if necessary, for 5 to 7 minutes, until fragrant and lightly toasted.

- If you plan to frost the muffins, we suggest that you omit the nuts.

SWEET POTATO DATE MUFFINS

MAKES 12 MUFFINS

1 ¾ cups (425 mL) quinoa flour

1 tsp (5 mL) baking powder

1 tsp (5 mL) baking soda

¼ tsp (1 mL) salt

¼ tsp (1 mL) ground cloves

¼ tsp (1 mL) nutmeg

⅓ cup (75 mL) unsalted butter, softened

⅓ cup (75 mL) organic cane sugar or white sugar

2 Tbsp (30 mL) pure maple syrup

2 large eggs

2 cups (500 mL) mashed cooked sweet potato

¾ cup (175 mL) chopped pitted dates

Light quinoa flour, moist sweet potatoes and soft dates make a tasty combination in these fluffy, satisfying muffins.

Preheat the oven to 375°F (190°C). Lightly grease a 12-cup muffin pan or line with paper liners.

In a large bowl, whisk together the quinoa flour, baking powder, baking soda, salt, cloves and nutmeg. In a medium bowl, cream the butter, sugar and maple syrup. Beat in the eggs, 1 at a time. Whisk in the sweet potato. Add this mixture to the flour mixture and stir just until blended. Add the dates, mixing until well distributed. Use a large spoon or ice-cream scoop to divide the batter evenly among the muffin cups.

Bake for 18 to 20 minutes or until a toothpick inserted into the center of a muffin comes out clean. Cool in the pan.

Store in a sealed container in the refrigerator for up to 1 week.

PER SERVING: Energy 230 calories; Protein 4 g; Carbohydrates 37 g; Dietary Fiber 4 g; Fat 7 g; Sugar 16 g; Cholesterol 45 mg; Sodium 230 mg

PUMPKIN CUPCAKES

These cupcakes are soft, moist and bursting with pumpkin flavor. Plain or topped with cream cheese frosting, pumpkin is always in season! Decorate to match all of your year-round celebrations, including birthdays, Halloween and even Valentine's Day.

Preheat the oven to 375°F (190°C). Lightly grease a 12-cup muffin pan or line with paper liners.

In a medium bowl, whisk together the quinoa flour, baking powder, baking soda, salt, cinnamon, ginger, cloves and nutmeg. In a large bowl, beat the eggs; add the pumpkin, sugar, buttermilk, apple-sauce and oil. Whisk until smooth. Add the pumpkin mixture to the flour mixture; gently stir just until blended. Use a large spoon or ice-cream scoop to divide the batter evenly among the muffin cups.

Bake for 15 minutes or until a toothpick inserted into the center of a muffin comes out clean. Cool in the pan. If frosting, refrigerate for 2 hours beforehand.

Store in a sealed container in the refrigerator for up to 1 week.

PER SERVING: Energy 170 calories; Protein 4 g; Carbohydrates 29 g; Dietary Fiber 3 g; Fat 4.5 g; Sugar 13 g; Cholesterol 30 mg; Sodium 280 mg

MAKES 12 CUPCAKES

2 cups (500 mL) quinoa flour

2 ½ tsp (12 mL) baking powder

½ tsp (2 mL) baking soda

½ tsp (2 mL) salt

1 tsp (5 mL) cinnamon

1 tsp (5 mL) ground ginger

½ tsp (2 mL) ground cloves

½ tsp (2 mL) nutmeg

2 large eggs

1 cup (250 mL) pumpkin purée

¾ cup (175 mL) organic
    cane sugar or white sugar

½ cup (125 mL) buttermilk

⅓ cup (75 mL) unsweetened
    applesauce

2 Tbsp (30 mL) vegetable oil

Really want to celebrate? Turn this into a double layer cake by evenly dividing the batter between 2 greased 8-inch (1.2 L) cake pans and bake for 20 to 22 minutes.

CHOCOLATE CREAM MINI CUPCAKES WITH AVOCADO ICING

These quinoa cupcakes will definitely satisfy your sweet tooth. The cupcakes can be made the day before, but the avocado icing is best made fresh on the day you are going to serve them.

Preheat the oven to 350°F (180°C). Line a 24-cup mini muffin pan with paper liners.

For the cupcakes, in a medium saucepan, bring the water and quinoa to a boil. Reduce to a simmer, cover and cook for 15 minutes. Remove from the heat and let sit with the cover on for another 15 minutes. The quinoa must be extra-fluffy.

In a blender, combine the sour cream, honey, egg, egg white, oil and vanilla. Blend until combined. Add ¼ cup (60 mL) of the quinoa and blend until completely smooth. Repeat adding ¼ cup (60 mL) quinoa, puréeing after each addition, until all the quinoa has been added.

In a medium bowl, whisk together the cocoa, baking powder, baking soda and salt until no lumps of cocoa powder remain. Add the puréed mixture. Stir just until blended. Divide the batter evenly among the cupcake liners.

Bake for 12 to 15 minutes, until a toothpick inserted in the center of a cupcake comes out clean. Cool in the pan.

For the icing, peel the avocado and in a small bowl, mash it with a fork until no big lumps remain. Place in a blender with the honey and vanilla. Purée until smooth. Add the cocoa powder and blend until completely incorporated. Transfer the icing to a piping bag (or a resealable plastic bag, then cut off one corner). Pipe the icing onto the cooled cupcakes.

Store in a sealed container in the refrigerator for up to 4 days (with the avocado icing).

PER SERVING (with icing): Energy 60 calories; Protein 1 g; Carbohydrates 7 g; Dietary Fiber 1 g; Fat 4 g; Sugar 3 g; Cholesterol 10 mg; Sodium 60 mg

MAKES 24 MINI CUPCAKES

CUPCAKES

⅔ cup (150 mL) water

⅓ cup (75 mL) white quinoa

¼ cup (60 mL) reduced-fat sour cream (gluten-free if required)

¼ cup (60 mL) liquid honey

1 large egg

1 large egg white

3 Tbsp (45 mL) grapeseed oil or light-tasting vegetable oil

½ tsp (125 mL) pure vanilla extract

⅓ cup (75 mL) sifted unsweetened cocoa powder

¾ tsp (4 mL) baking powder

¼ tsp (1 mL) baking soda

¼ tsp (1 mL) salt

ICING

1 ripe avocado

1 Tbsp (15 mL) liquid honey

1 tsp (5 mL) pure vanilla extract

¼ cup (60 mL) unsweetened cocoa powder

APPLE CINNAMON ENERGY BARS

½ cup (125 mL) quinoa

2 ½ cups (625 mL) unsalted raw almonds chopped into ¼-inch (5 mm) pieces

¼ cup (60 mL) peanuts chopped into ¼-inch (5 mm) pieces

¼ cup (60 mL) raw sesame seeds

1 cup (250 mL) dried apple chopped into ¼-inch (5 mm) to ½-inch (1 cm) pieces

¼ cup (60 mL) chopped raisins or whole dried currants

¼ cup (60 mL) honey

¼ cup (60 mL) pure maple syrup

1 Tbsp (15 mL) unsalted butter

1 tsp (5 mL) cinnamon

1 tsp (5 mL) pure vanilla extract

Look no further for that healthful and tasty granola bar for your family. This perfect blend of cinnamon, apple and nuts will be the first thing you grab when you need something healthy for lunches, hiking, camping or keeping in the glove compartment for those times you're stuck in traffic.

Preheat the oven to 350°F (180°C). Line bottom and sides of a 13- × 9-inch (3 L) cake pan with parchment or waxed paper. Cut another piece to cover the top.

Place the quinoa in a resealable plastic bag and gently roll over it with a rolling pin to crack the seeds slightly. Spread the quinoa, almonds, peanuts and sesame seeds evenly on a baking sheet. Bake for 5 minutes, then stir. Bake for another 5 minutes or until lightly toasted and fragrant. Pour the mixture into a large bowl, then add the apple and raisins. Mix with your hands to separate the fruit pieces.

Combine the honey, maple syrup, butter, cinnamon and vanilla in a small saucepan. Heat on medium heat, stirring, until bubbling. Pour over the quinoa mixture and stir to coat thoroughly.

Pour into the prepared pan and spread evenly with a spatula. Place the piece of parchment or waxed paper on top and press firmly all over. Let cool for 2 to 3 hours, then cut into 16 bars.

Wrap individual bars in plastic wrap or store in a sealed container for up to 1 month.

PER SERVING: Energy 190 calories; Protein 5 g; Carbohydrates 21 g; Dietary Fiber 3 g; Fat 10 g; Sugar 12 g; Cholesterol 0 mg; Sodium 20 mg

CASHEW APRICOT ENERGY BARS

Hearty and loaded with flavor, these granola bars will definitely satisfy your hunger. They're especially great for that mid-afternoon snack.

Preheat the oven to 350°F (180°C). Line bottom and sides of a 13- × 9-inch (3 L) cake pan with parchment or waxed paper. Cut another piece to cover the top.

Place the quinoa in a resealable plastic bag and gently roll over it with a rolling pin to crack the seeds slightly. Spread the quinoa, cashews, almonds, coconut and sunflower seeds evenly on a baking sheet. Bake for 5 minutes, then stir. Bake for another 5 minutes or until lightly toasted and fragrant. Stir again and set aside to cool slightly.

Pour the quinoa mixture into a large bowl, then add the apricots. Mix with your hands to separate the apricot pieces.

Heat the honey and vanilla in a small saucepan on medium heat, stirring often. Remove from the heat when honey is bubbling. Pour over the quinoa mixture and stir until evenly distributed.

Pour into the prepared pan and spread evenly with a spatula. Place the piece of parchment or waxed paper on top and press firmly all over. Let cool for 2 to 3 hours, then cut into 18 bars.

Wrap individual bars in plastic wrap or store in a sealed container for up to 1 month.

PER SERVING: Energy 160 calories; Protein 4 g; Carbohydrates 20 g; Dietary Fiber 2 g; Fat 9 g; Sugar 12 g; Cholesterol 0 mg; Sodium 0 mg

MAKES 18 BARS

½ cup (125 mL) quinoa

1 cup (250 mL) unsalted raw cashews, finely chopped (same size as a sunflower seed)

1 cup (250 mL) unsalted raw almonds, finely chopped (same size as a sunflower seed)

½ cup (125 mL) unsweetened shredded coconut

¼ cup (60 mL) unsalted raw sunflower seeds

1 cup (250 mL) finely chopped dried apricots

½ cup (125 mL) honey

¼ tsp (1 mL) pure vanilla extract

MIXED BERRIES WITH BLACK QUINOA & BLACK CURRANT YOGURT

SERVES 4

⅔ cup (150 mL) water

⅓ cup (75 mL) black quinoa

2 cups (500 mL) fresh raspberries

1 cup (250 mL) fresh blackberries

1 Tbsp (15 mL) organic
    cane sugar or white sugar

1⅓ cups (325 mL) low-fat
    plain yogurt

1 Tbsp (15 mL) pure maple syrup

5 Tbsp (75 mL) Ribena black
    currant concentrate or 3 Tbsp
    (45 mL) crème de cassis +
    1 Tbsp (15 mL) sugar

A light dessert with a sophisticated flavor and a dramatic appearance.

Bring the water and quinoa to a boil in a medium saucepan. Reduce to a simmer, cover and cook for 15 minutes. Fluff with a fork and set aside to cool completely.

Combine the quinoa, 1½ cups (375 mL) of the raspberries and ¾ cup (175 mL) of the blackberries in a medium bowl. Sprinkle on the cane sugar and toss gently. Set aside for about 5 minutes to draw out the juices.

In another bowl, stir together the yogurt, maple syrup and black currant concentrate until combined. Spoon the fruit mixture into 4 dessert bowls. Divide the yogurt on top of each serving and garnish with the remaining raspberries and blackberries. Serve chilled.

PER SERVING: Energy 200 calories; Protein 8 g; Carbohydrates 37 g; Dietary Fiber 6 g; Fat 2.5 g; Sugar 22 g; Cholesterol 5 mg; Sodium 60 mg

For a yummy alternative, try this recipe with 2 ripe peaches, pitted and sliced.

CHOCOLATE CHIP FRUIT GRANOLA BARS

MAKES 12 BARS

½ cup (125 mL) rice syrup or liquid honey

¼ cup (60 mL) grapeseed oil or vegetable oil

1 tsp (5 mL) pure vanilla extract

3 cups (750 mL) quinoa flakes

½ cup (125 mL) sweetened dried cranberries

¼ cup (60 mL) semisweet mini chocolate chips or mini carob chips

Easy to make, no-fuss bars. Switch up the fruit for variety—try coarsely chopped dried cherries or dried blueberries, or even peanuts. Rice syrup is a nice alternative to the usual sweeteners because it has a milder sweetness. Mini chocolate chips are essential, as larger chips will make the bar crumbly.

Preheat the oven to 350°F (180°C). Line an 8-inch (2 L) square cake pan with a piece of parchment large enough to come up sides of pan.

In a large bowl, stir together the syrup, oil and vanilla until well blended. Add the quinoa flakes, dried cranberries and chocolate chips. Stir until the flakes are completely covered with syrup and the chocolate chips and cranberries are evenly dispersed. Press evenly and firmly into the baking dish, using another piece of parchment over the top. (The mixture is very sticky.) Once firmly packed, remove and discard the top piece of parchment.

Bake for 20 minutes. Let cool for 30 minutes, then remove from the pan by lifting the parchment. Transfer to a cutting board and remove the parchment. Cut into 12 bars.

Store in a sealed container for up to 2 weeks.

PER SERVING: Energy 230 calories; Protein 4 g; Carbohydrates 40 g; Dietary Fiber 2 g; Fat 7 g; Sugar 13 g; Cholesterol 0 mg; Sodium 280 mg

APPLE SPICE CAKE

Full of apple-spiced goodness, this tasty cake is moist and gluten-free!

Combine the water and quinoa in a medium saucepan and bring to a boil. Reduce to a simmer, cover and cook for 15 minutes. Remove from the heat and let sit, covered, for another 10 minutes. The quinoa should be fluffy. Fluff with a fork and set aside to cool.

Preheat the oven to 350°F (180°C). Lightly grease or spray with cooking oil a 9- or 10-inch (2 or 3 L) Bundt pan.

Combine the eggs, egg whites, butter, applesauce and vanilla in a blender. Blend until smooth. Add ½ cup (125 mL) of the cooked quinoa and blend until smooth. Add 3 more ½-cup (125 mL) portions of quinoa, for a total of 2 cups (500 mL), blending until smooth after each addition.

In a medium bowl, whisk together the sugar, cornstarch, baking powder, baking soda, salt, cinnamon, allspice and nutmeg. Stir in the grated apple, raisins and walnuts (if using). Pour the quinoa purée into the bowl and stir just until combined. Pour the batter into the prepared pan and spread evenly.

Bake for 45 minutes or until a toothpick inserted in the cake comes out clean. Let the cake rest in the pan for about 15 minutes. (The cake may fall slightly after it's removed from the oven.) Turn upside down onto a large plate and lift off the pan. While still warm, drizzle the cake with maple syrup and lightly sprinkle with icing sugar. Serve warm.

Store in a sealed container in the refrigerator for up to 1 week.

PER SERVING: Energy 220 calories; Protein 4 g; Carbohydrates 33 g; Dietary Fiber 2 g; Fat 9 g; Sugar 19 g; Cholesterol 50 mg; Sodium 320 mg

SERVES 10

1⅓ cups (325 mL) water

⅔ cup (150 mL) white quinoa

2 large eggs

2 large egg whites

¼ cup (60 mL) unsalted butter, melted and cooled to room temperature

¼ cup (60 mL) unsweetened applesauce

1 tsp (5 mL) pure vanilla extract

½ cup (125 mL) organic cane sugar or white sugar

⅓ cup (75 mL) cornstarch

2½ tsp (12 mL) baking powder

½ tsp (2 mL) baking soda

½ tsp (2 mL) salt

1½ tsp (7 mL) cinnamon

1 tsp (5 mL) ground allspice

½ tsp (2 mL) nutmeg

1½ cups (375 mL) peeled and grated Granny Smith apples (about 2)

⅓ cup (75 mL) raisins

⅓ cup (75 mL) chopped walnuts (optional)

3 Tbsp (45 mL) pure maple syrup

Icing sugar for garnish

Cooked quinoa already on hand? Purée 2 cups (500 mL) extra-fluffy cooked quinoa in this recipe.

CHERRY LAVENDER CAKE

SERVES 9

¼ cup (60 mL) organic
cane sugar or white sugar

¼ cup (60 mL) water

1 Tbsp (15 mL) lemon juice

1 tsp (5 mL) cornstarch

2 cups (500 mL) pitted
fresh cherries

1 cup (250 mL) quinoa flour

⅓ cup (75 mL) organic
cane sugar or white sugar

1 Tbsp (15 mL) chopped dried
lavender leaves (edible grade)

1 ¾ tsp (8 mL) baking powder

1 tsp (5 mL) salt

1 large egg

½ cup (125 mL) whole milk

¼ cup (60 mL) unsalted butter,
melted and cooled

¼ cup (60 mL) unsweetened
applesauce

Lavender—both the leaves and the flowers—is the latest trend in new and unusual baking ingredients. An edible herb, it contains vitamin A, calcium and iron. A touch of lavender adds a new dimension to this fluffy quinoa cake. Similar to a pudding cake, it is saucy and loaded with baked fresh cherries. It makes a completely different, sweet surprise for your afternoon tea. If you're new to lavender in baking and unsure if you'll like the taste, you may want to use half the amount given in the recipe the first time you make it.

Preheat the oven to 375°F (190°C). Grease or lightly spray with cooking oil a 9-inch (2 L) square cake pan.

In a medium saucepan, whisk together the sugar, water, lemon juice and cornstarch. Add the cherries and bring to a boil. Reduce to a simmer and stir until the mixture thickens slightly, 4 to 5 minutes. Remove from the heat and set aside.

In a medium bowl, whisk together the flour, sugar, lavender, baking powder and salt. In a small bowl, beat the egg, then whisk in the milk, butter and applesauce. Add the egg mixture to the flour mixture, mixing just until combined. Spread the batter in the prepared pan. Pour the cherry mixture evenly over the top.

Bake for 25 minutes, or until a toothpick inserted in the center comes out clean. Serve warm.

Store in a sealed container in the refrigerator for up to 3 days.

PER SERVING: Energy 190 calories; Protein 3 g; Carbohydrates 29 g; Dietary Fiber 3 g; Fat 7 g; Sugar 18 g; Cholesterol 35 mg; Sodium 280 mg

HUMMINGBIRD COFFEE CAKE

Here is a new version of hummingbird cake, made with bananas, pineapple and pecans. It is perfect during coffee with friends. Decorate with cream cheese icing, if you like.

Preheat the oven to 350°F (180°C). Lightly grease or spray with cooking oil a 9-inch (2.5 L) square cake pan.

In a medium bowl, whisk together the flour, potato starch, baking powder, baking soda and cinnamon. Stir in the pecans. In a small bowl, beat the eggs, then whisk in the pineapple, bananas, sugar, oil and vanilla. Pour banana mixture into the flour mixture and stir just until combined. Pour batter into the prepared pan.

Bake for 40 to 45 minutes or until a toothpick inserted in the center comes out clean. Cool in the pan. Frost with your favorite light cream cheese icing recipe, if desired.

Store in a sealed container in the refrigerator for up to 1 week.

PER SERVING (unfrosted): Energy 140 calories; Protein 2 g; Carbohydrates 19 g; Dietary Fiber 2 g; Fat 7 g; Sugar 7 g; Cholesterol 25 mg; Sodium 105 mg

SERVES 16

¾ cup (175 mL) quinoa flour

½ cup (125 mL) potato starch
 or fine rice flour

2 ½ tsp (12 mL) baking powder

¼ tsp (1 mL) baking soda

1 ¼ tsp (6 mL) cinnamon

½ cup (125 mL) chopped pecans

2 large eggs

1 can (8 oz/227 g) crushed
 pineapple, drained well

1 ½ cups (375 mL) mashed bananas

¼ cup (60 mL) organic
 cane sugar or white sugar

¼ cup (60 mL) grapeseed oil
 or vegetable oil

1 ½ tsp (7 mL) pure vanilla extract

ORANGE GINGERBREAD

SERVES 10

GINGERBREAD

1½ cups (375 mL) quinoa flour

1½ cups (375 mL) almond flour

⅓ cup (75 mL) organic
cane sugar or white sugar

1½ tsp (7 mL) baking soda

½ tsp (2 mL) salt

1 tsp (5 mL) ground ginger

2 large eggs, lightly beaten

¾ cup (175 mL) buttermilk

½ cup (125 mL) unsweetened
applesauce

¼ cup (60 mL) vegetable oil

¼ cup (60 mL) fancy molasses

1 Tbsp (15 mL) grated orange zest

1 Tbsp (15 mL) freshly
squeezed orange juice

GLAZE

(OPTIONAL)

1¼ cups (300 mL) icing sugar

3 Tbsp (45 mL) freshly
squeezed orange juice

This classic gingerbread has the goodness of quinoa and a rustic texture from almond flour. It is moist and fluffy, with the slight scent of orange. For an extra bit of sweetness, drizzle with the optional orange glaze.

Preheat the oven to 350°F (180°C). Lightly grease or spray with cooking oil a 9- × 5-inch (2 L) loaf pan.

For the gingerbread, in a large bowl, whisk together the quinoa flour, almond flour, sugar, baking soda, salt and ginger. Add the eggs, buttermilk, applesauce, oil, molasses, orange zest and orange juice. Mix well. Pour into the prepared pan.

Bake for 45 to 50 minutes or until a toothpick inserted in the center comes out clean. Cool completely in the pan.

For the glaze (if using), whisk together the icing sugar and orange juice. Turn the gingerbread out of the pan and poke holes in the top of the loaf. Cover with glaze.

Store in a sealed container in the refrigerator for up to 1 week.

PER SERVING (without glaze): Energy 300 calories; Protein 8 g; Carbohydrates 31 g; Dietary Fiber 4 g; Fat 16 g; Sugar 14 g; Cholesterol 40 mg; Sodium 350 mg

COUNTRY APPLE PECAN PIE

A homemade treat! The wonderful aroma of tender apples, cinnamon and toasted pecans will fill your whole home. Serve à la mode if desired. Cripps Pink apples are also sold as Pink Lady.

Place a baking sheet on the lowest rack of the oven and preheat the oven to 350°F (180°C). Lightly grease or spray with cooking oil a 9-inch (23 cm) pie plate. Roll out the pastry and line the pie plate (see page 190).

In a medium bowl, toss the apples with the lemon juice. Pour in the maple syrup and add the cornstarch, cinnamon and salt (if using). Toss well. Pour the apples into the pie shell, evenly distributing and flattening them.

In a small bowl, whisk together the oats, pecans, brown sugar, cornstarch and cinnamon. With your fingers, rub in the butter until evenly distributed. Sprinkle the topping evenly over the apples, then use the palm of your hand to gently press it onto the pie.

Bake for 60 to 70 minutes or until the apples are tender. Place foil over the pie if the crust becomes too dark. Let sit for 30 minutes before serving.

Store in a sealed container in the refrigerator for up to 1 week.

PER SERVING: Energy 380 calories; Protein 3 g; Carbohydrates 55 g; Dietary Fiber 5 g; Fat 18 g; Sugar 21 g; Cholesterol 35 mg; Sodium 190 mg

SERVES 8

1 unbaked single Flaky Pie Crust (page 190)

6 cups (1.5 L) peeled, cored and thinly sliced Golden Delicious or Cripps Pink apples

1 Tbsp (15 mL) lemon juice

¼ cup (60 mL) pure maple syrup

2 Tbsp (30 mL) cornstarch

½ tsp (2 mL) cinnamon

Pinch of salt (optional)

½ cup (125 mL) quick-cooking rolled oats (gluten-free if required)

⅓ cup (75 mL) chopped toasted pecans

3 Tbsp (45 mL) brown sugar

1 Tbsp (15 mL) cornstarch

¼ tsp (1 mL) cinnamon

1 Tbsp (15 mL) salted butter, softened

To toast nuts, preheat the oven to 350°F (180°C). Spread the nuts on a baking sheet and toast in the oven, stirring once if necessary, for 5 to 7 minutes, until fragrant and lightly toasted.

FLAKY PIE CRUST

½ cup (125 mL) quinoa flour

½ cup (125 mL) brown rice flour

½ cup (125 mL) potato starch

1 Tbsp (15 mL) organic
   cane sugar or white sugar

¼ tsp (1 mL) salt

½ cup (125 mL) cold unsalted
   butter, cut into pieces

⅓ cup (75 mL) + 2 Tbsp (30 mL)
   cold water

This flaky pie crust has a blend of flours for a mild, pleasing flavor. It can be used for a variety of sweet or savory fillings. If you need a top crust, simply double the recipe.

Combine the quinoa flour, rice flour, potato starch, sugar and salt in a medium bowl. Whisk together well. Add the cold butter. Cut in the butter with a pastry blender or two knives until the butter is in pea-sized pieces. While gently stirring, add the cold water slowly just until combined. Form dough into a ball and flatten into a disk. Wrap with plastic wrap and place in the refrigerator for 1 hour.

Let the dough sit at room temperature until soft enough to be rolled. Dust your work surface with potato starch or flour and place the pastry dough on top. Lightly dust the top of the pastry with potato starch or flour. Roll from the center out, turning every two or three rolls to ensure the bottom does not stick to your rolling surface. Roll into a round ³⁄₁₆ inch (5 mm) thick and at least 12 inches (30 cm) wide.

Drape the pastry over the rolling pin and gently unroll it over the pie plate. Press the pastry into the bottom of the plate. Press any tears or cracks together, then trim the edge with a knife, allowing ½ inch (1 cm) overhang. For a single pie crust, flute the edges by pressing the dough from the inside with one finger and pinching it gently between two fingers on the outside.

MAKING A DOUBLE-CRUST PIE Roll out the second disk of dough on a piece of parchment until it is ³⁄₁₆ inch (5 mm) thick (so it will brown and bake properly). Turn the crust over onto the filled pie shell and peel off the parchment. Press the edges together and flute them (see above). Brush all over with egg wash (1 egg beaten with 1 tsp/5 mL water). Cut several steam vents in the top.

BAKING AN UNFILLED SINGLE PIE CRUST Pierce crust on sides and bottom. Bake an unfilled single pie shell at 450°F (230°C) for 15 minutes or until crust is a very light brown.

BAKING WITH FILLING OR A DOUBLE CRUST Bake a single pie crust with filling or a double-crust fruit pie on the bottom oven rack at 450°F (230°C) for 10 minutes, then reduce the temperature to 350°F (180°C) and bake for another 30 to 60 minutes, depending on the filling. Cooked fillings generally take 30 minutes, while fillings that need to cook can take up to 60 minutes.

PER SERVING (⅛ pie, single crust, without filling): Energy 210 calories; Protein 2 g; Carbohydrates 24 g; Dietary Fiber 1 g; Fat 12 g; Sugar 2 g; Cholesterol 30 mg; Sodium 180 mg

OLD-FASHIONED SWEET POTATO PIE

SERVES 8

1 unbaked single Flaky
    Pie Crust (page 190)

1½ cups (375 mL) mashed
    cooked sweet potato

¾ cup (175 mL) 2% evaporated milk

⅓ cup (75 mL) light brown sugar

2 Tbsp (30 mL) pure maple syrup

1½ tsp (7 mL) cinnamon

1 tsp (5 mL) pure vanilla extract

1 large egg

1 large egg white

Traditionally served for Thanksgiving dinner, this pie is now being enjoyed throughout the year because of the nutrition of sweet potatoes. They are rich in vitamin A, beta-carotene and vitamin C. Serve this pie with whipped cream sweetened with maple syrup, if desired.

Position oven rack on the bottom level and preheat the oven to 450°F (230°C). Lightly grease or spray with cooking oil a 9-inch (23 cm) pie plate. Roll out the pastry and line the pie plate (see page 190).

In a medium bowl, combine the sweet potato, evaporated milk, brown sugar, maple syrup, cinnamon, vanilla, egg and egg white. Beat with an electric mixer on medium speed until filling is smooth and uniform. Pour into the prepared crust.

Bake for 20 minutes, then reduce temperature to 325°F (160°C) and bake for another 30 minutes or until a knife inserted in the center comes out clean. If the crust begins to get too dark, cover the edges with a piece of foil.

Serve cool or at room temperature with whipped cream, if desired.

Store in a sealed container in the refrigerator for up to 1 week.

PER SERVING: Energy 330 calories; Protein 5 g; Carbohydrates 47 g; Dietary Fiber 3 g; Fat 13 g; Sugar 16 g; Cholesterol 60 mg; Sodium 240 mg

BLACKBERRY BRÛLÉE

Fluffy quinoa is puréed silky smooth with whole milk or cream, loaded with blackberries and topped with a sweet, crunchy caramelized topping. A decadent dessert that's packed with nutrition.

Lightly grease four 1-cup (250 mL) ramekins or an 8-inch (2 L) square baking dish.

Combine the water and quinoa in a medium saucepan. Bring to a boil, reduce to a simmer, cover and cook for 15 minutes. The quinoa must be extra-fluffy. Fluff with a fork and set aside to cool.

Position oven rack at the center of the oven. Preheat the broiler to 500°F (260°C).

In a blender or food processor, combine the cooked quinoa, milk, ¼ cup (60 mL) brown sugar, cinnamon and vanilla. Purée well, for at least 2 to 3 minutes. The mixture should be thick and very smooth. Pour into a small bowl and toss with the blackberries. Scoop into ramekins or the baking dish. Top evenly with 3 Tbsp (45 mL) brown sugar.

Broil for 6 to 8 minutes, until the brown sugar topping is caramelized. Serve warm.

Store in a sealed container in the refrigerator for up to 4 days.

PER SERVING: Energy 180 calories; Protein 5 g; Carbohydrates 35 g; Dietary Fiber 3 g; Fat 3 g; Sugar 19 g; Cholesterol 5 mg; Sodium 25 mg

SERVES 4

1 cup (250 mL) water

½ cup (125 mL) quinoa

¾ cup (175 mL) whole milk or cream

¼ cup (60 mL) + 3 Tbsp (45 mL) brown sugar

1 tsp (5 mL) cinnamon

½ tsp (2 mL) pure vanilla extract

¾ cup (175 mL) whole fresh blackberries

Cooked quinoa already on hand? Add 1½ cups (375 mL) extra-fluffy cooked quinoa to the milk mixture and proceed from there.

CAFÉ MOCHA PUDDING

Here, quinoa is simmered in bold coffee, then blended into a rich and creamy chocolate pudding. If children won't be eating it and you prefer the kick of caffeine, you can swap out the decaf for the real thing.

Combine the coffee and quinoa in a medium saucepan. Bring to a boil, reduce to a simmer, cover and cook for 25 minutes. The quinoa should be extra-fluffy. Fluff with a fork and set aside to cool.

In a blender or food processor, combine the quinoa, milk, sugar, cocoa and vanilla. Purée well, for at least 2 to 3 minutes. The mixture should be very thick and smooth. Scoop into individual serving dishes. Chill for at least 1 hour (or overnight) before serving. Serve garnished with vanilla whipped cream (if using).

Store in a sealed container in the refrigerator for up to 4 days.

PER SERVING: Energy 180 calories; Protein 6 g; Carbohydrates 36 g; Dietary Fiber 4 g; Fat 3 g; Sugar 17 g; Cholesterol 5 mg; Sodium 20 mg

SERVES 4

1 ½ cups (375 mL) strong decaffeinated coffee or espresso

½ cup (125 mL) quinoa

½ cup (125 mL) whole milk

⅓ cup (75 mL) organic cane sugar or white sugar

⅓ cup (75 mL) unsweetened cocoa powder

½ tsp (2 mL) pure vanilla extract

Whipping cream whipped with ¼ tsp (1 mL) pure vanilla extract for garnish (optional)

CHOCOLATE HAZELNUT CREAM

SERVES 6

1 cup (250 mL) water

½ cup (125 mL) quinoa

½ cup (125 mL) toasted
    flaked hazelnuts

½ cup (125 mL) unsweetened
    cocoa powder

⅓ cup (75 mL) organic
    cane sugar or white sugar

½ tsp (2 mL) pure vanilla extract

1¼ cups (300 mL) whole milk

Whipped cream for garnish
    (optional)

Fluffy quinoa is puréed into a thick, decadent pudding with whole milk, cocoa and toasted hazelnuts. A superb dessert with a wow factor that makes you completely forget it's good for you!

Combine the water and quinoa in a medium saucepan. Bring to a boil, reduce to a simmer, cover and cook for 15 minutes. The quinoa should be extra-fluffy. Fluff with a fork and set aside to cool.

Set aside 1 Tbsp (15 mL) of the hazelnuts for garnish. In a blender or food processor, combine the remaining hazelnuts, quinoa, cocoa, sugar and vanilla. Add milk ¼ cup (60 mL) at a time, blending well and scraping down the sides (when necessary) after each addition. Purée well, for at least 2 to 3 minutes. The mixture should be very thick and smooth. Scoop into individual serving dishes. Chill for 1 hour before serving. Serve garnished with the remaining hazelnuts and whipped cream (if using).

Store in a sealed container in the refrigerator for up to 4 days.

PER SERVING: Energy 200 calories; Protein 6 g; Carbohydrates 28 g; Dietary Fiber 4 g; Fat 9 g; Sugar 14 g; Cholesterol 5 mg; Sodium 25 mg

- Cooked quinoa already on hand? Use 1½ cups (375 mL) of extra-fluffy cooked quinoa in this recipe.

- To toast nuts, preheat the oven to 350°F (180°C). Spread the nuts on a baking sheet and toast in the oven, stirring once if necessary, for 5 to 7 minutes, until fragrant and lightly toasted.

PERFECT PUMPKIN PUDDING

Enjoy the taste of pumpkin pie without the crust (and extra calories). This perfect blend of spices in a creamy quinoa pudding makes for a thick, delicious and healthy option. Top each slice with maple whipped cream and toasted pecans. This dessert can be made the day before serving.

For the pudding, combine the water and quinoa in a medium saucepan and bring to a boil. Reduce to a simmer, cover and cook for 17 minutes. The quinoa should be extra-fluffy. Fluff with a fork and set aside to cool.

Preheat the oven to 400°F (200°C). Lightly grease an 8-inch (2 L) square baking dish.

In a medium bowl, beat the egg. Add the pumpkin and whisk until thoroughly combined.

In a medium saucepan, combine the milk, sugar, cinnamon, ginger, cloves, cardamom and salt. Bring to a boil on medium heat, stirring constantly. Whisk in the pumpkin mixture and continue to heat, stirring, until bubbling and thickened slightly, about 2 minutes. Stir in the quinoa and vanilla. Pour into the baking dish.

Bake for 30 minutes or until set. Let cool. Cut into 8 pieces.

For the topping (if using), in a medium bowl, whip the cream with the maple syrup until stiff peaks form.

Serve pudding topped with maple cream and garnished with a candied or toasted pecan.

Store in a sealed container in the refrigerator for up to 4 days.

PER SERVING: Energy 230 calories; Protein 9 g; Carbohydrates 39 g; Dietary Fiber 2 g; Fat 3.5 g; Sugar 23 g; Cholesterol 55 mg; Sodium 150 mg

SERVES 4

PUDDING
1 cup (250 mL) water

½ cup (125 mL) white quinoa

1 large egg

1 cup (250 mL) pumpkin purée

2 cups (500 mL) 1% milk

⅓ cup (75 mL) organic cane sugar or white sugar

½ tsp (2 mL) cinnamon

¼ tsp (1 mL) ground ginger

Pinch each of ground cloves, ground cardamom and salt

1 tsp (5 mL) pure vanilla extract

TOPPING
(OPTIONAL)
¾ cup (175 mL) whipping cream

2 Tbsp (30 mL) pure maple syrup

8 toasted pecans

- Cooked quinoa already on hand? Add 1½ cups (375 mL) extra-fluffy cooked quinoa to the pudding mixture.
- To toast nuts, preheat the oven to 350°F (180°C). Spread the nuts on a baking sheet and toast in the oven, stirring once, for 5 to 7 minutes, until fragrant and lightly toasted.

RASPBERRY ALMOND CUSTARD

SERVES 4

1 cup (250 mL) water

½ cup (125 mL) white quinoa

1 can (12 ounces/370 mL)
    evaporated partly
    skimmed milk

¼ cup (60 mL) brown sugar

1 large egg

1 large egg white

1 tsp (5 mL) pure almond extract

½ cup (125 mL) fresh raspberries

¼ cup (60 mL) toasted
    sliced almonds

A new twist on custard. This creamy custard is made with quinoa and topped with fresh raspberries and toasted almonds.

Combine the water and quinoa in a small saucepan. Bring to a boil, reduce to a simmer, cover and simmer for 15 minutes. The quinoa should be extra-fluffy. Fluff with a fork and set aside to cool.

Heat the evaporated milk and brown sugar in a medium saucepan on medium-high heat. In a small bowl, beat the egg and egg white. Whisk a spoonful of the warm milk into the egg to temper it. Continue with 6 more spoonfuls of milk, whisking after each addition. Whisk the egg mixture gently into the milk mixture. Continue to heat for 3 minutes, stirring constantly. Stir in 1½ cups (375 mL) of the cooked quinoa and the almond extract. Remove from the heat and divide among 4 individual ramekins. Place plastic wrap directly on surface of custard and refrigerate until cool. Serve topped with fresh raspberries and toasted almonds.

Store in a sealed container in the refrigerator for up to 4 days.

PER SERVING: Energy 310 calories; Protein 14 g; Carbohydrates 36 g; Dietary Fiber 3 g; Fat 13 g; Sugar 20 g; Cholesterol 75 mg; Sodium 140 mg

To toast nuts, preheat the oven to 350°F (180°C). Spread the nuts on a baking sheet and toast in the oven, stirring once if necessary, for 5 to 7 minutes, until fragrant and lightly toasted.

STEWED SUMMER FRUIT WITH CINNAMON & LEMON

Each European country has its own version of a fruit "soup" made of delicious combinations of fresh and dried fruit and served with cream. While very tasty, traditionally these recipes can have a large amount of unnecessary sugar. Not this one! We've revamped it so you can enjoy this refreshing dessert worry-free. Enjoy it hot or cold.

In a large saucepan, combine the water, quinoa, rhubarb, strawberries, prunes, raisins, lemon, honey and cinnamon stick. Bring to a boil, reduce to a simmer, cover and cook, stirring occasionally, for 45 minutes or until the strawberries and rhubarb have cooked down and become part of the sauce. Remove from the heat, stir and remove the cinnamon stick and lemon pieces. Let cool slightly before serving, or chill, if desired.

Stir the yogurt and maple syrup together in a small bowl. Spoon stewed fruit into individual serving dishes. Serve hot or cold, topped with the maple yogurt.

Store in a sealed container in the refrigerator for up to 4 days.

PER SERVING: Energy 160 calories; Protein 5 g; Carbohydrates 33 g; Dietary Fiber 3 g; Fat 1 g; Sugar 17 g; Cholesterol 0 mg; Sodium 15 mg

SERVES 8

3 ⅓ cups (825 mL) water

⅔ cup (150 mL) quinoa

1 ½ cups (375 mL) sliced fresh or frozen unsweetened rhubarb

1 ½ cups (375 mL) halved fresh or frozen strawberries

½ cup (125 mL) quartered pitted prunes

⅓ cup (75 mL) seedless raisins or dried currants

½ lemon (see Tip)

3 Tbsp (45 mL) honey

1 cinnamon stick

1 cup (250 mL) nonfat plain thick Greek yogurt

1 Tbsp (15 mL) pure maple syrup

If you would like to keep the lemon in the stewed fruit mixture, slice it thinly. However, if you want the option of removing it before serving, slice it very thick so it is easy to pull out.

LEMON GINGER BLUEBERRY CRISP

SERVES 6

6 cups (1.5 L) fresh or thawed
frozen blueberries

¼ cup (60 mL) lightly packed
brown sugar

1 tsp (5 mL) cinnamon

1 tsp (5 mL) grated lemon zest

1 Tbsp (15 mL) lemon juice

1¼ cups (300 mL) quinoa flakes

½ cup (125 mL) sliced almonds

2 Tbsp (30 mL) unsalted
butter, melted

1 Tbsp (15 mL) brown sugar

½ tsp (2 mL) ground ginger

A lively dessert, with a delightful combination of lemon and blueberries and a hint of ginger. Top with ice cream, if desired.

Preheat the oven to 350°F (180°C). Lightly grease or spray with cooking oil an 11- × 7-inch (2 L) baking dish.

Combine the blueberries, brown sugar, cinnamon, lemon zest and lemon juice in a medium bowl. Toss until blueberries are evenly coated. Pour into the baking dish and spread evenly.

In the same bowl, combine the quinoa flakes, almonds, butter, brown sugar and ginger. Stir until the flakes are coated with the butter mixture. Sprinkle evenly over the blueberries.

Bake for 30 minutes or until the blueberry filling is hot. Serve warm with ice cream, if desired.

Store in a sealed container in the refrigerator for up to 4 days.

PER SERVING: Energy 280 calories; Protein 6 g; Carbohydrates 49 g; Dietary Fiber 6 g; Fat 10 g; Sugar 22 g; Cholesterol 10 mg; Sodium 210 mg

ACKNOWLEDGMENTS

MOST importantly, our deepest gratitude to our family, Paul and Ian, and always our amazing Sydney, Alyssa and Aston. We are also grateful for the support of Vera Friesen, Swen Runkvist and the Green family.

Thank you to numerous industry advisors, supporters and friends: Sergio Nuñez de Arco, Tania Petricevic, Marcos Guevara, Laurie Scanlin & Claire Burnett, Jeffrey & Amy Barnes, Marjorie & Bob Leventry, Francisco & Magdalena Diez-Canseco, Olivier & Didier Perreol, Gordon Kirke, Jocelyn Campanaro & Craig Billington, Stefani Farkas, Terry Paluszkiewicz, Annica Sjoberg, Rose Gage, the Addersons, Brenda & Ingrid Wicklund, Linda Beaudoin, Theresa Kyi, Frank Dyson, Shela Shapiro, Shaundra Carvey-Parker, Heather Dyer, Bert Leat & Julie Roberts, Sara & Jim Busby, Kerri Rosenbaum Barr, Billijon Morgan, Jeanette Young-Laroque, Liz Boily, Megan Portello & family, the Vanderwater family, the Atom Girls Hockey Family (you know who you are), Terri Peters, Tammy Martel, Vitaliy Prokopets, Grant & Patricia Wood, Nancy Midwicki, Shannon Goodspeed, Ryan Szulc, Madeleine Johari and Uncle John & Aunt Beryl and all of those brilliant Barbers in England!

We must acknowledge Verna Deason and the entire Deason family. We were always watching, listening and inspired by you. You have all been a tremendous influence on us, and we thank you.

INDEX

THE *ultimate*
PAPERCRAFT
AND
ORIGAMI
Book

THE *ultimate*
PAPERCRAFT
AND
ORIGAMI
Book

PAUL JACKSON AND
ANGELA A'COURT
WITH
MARION ELLIOT

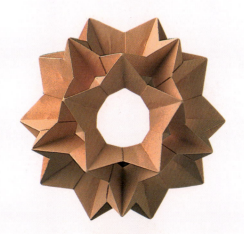

SMITHMARK

PUBLISHER'S NOTE

No occupation is gentler than papercraft, but some general points should be remembered for safety and care of the environment.

▌ Always choose non-toxic materials whenever possible; for example PVA, strong clear glue, non-toxic varnishes and poster paints.

▌ Craft knives, scissors and all cutting implements should be used with care. Children love papercrafts, but should only be allowed to use sharp tools under supervision.

▌ Always use a cutting board or cutting mat to avoid damage to household surfaces (it is also safer to cut onto a firm, hard surface).

▌ Protect surfaces from paint, glue and varnish splashes by laying down old newspapers.

This edition published in 1992
by SMITHMARK Publishers Inc.,
16 East 32nd Street,
New York,
NY 10016,
USA

SMITHMARK books are available for bulk purchase for sales promotion and premium use.
For details write or call the manager of special sales, SMITHMARK Publishers Inc.,
16 East 32nd Street,
New York,
NY 10016;
(212) 532-6600

© Anness Publishing Limited 1992
Boundary Row Studios
1 Boundary Row
London SE1 8HP
United Kingdom

ISBN 0-8317-8193-9

Editorial Director: Joanna Lorenz
Project Editor: Penelope Cream
Art Director: Peter Bridgewater
Designer: Michael Morey
Photographer: Martin Norris
Illustrator: Lorraine Harrison

Printed and bound in Hong Kong

CONTENTS

INTRODUCTION

Paper is everywhere: our lives would be impossible without wrappings, letters,
magazines, cards, packaging, leaflets, posters, newspapers and notepads.
It is one of the most inexpensive and readily available of materials, yet it is
commonly neglected as a craft, art and hobby medium. With know-how,
imagination and enthusiasm, papercraft skills, origami techniques and
papier-mâché artistry can transform this simple, functional and cost-effective
material into fantastic gifts, wonderful shapes, delightful stationery and
beautiful objects, such as toys, bags, jewellery and boxes.

Decorative Papercrafts

■ N A T T Y   N A P K I N S

Here is a very quick way to add your own style to ordinary napkins and add a sparkle to the tone of your meal! Even a squiggle, a dot, or a circle can transform the napkin. Try experimenting with different shapes, and perhaps give everybody their own design.

YOU WILL NEED
Plain coloured paper napkins
Pen
Gold and silver metallic pens

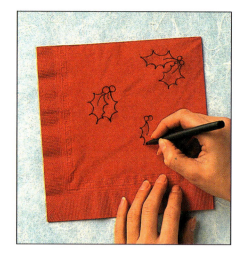

1 For a Christmas feel use a plain red napkin and lightly mark out a holly leaf and berry sprig in pen.

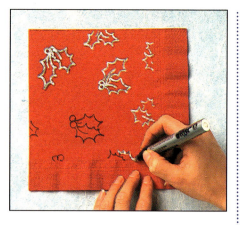

2 Then take a silver metallic pen with a medium nib and carefully trace over the pen lines.

3 For a Hallowe'en evening take a black napkin and draw gold stars and half moons with a gold pen.

■ TWO-TONE GIFTWRAP

Here is another way to make your own wrapping paper, this time using two layers of co-ordinating crêpe paper.

YOU WILL NEED
Crêpe paper in two contrasting colours
Glue

1 First work out how much paper you will need in order to cover the gift. Now cut a piece of paper to this size in each of your two chosen colours. Decide which colour will be on top and pleat it lengthwise.

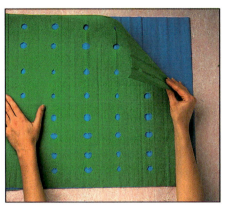

2 Now cut circles out through all the layers along both sides of the pleat.

3 Open up the top paper and glue it onto the bottom. It is exciting to see how the colour of the bottom layer shows through. If you want a really elaborate design, add cut-out pieces in a further colour, leaving openings large enough to reveal the colours beneath. Now wrap your gift up in the two-tone dotty paper.

BAROQUE BAUBLES

We have used a polystyrene ball for this decoration. They can be found, in a range of sizes, in craft shops and are used for making dolls' heads.

YOU WILL NEED
Polystyrene ball
Gouache paint
Gold doily
Glue
Brass paper fastener
Gold thread

1 First of all, paint the bauble with some gouache in a suitable colour.

2 When the paint has dried, cut out pieces from a doily. Decide how they are to be arranged on the bauble and glue them into position.

3 Cut out a further motif from the doily and take a brass paper fastener and push it through the centre. Now push this into the top of the ball.

4 Taking some gold thread, wrap it around the brass fastener so that it is ready to be hung on the Christmas tree.

■ ORIENTAL FAN

Here is an easy way to make a beautiful fan to cool yourself on a hot summer's day. This fan is loosely designed on a Japanese fan and so we have made it with Japanese rice paper.

YOU WILL NEED
Thin card
Craft knife
Glue
Double-sided tape
Rice paper or tissue paper

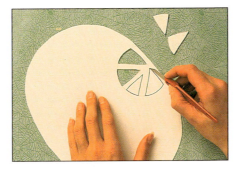

1 Cut out an oval piece of thin card. Make sure that the card is not too thick so that it is flexible for fanning. Cut out the bottom area of the fan with a craft knife.

2 Next cut thin strips of card and lining them up at the base, stick them on both sides of the fan so that they follow the cut out lines.

3 To make the handle, cut out two strips of thicker card measuring 14 × 1½ cm (5½ × ½ in). Taper the ends and stick double-sided tape onto both pieces. Attach them to either side of the base part of the fan.

4 Now cover the fan in rice paper by gluing round the edge and along the struts. We have used a different colour paper on either side for variety. If you cannot find rice paper, use tissue paper instead. Trim the edges with scissors.

5 Cover the handle by wrapping it with a long strip of rice paper and gluing it at the bottom.

WELL-DRESSED NAPKIN

Here is a quick and simple way to dress up a napkin using coloured card. You can make the holder in contrasting or a toning coloured card to suit the setting.

YOU WILL NEED
Paper napkins
Thin card in two contrasting colours
Glue

1 First cut a square of card to the same size as the folded napkin.

2 Fold the card diagonally with the front fold half-way up. Cut a triangle in contrasting coloured card slightly smaller than the front triangle. Cut out a zigzag edge along two sides.

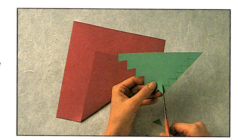

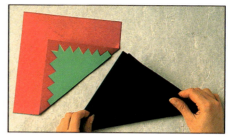

3 Now fold the napkin in half and place it into the napkin holder. Why not experiment with different designs on the front, or leave it plain and glue on a cut out motif from a magazine.

▮ GIFT BOX

Here is an easy and stylish way to present an awkwardly-shaped gift. It also makes a lovely box to use afterwards to keep things in.

YOU WILL NEED
Empty shoe box with lid
Patterned and plain wrapping paper
Glue
Tissue paper

1 Wrap the outside of the box in the patterned paper.

2 Now line the inside of the box with plain paper.

3 Cover the lid of the box on the top and inside in the plain paper. Take some tissue paper in a co-ordinating colour, softly scrunch it up and arrange it in the bottom of the box. Place the gift inside and put the lid on.

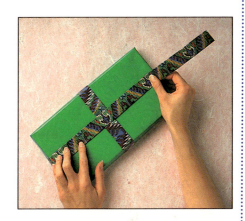

4 As a further decoration, enhance the top by attaching paper strips cut from the patterned paper to suggest ribbons.

CLASSIC
LINES

If you want to write a letter in a hurry, but still want it to be stylish, here are a couple of quick ways to make some beautiful writing paper. You will need some lightly coloured wrapping paper in a classical design.

YOU WILL NEED
Pale wrapping paper
Tracing paper
Glue
Sheet of white paper

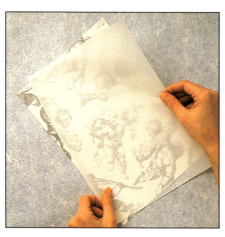

1 Cut out a rectangle of wrapping paper to the size of writing paper, and cut a piece of tracing paper to the same size. Stick the tracing paper on top of the wrapping paper, smoothing out any bubbles. Use a black felt-tip pen to write your letter so that it shows up clearly.

2 If you have a bit more time you could select one particular motif from the paper and cut this out.

3 Glue the motif to a sheet of white paper.

4 As before, glue a sheet of tracing paper on top to give an elegant double layer. You could make a collection of writing paper by cutting out different motifs from one sheet of wrapping paper.

PAINT AND PAPER

Have fun turning an ordinary piece of black paper into bright and jazzy wrapping paper. You could of course vary the colour of the paper and paints.

YOU WILL NEED
Plain paper
Paints

2 Add more colours as you wish until the paper is brightly decorated.

1 Take a piece of black paper large enough to cover your present. Now choose the paint colours you are going to use. This example uses fuchsia pink, orange and gold paints to contrast with the black background. After preparing the paint on a saucer, decorate the paper with random 'blobs', working with one colour at a time.

3 For a more regular painted pattern, the present can be wrapped first and then, following the shape of the gift, painted with wavy lines.

SOAP-BOX

Guest soaps come in all shapes and colours. Decorate a box in pretty shades to match your soaps for an attractive present.

YOU WILL NEED
Empty circular box
Assorted coloured card
Glue
Tissue paper
Soaps

1 Cover the outside of the box by gluing a strip of coloured card around the side.

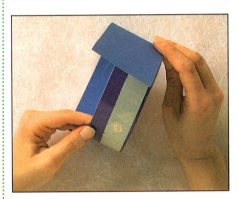

2 This particular gift uses shell-shaped soaps, so draw shell shapes onto coloured cards that complement the colours of the soaps.

3 Cut out the shell shapes and stick them onto the outside of the box.

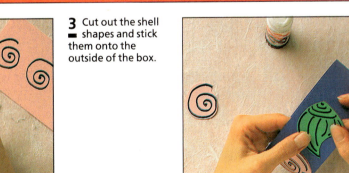

4 Scrunch up a large piece of tissue paper and arrange it inside the box. Place the soaps on top of the tissue paper.

BOWLED OVER

This bowl is made by a traditional method where layers of papier-mâché are laid into a greased mould and removed when dry. For this project, an ordinary china bowl has been used, but all sorts of items can make interesting moulds – just remember to grease them first, otherwise they will be permanently lined with paper!

YOU WILL NEED
Bowl suitable for using as a mould
Petroleum jelly
Newspaper
Diluted PVA glue
Heavy corrugated card
Strong clear glue
Masking tape
Fine sandpaper
White paint
Assortment of poster paints
Non-toxic clear gloss varnish

1 Coat the inside of the bowl with five layers of PVA-soaked newspaper strips, allowing for an overlap of 2½ cm (1 in). Leave to dry in a warm place for 48 hours.

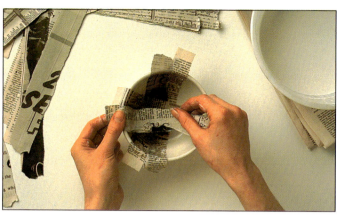

2 Gently prise the paper bowl from its mould with a blunt knife, and leave it upside down to dry for a few hours.

3 Trim the ragged edge to about ½ cm (¼ in).

4 Cut a zigzag bowl rim from the thick cardboard and lay it on the top of the papier-mâché bowl rim. Stick the rim on the bowl with strong clear glue, and hold it in place with masking tape. Allow the glue to dry for an hour or so and then paper over the rim, covering the joins carefully.

5 Paper the underside of the rim in the same way. Leave the bowl to dry for 24 hours. Lightly sand down the surface of the bowl, and then prime it with two coats of white paint.

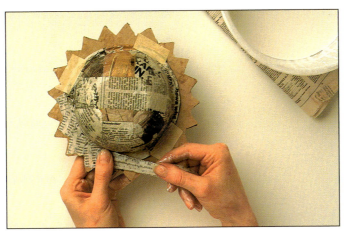

6 Draw in any decoration with pencil first, and then decorate the bowl with poster paints. Let the bowl dry thoroughly, and then seal it with two coats of clear gloss varnish.

TAKE A
LETTER

As well as paper and card, this letter rack also requires a block of wood to give it a firm base. Cover it in patterned paper to match your desk accessories.

YOU WILL NEED
Block of wood 19½ × 4½ × 2 cm
(7½ × 1¾ × ¾ in)
Patterned paper
Glue or waterbased wood adhesive
Mounting card

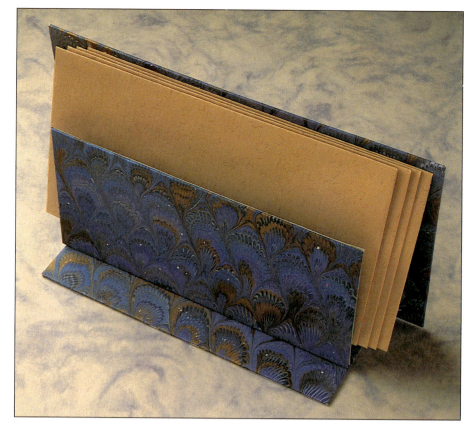

1 Entirely cover the block of wood in the patterned paper and glue in place. Trim it where necessary.

2 Cut three pieces of mounting card, one piece measuring 25 × 13 cm (10 × 5 in) and the other two measuring 20 × 9 cm (8 × 3½ in). With each bit of card, measure and cut out a piece of paper slightly larger than the card itself. Glue the paper onto the card, and mitre the corners carefully by snipping off the corners diagonally and folding the turnings on to the back, making sure that they are well stuck down. Repeat with each piece of card.

3 Now stick a piece of paper slightly smaller than the card onto the back.

4 Using a strong glue or waterbased wood adhesive stick the smaller, front card to the narrow edge of the covered piece of wood, making sure it is centred. Glue the back card in the same way.

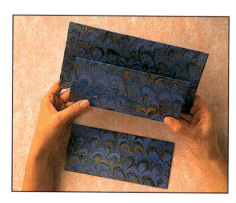

5 To complete the letter rack, position and glue it onto the covered base.

ADVENT CALENDAR

Make the countdown to Christmas even more exciting with this beautiful tree advent calendar. The windows are decorated with pictures cut out from old Christmas cards.

YOU WILL NEED
Red, green and orange card
Thin cardboard
Craft knife
Old greetings cards
Glue
Silver metallic pen

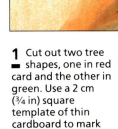

1 Cut out two tree shapes, one in red card and the other in green. Use a 2 cm (¾ in) square template of thin cardboard to mark out 25 windows at random on the green tree. Now cut along three sides of each window with a craft knife.

2 Place the green tree onto the red tree so that it is slightly higher and gives the green tree a red line on the bottom edges.

Carefully open each window and mark their position on the red tree in pencil. Remove the green tree. Cut out 25 small pictures from old Christmas cards and glue them onto the pencilled squares on the red Christmas tree.

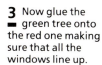

3 Now glue the green tree onto the red one making sure that all the windows line up.

4 Decorate the tree with cut-out circles of red and orange card to suggest the Christmas tree baubles.

5 Using a silver pen draw a bow above each bauble and then number the windows 1 to 25.

WASTE PAPER BOX

Waste paper boxes can make elegant gifts that can be put to use straight away. They can be covered in paper that matches the decor of the room they are intended for, or else in paper of your favourite design.

YOU WILL NEED
Thick card
Dark contrasting or toning paper
Impact adhesive
Decorative paper

1 For this waste paper box, cut out one square in thick card measuring 20 cm (9 in). Now measure and cut out from the same type of card the four sides so that they are 20 cm (9 in) wide, with a height of 25 cm (11 in). Cover one side of all these pieces with a dark toning paper.

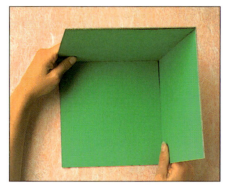

2 Next glue the sides onto the base and to each other using an impact adhesive.

3 Now cut out a square of decorative paper measuring 24 cm (10 in). Firmly glue it onto the base and cut the corners diagonally. Glue the turnings around and up onto the sides of the container to give the box extra strength.

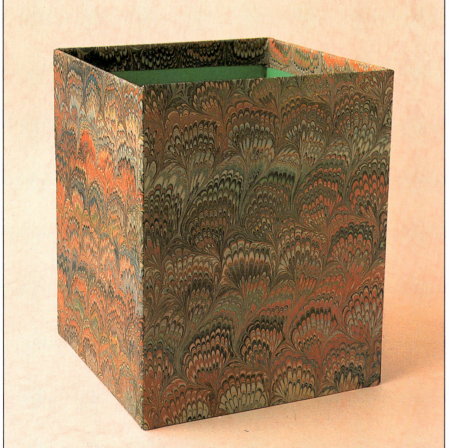

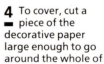

4 To cover, cut a piece of the decorative paper large enough to go around the whole of the box. Stick it on and trim where necessary at the base to create a neat finish.

5 At the top, turn the excess paper over and glue down onto the inside of the box, after mitring the corners. This will produce a very professional look.

ELEGANT LAMPSHADE

Add a designed look to your room by using a left-over piece of wallpaper, or a paper of a complementary colour, to make this lampshade.

YOU WILL NEED
Lampshade frame
Coloured paper or wallpaper
Craft knife
Coin
Glue

1 First of all take a lampshade frame and place it onto your chosen paper. Draw around the shape while slowly moving the frame round to obtain the correct measurement. Now cut out the shape slightly outside the drawn line using scissors or a craft knife to give a piece of paper larger than the frame. Using a coin, draw a scalloped edge along the bottom edge.

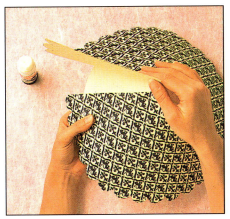

2 Then cut along it until the edging is complete.

3 Now apply a layer of glue to the frame and carefully attach the paper to it, smoothing it out to avoid bumps or creases.

4 Finally, cut small darts around the top and glue them down, working around until the frame is completely covered and the shade ready to be fitted to a lamp.

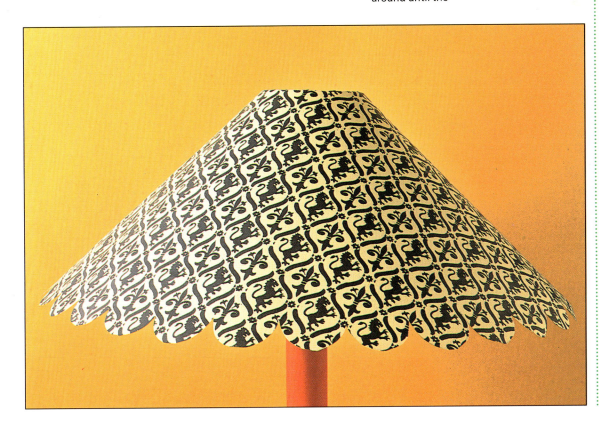

DESIGNER PENCIL POT

This pencil pot is a lovely idea to cheer up your own desk, or it can make a beautiful personalized gift for a friend. The matching pencils add an artistic touch.

YOU WILL NEED
Empty cardboard tube or salt
*   *container*
Patterned paper
Glue
Pencils

1 First of all you will need to cover the inside of the container. Measure the height and circumference of the pot and cut out two pieces of paper, slightly larger. You could use wallpaper, wrapping paper or marbled paper.

2 Take one of the pieces, glue it and carefully slot it into the inside of the pot, pressing it around the inside walls.

3 Cut darts on the excess paper at the top and glue them down to the outside one by one.

4 Take the other piece of paper and stick it to the outside so that the edge is flush with the top of the pot.

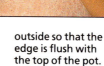

5 Once again cut darts into the excess length at the bottom and glue them onto the base.

6 Now draw around the base of the pot onto the patterned paper and cut out a circle slightly smaller. Glue this and drop it inside the bottom.

7 Cut out another circle and glue it to the outside base.

8 To make the matching pencils, cut out a strip of the same patterned paper the length of the pencils and approximately twice the width. Glue it and place the pencil at one edge and roll. Trim the paper where necessary.

DESK BLOTTER

To make the blotter special it is a good idea to select a wrapping paper to suit the type of desk area. You could choose a hand-made marbled paper for a very traditional look, or an abstract paper or two co-ordinating plain papers for a more modern effect.

YOU WILL NEED
Thick card
Patterned paper
Glue
Thin card
Coloured paper
Blotting paper

1 Cut a piece of thick card 46 × 30 cm (18 × 12 in). This will be the finished size of the blotter. Cut your chosen paper 3 cm (1 in) larger all around than the card.

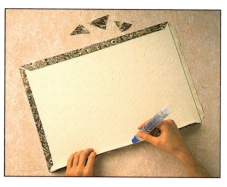

2 Next fold and glue the edges onto the back of the card, mitring the corners by trimming them diagonally.

3 For the corner pieces cut four triangles in thin card measuring 10 × 10 × 14 cm (4 × 4 × 5½ in) and cover them in coloured paper cut to the same size first. Glue and turn down the bottom edge and the top point. Repeat this for all four corner pieces.

4 Position the corner pieces onto the corners of the blotter. Turn the board over and fold the edges around, gluing them securely.

5 Cut another piece of coloured paper the same size as the blotter and glue it on to the back. Trim where necessary.

6 Insert a piece of blotting paper under the corners.

∎ S W E E T   T H O U G H T

Chocolates are always a treat, especially when they are gift-wrapped. Simply cover an empty container with vibrant tissue paper and fill with sweets.

YOU WILL NEED
Empty bowl-shaped food container
Tissue paper
Glue or tape
Metallic card
Pencil or paint brush

1 Cover the bowl with tissue paper by placing the centre of the paper inside, pushing it down and then moulding it out and around the sides.

2 Glue or tape the tissue paper to the underside, trimming where necessary.

3 Now cut two strips measuring 3 × 50 cm (1¼ × 20 in) of coloured metallic card. Tightly roll each end of the card strips around a pencil or paint brush so that it curls.

4 Now glue the centre of the cards and place them into the bowl at right angles. Place another piece of tissue paper that has been scrunched up into the bottom of the container, and arrange the chocolates on the top.

■ N E C K L A C E   A N D   E A R R I N G S

This beautiful necklace with matching earrings is created from only a small piece of decorative paper. A printed feather marbled pattern is used here.

YOU WILL NEED
Patterned paper
Pair of earring fittings
Leather cord
Glue

1 For the earrings, cut out two tab shapes from the decorative paper, using the template as a guide to the shape. Now fold the tab in half to the point and continue to pleat out from the centre.

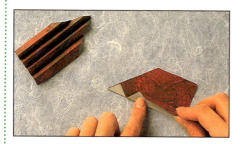

2 Pierce the top and push an earring fitting through to create a fan shape. Make a second earring in the same way.

3 For the necklace you will need to make five 'fans' in the same way and then pierce them at the top.

4 To make the beads which sit inbetween the fans, cut 30 cm (12 in) strips of paper into elongated triangles measuring 4 cm (1½ in) at the base and tapering to 1 cm (½ in) at the tip. Starting at the wide end, roll up the strips around a pencil and glue the end. Now thread a piece of leather cord through the tops of the fans, alternating them with the beads.

■ FESTIVE CRACKERS

Here is an economical way to make your own festive crackers as well as to give your guests a personal surprise present by adding a small gift.

YOU WILL NEED

Crêpe paper in two colours
Thin writing paper
Cracker snaps
Thin card
Two cardboard tubes
Glue
Strong thread
Double-sided tape

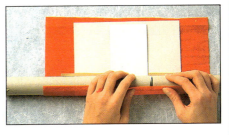

1 First of all cut a length of crêpe paper measuring 35 × 20 cm (14 × 8 in). Lay it flat and place a piece of thin writing paper centrally on top. Place a cracker snap on top and then place a piece of card measuring 15 × 8 cm (6 × 3 in), across the centre.

2 Place two cardboard tubes onto the papers so that their ends meet in line with the right hand side of the piece of card. Roll the crêpe paper around and glue at the edges.

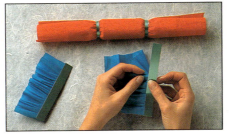

3 Pull the right hand tube out slightly and use some strong thread to tie inbetween the tubes and gather the paper as illustrated. Now pop your gift in at the other end. Pull the other cardboard tube so that you can feel a gap between the tube and the inner card, and tie the end as before with some strong thread.

4 Remove the cardboard tubes and, using a strip of contrasting coloured card, stick over the threads to neaten. Now cut another strip of the same card and a strip of contrasting coloured crêpe paper twice this length. Put double-sided tape on the back of the card and gather up the crêpe paper onto it.

5 To finish off decorate the cracker with a diamond of card.

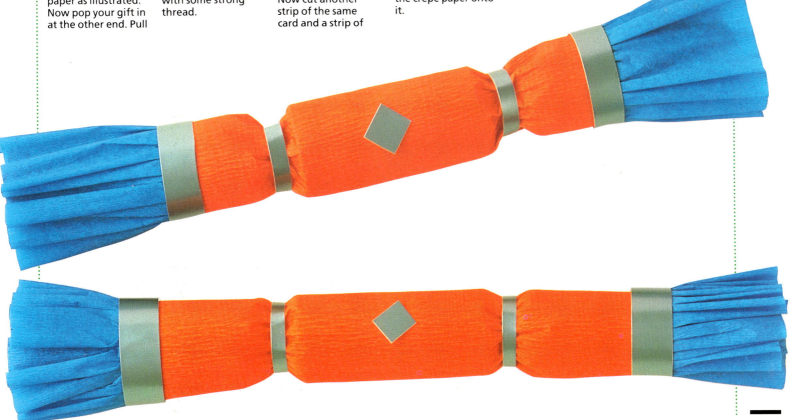

SUNNY MOBILE

Mobiles come in many forms, from very simple brightly coloured abstract shapes, to highly sophisticated motor-driven extravaganzas. This one is made in a traditional way and features a soothing arrangement of the sun with clouds, which will move gently if hung in a breeze.

YOU WILL NEED
Thin card
*Thin wire jewellery hangers, one for
    each piece of mobile*
Strong clear glue
Masking tape
Newspaper
Diluted PVA glue
Fine sandpaper
White paint
Assortment of poster paints
Black ink (optional)
Non-toxic clear gloss varnish
Fishing line or similar nylon cord
Thin florists' or model-makers' wire

Son

Cloud

1 Scale up the mobile shapes from the template to the size required and transfer them to the thin card. Make a total of four cloud shapes. Cut out each shape. Stick a wire hanger to the back of each mobile piece with strong clear glue, and secure the hangers with a piece of masking tape.

2 Let the glue dry for an hour, and then cover each card shape with three layers of papier-mâché, using short, narrow strips of newspaper soaked in diluted PVA glue. Allow the shapes to dry overnight in a warm place.

3 Lightly sand down each piece of mobile, and then prime them with two even coats of white paint.

4 Draw in any design with pencil first, and then decorate the mobile shapes with poster paint. Accentuate details with black ink if desired. When the decoration has thoroughly dried, seal all the pieces with two coats of clear gloss varnish.

To assemble the mobile, cut two pieces of thin florists' or model-makers' wire to a length of about 15 cm (6 in). Suspend one piece of wire from the centre of the other. Attach the shapes to the wires using short lengths of nylon cord tied through the fasteners. Attach a length of cord to the middle of the top wire and hang the mobile in place.

■ WINDMILL

This traditional toy is easy to make as well as being fun to watch turn in the wind. For a children's party you could make one for each guest in a variety of colours.

YOU WILL NEED
Square of stiff paper
Map pin
Empty ballpoint pen casing
Piece of cork
Plastic drinking straw or short bamboo cane

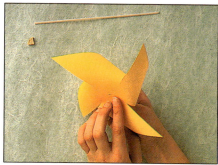

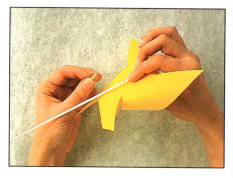

1 First, scale up the ■ pattern from the template to the size required and transfer it to the square of paper. Cut along the lines from each corner nearly to the centre. Bend each alternate corner to the centre, securing each one with a map pin. It is easier to create the pin hole when the sheet is flat.

2 Next, push the ■ pin through the centre of the windmill to the back.

3 Cut a small piece ■ off the end of a ballpoint pen ink casing to act as a bearing, and put it onto the point of the pin behind the paper. Push the pin through a drinking straw, and then into a small piece of cork for safety.
Alternatively, push the pin into a garden cane, making sure the point is well inside the wood so that no sharp end is protruding.

DANCING FINGER PUPPETS

Finger puppets are traditional toys that have been made to amuse children (and adults!) for many years. Here are a flying Scotsman and a member of the corps de ballet for you to make.

YOU WILL NEED
Thick white paper
Felt-tip pens or coloured pencils
Glue
Thin card
Craft knife

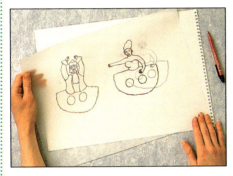
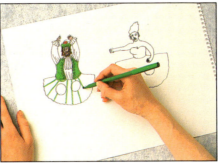

1 Scale up the puppet designs from the template to the size required and transfer them to the paper.

2 Colour in the Scotsman and the ballerina with felt-tip pens or coloured pencils.

3 Then stick the puppets onto the thin card, and cut carefully around each one with a craft knife. Cut out the finger holes with a craft knife, and your puppets are ready to dance the night away!

NECK TIES AND BOW-TIES

A tie always creates a good impression, and these paper ties add a touch of fun without the formality. All you need is a sheet of wrapping paper or crêpe paper.

YOU WILL NEED
Neck tie
Wrapping paper
Glue
String or elastic
Crêpe paper
Double-sided tape

1 To make this party tie cut out a piece of suitable wrapping paper using the front part of a real neck tie as a guide. Make sure that the paper is slightly larger all round to allow for turnings.

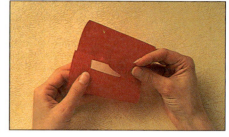

2 Glue and fold back the turnings to get a good finish.

 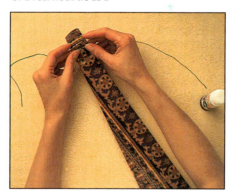

3 To make the 'knot', cut out a fairly large rectangle of paper. Cut a piece of string or elastic long enough to go around your neck, and place it across the rectangle. Glue and fold the rectangle in half. Now glue the 'knot' to the top of the tie and knot the elastic at the ends.

4 To make a bow-tie, use some crêpe paper, measuring 25 × 10 cm (10 × 4 in). Join the ends together to form a ring with double-sided tape.

5 Gather in the centre and cut a thin strip of crêpe paper and wind it around the middle. Apply glue to the end, but before sticking it down, insert a neck-length of elastic.

6 Glue on coloured spots to make an impression at the party!

■ PAPER PEAR

You could make any sort of fruit or vegetable from papier-mâché using this method. It is possible to make quite convincing shapes by 'sculpting' the crumpled newspaper with masking tape. You might even be inspired to attempt something really exotic, like a star fruit!

YOU WILL NEED
Newspaper
Masking tape
Diluted PVA glue
Fine sandpaper
White paint
Assortment of poster paints
Non-toxic clear gloss varnish

1 Loosely crumple a sheet of newspaper into a large egg shape. Twist and tape the paper. You may have to add smaller wedges of crumpled paper to achieve the shape you want.

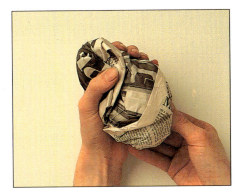

2 To make the stalk, roll a small piece of newspaper into a thin tube, bend the top over, and tape it firmly. Make a hole in the top of your pear, and push the stalk in, fixing it with masking tape.

3 Soak strips of newspaper in diluted PVA glue. Cover the pear with three layers of paper strips. Smooth its surface with your hands.

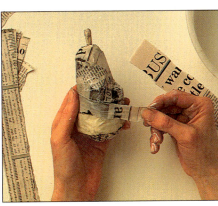

4 Let the pear dry overnight in a warm place, such as an airing cupboard. Lightly sand the surface of the fruit, and prime it with two coats of white paint.

5 Colour your pear with poster paints. When it has dried, seal the surface with two coats of clear varnish. You might like to use satin finish rather than gloss varnish to give a more naturalistic look.

DECORATIVE CUP

This papier-mâché cup is formed in an exotic style from heavy cardboard. This method of making a frame which can be built up with layers of papier-mâché allows great versatility of style: almost any design on paper can be reproduced in card with a little planning.

YOU WILL NEED
Heavy cardboard
Diluted PVA glue
Masking tape
Newspaper
Fine sandpaper
White paint
Selection of poster paints
Non-toxic clear gloss varnish

1 Scale up the cup pieces from the template to the size required and transfer them onto heavy cardboard. Assemble the cup by first sticking the three triangles of card together using PVA glue. Strengthen with strips of masking tape, and then assemble the base.

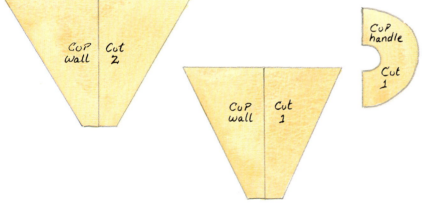

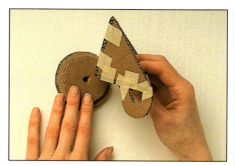

2 Stick the handle to one side of the cup and secure with masking tape. To stick the bowl and base together, make a hole in the centre of the base using a sharp pencil. Apply glue to the 'point' of the bowl and rest this on the base. Finally, fix in place with masking tape for extra strength.

3 Next, paint the cup with one coat of diluted PVA glue to prevent it from warping, and then cover it with four layers of papier-mâché. Use short thin pieces of newspaper soaked in diluted PVA glue. Make sure the pieces of newspaper are thin enough to go around the handle.

4 Leave the cup to dry overnight in a warm place. Then lightly sand down the dried cup, and prime it with two coats of white paint.

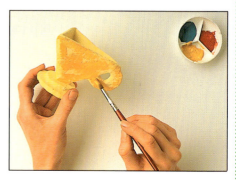

5 Decorate the cup with poster paint. When the paint has dried thoroughly, apply a coat of clear gloss varnish.

MASKED BALL

Keep the guests at the party guessing with this stylish evening mask. Choose crêpe paper to match your ballgown and trim with matching ribbon.

YOU WILL NEED
Gold foil card
Gold doily
Glue
Foil crêpe paper
Sticky tape
Doweling rod
Ribbon

1 Scale up the template to the size required and cut out a mask shape in gold foil card.

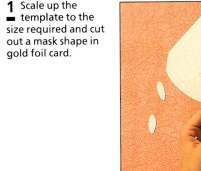

2 Now cut the scalloped edge from a gold doily and glue it to the top of the mask.

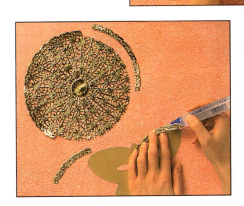

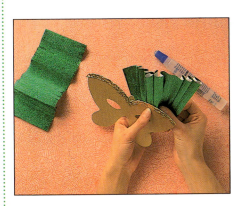

3 Gather a strip of foil crêpe paper and stick it to the back of the mask along the top edge. You might need to secure this further with some tape.

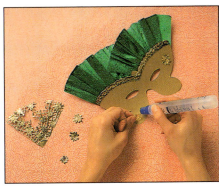

4 Now cut out some other motifs from the doily and stick them onto the mask front to decorate.

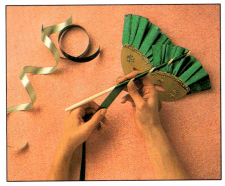

5 Take a piece of doweling rod, wrap a length of ribbon around it and glue the ends. Curl further pieces of ribbon and stick them to the top of the doweling. Tape the doweling rod onto one side of the mask and set off for the ball.

INDIAN CHIEF

Transform a strip of card into an exciting headband fit for an Indian chief. Why not make one each for the whole tribe?

YOU WILL NEED
Coloured card
Assorted coloured card
Glue
Sticky tape

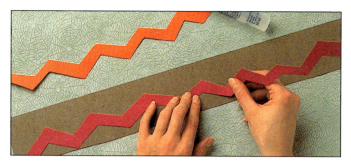

1 First of all cut out a length of stiff coloured card measuring 60 × 6 cm (24 × 2½ in). Now decorate it by cutting out zigzag lines from brightly-coloured card and sticking them onto the band.

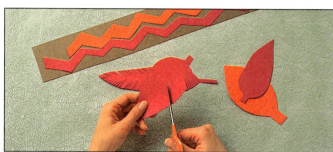

2 Draw and cut out feather shapes from the brightly coloured card and make lots of small scissor cuts along the sides of the feathers to make them more realistic.

3 Apply glue to the inside of the band and stick the feathers in place. To secure them really well use a strip of tape on top.

4 Fold the two ends together, adjust the size and tape to fit.

■ SUNFLOWER

Brighten up a room with some crêpe paper sunflowers that will bring a ray of sunshine all year round.

YOU WILL NEED
Brown card
Brown and green crêpe paper
Glue
Bright yellow paper
Doweling rod
Green paper
Sticky tape

1 Cut out two 10 cm (4 in) diameter circles from brown card. Next cut 4 cm (1½ in) squares of brown crêpe paper and attach them to one side of one of the brown circles by screwing up each one and gluing it on.

2 Using the petal template, scaled up to the size required, cut out petals in bright yellow paper.

3 Pleat and glue them into position onto the back of the covered brown circle so that they follow the edge.

4 To make the stem take a piece of doweling rod approximately 50 cm (20 in) long. Cut leaf shapes in green paper and twist the ends to make a small stem.

5 Attach the leaf stems to the doweling rod at intervals, securing with tape.

6 Cover the stick completely by winding a long strip of green crêpe paper around it.

7 Tape the flower head to the front of the stick, then turn over and glue the remaining brown circle to the back to neaten.

FLYING IN THE WIND

This regal kite will look very grand flying in a blue sky with its gold bows trailing behind. If it is made with fairly stiff paper, it should withstand quite strong gusts of wind. It is possible to make the kite in a variety of sizes: just follow the basic rule that the cross bar is two-thirds the length of the long doweling rod.

YOU WILL NEED
Two lengths of wooden doweling rod, one measuring 40 cm (16 in) and one 60 cm (24 in)
Lengths of strong thin string
Craft knife
Large sheet of stiff coloured paper
Strong glue
Curtain ring
Ball of kite string
Contrasting scraps of coloured paper for decoration and tail ribbons
Length of coloured ribbon for kite tail

1 First, take the two pieces of doweling rod. Using a pen, mark the shorter piece halfway along its length. Mark the longer piece a third of the way down its length. Join the pieces of doweling rod together so that the marks touch; the shorter piece should lie horizontally across the longer, forming a cross. Tie the sticks tightly together with thin string.

2 Using a craft knife, make a notch at the end of each piece of doweling rod. Then tie the end of a length of string around the notch in the top of the kite frame, and wind the string around the outside, securing it around each notch in turn. Tie the ends of the string together when you reach the top of the frame again.

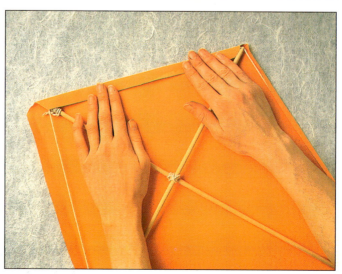

3 Next, place the kite frame on the large piece of coloured paper and cut around it, leaving 1 cm (½ in) of paper spare outside the edges of the string. Cut the corners of the paper back to the ends of each piece of doweling rod, and then smear glue along the edges of the paper, folding them over to enclose the string.
Tie a length of string to each end of the short rod, and a piece to either end of the long one. Pull the strings together so that they overlap, and secure them where they touch with a curtain ring. Tie the ball of kite string to the curtain ring.

4 Decide on the colour of the tail decoration and stick it to the front of the kite with strong glue. Secure the tail ribbon at the bottom of the kite frame, and stick paper bows in place along its length with a dab of glue or small pieces of tape. Alternatively, tie the kite tail around each bow to keep them firmly in place.

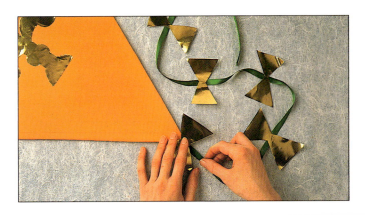

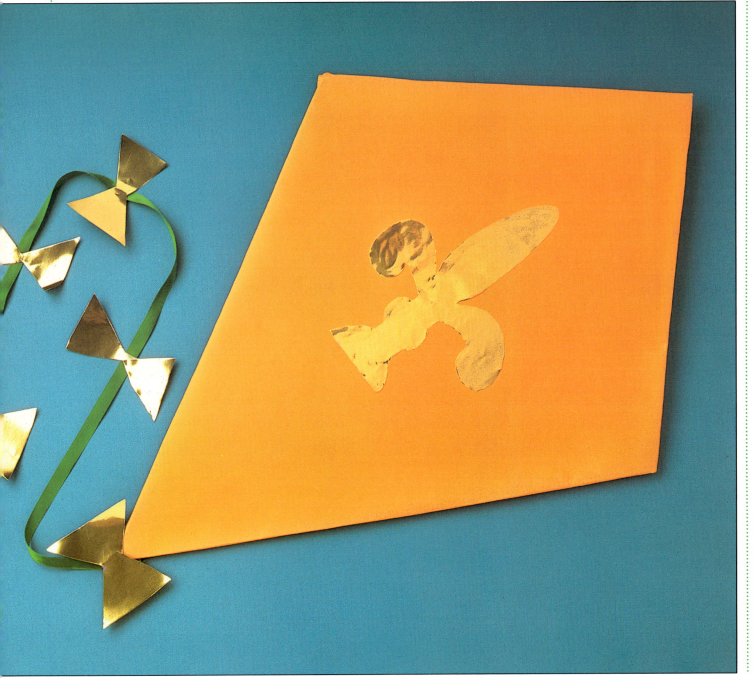

CANDLE DECORATIONS

This is a very quick and decorative way to display candles, but remember that lit candles should never be left unattended under any circumstances.

YOU WILL NEED
Oasis or florist's sponge
Tissue paper
Candle
Thin paint brush

1 To make the candle holder, first cut a block of oasis or florist's sponge to the size that you require.

2 Now cut out small squares of tissue paper. This tissue paper is black on one side and gold on the other so that it has a two-tone effect, intended to match the elegant black candles used.

3 Push the base of the candle into the oasis so that it can stand by itself.

4 Taking a square of tissue paper, place the end of a paint brush in the centre of the paper and poke it into the oasis so that it is held in place. Continue to do this until the block is covered.

STAR GARLAND

For this star garland you will need lots of different colours of tissue paper. Four colours have been used here, but it is up to you how many you choose.

YOU WILL NEED
Coloured tissue paper
Double-sided tape

1 First of all fold up the sheets of tissue paper in individual colours and draw a star shape on top. Now cut out the stars and repeat in all the colours.

2 Stick double-sided tape onto four points of one star and place another star of a different colour on top.

3 Put a further piece of double-sided tape into the centre of the second star and place the next coloured star on top of this. Continue to build up the garland, sticking the stars alternately at sides and centre, until you have a chain long enough for the length that you require.

SPACE ALIEN

A hair band simply covered in shiny paper makes an effective alien headdress. Team with T-shirt or leotard and tights for a double-quick space outfit.

YOU WILL NEED
Rigid hair band
Blue metallic crêpe paper
Glue
Sticky tape

1 Use an old hair band and wind a strip of blue metallic crêpe paper around it, taking care not to tear the paper. Secure the end with glue or sticky tape.

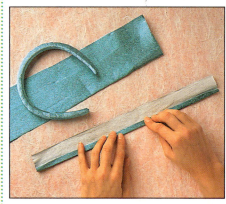

2 Next cut two lengths of the crêpe paper and roll them up lengthways, gluing them to make a tube.

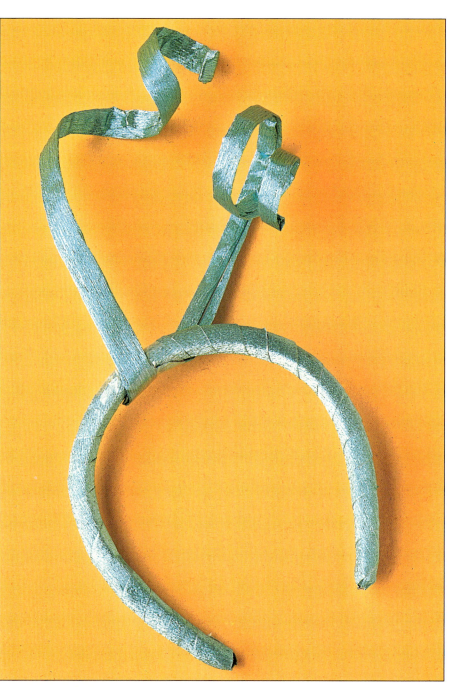

3 Now tightly wind the top part of the tube around a pencil or paint brush to make it curl. Repeat with the other length. Fix the Space Alien 'antennae' onto the hair band with clear tape and mould into a suitable shape.

CHRISTMAS TREE GIFT BOX

Here is a way to make a very attractive Christmas decoration to hang on the tree. Pop a sweet or small gift inside or leave it empty simply for decoration.

YOU WILL NEED
White card
Craft knife
Ruler
Glue
Wrapping paper
Ribbon

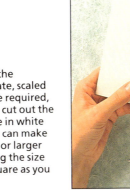

1 Using the template, scaled to the size required, draw and cut out the box shape in white card. You can make it smaller or larger by altering the size of the square as you like.

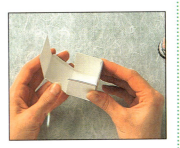

2 Score along all the lines using a craft knife and ruler, taking care not to cut through the card completely.

3 Shape the box by folding the sides up along the scored lines. Apply glue to the tabs and hold the box in position until it is fixed.

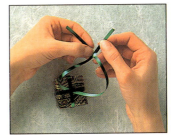

4 Now cover the box in an appropriate wrapping paper.

5 Finish off by tying a ribbon decoratively, and making a loop to hang the box on the tree.

▪ SPARKLING FRAME

This frame is decorated with two different coloured foils, and will take standard-sized photographs. It opens at the side and could easily be made larger to accommodate bigger pictures.

YOU WILL NEED
Heavy corrugated cardboard
Thin corrugated cardboard
Strong clear glue
Diluted PVA glue
2 picture hangers
Masking tape
Newspaper
Fine sandpaper
White paint
Silver foil
Gold foil
Cord for hanging

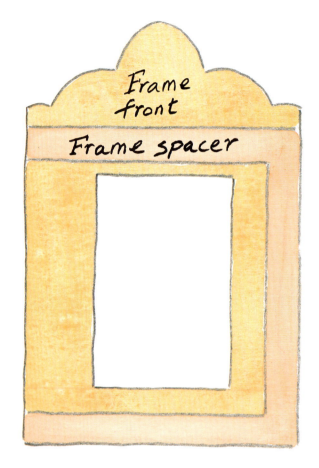

Frame front

Frame spacer

1 Scale up the frame pieces from the template to the size required. Transfer the front to heavy cardboard and the spacer to thin cardboard. Cut a rectangle in thick cardboard to form the back of the frame. Stick the spacer to three sides of the reverse of this rectangle and secure with tape. One side is left open for inserting the picture. When the glue is dry, prime the pieces with diluted PVA glue to help prevent warping. Allow to dry for three or four hours. Glue and tape the hangers to the back.

2 Now cover both pieces of frame with three layers of papier-mâché, using strips of newspaper about 2½ cm (1 in) wide. Let the papier-mâché dry overnight, and then sand the layers lightly with fine sandpaper.

3 When they are dry, prime the frame pieces with two coats of white paint *before* they are joined. Although the paint will eventually be covered, you will be able to see much more easily where to stick the foil if the surface of the frame is white. Stick the back to the front of the frame with strong, clear glue, and hold the joins together with tape. Cover the joins with two layers of papier-mâché strips, and apply another coat of white paint.

4 When everything is dry, decorate the frame. Cut strips of silver foil to fit on the frame and glue them in place. Make sure that you cover the inside edges of the frame. Next, cut shapes from gold foil and stick them around the frame. Finally, attach some cord to the back of the frame, around the hangers.

MOSAIC STYLE

Mosaic tiling is a very ancient form of art and was used as a practical way to decorate floors. It is also an attractive way to make a picture using paper. It does need patience and the finished result makes a beautiful piece to frame and display.

YOU WILL NEED
White and brown card
Coloured papers
Glue
Craft knife

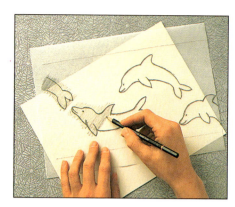

1 Scale up the design from the template to the size required and transfer it onto a piece of white card 30 × 20 cm (12 × 8 in).

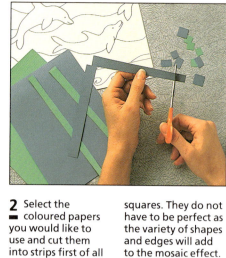

2 Select the coloured papers you would like to use and cut them into strips first of all and then into squares. They do not have to be perfect as the variety of shapes and edges will add to the mosaic effect.

3 Organize the various squares of colours into separate piles and start to glue them onto the picture.

4 Continue to build up the squares in colour sections. In order to achieve a smooth line, it may be necessary to use a craft knife to trim the edges of the squares once they have been glued.

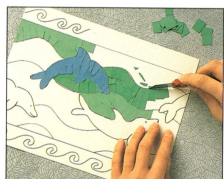

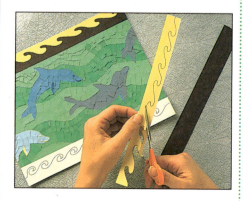

5 To make the border, cut two strips of the brown card 3 cm (1¼ in) wide and the length of the white board. Cut two yellow strips of paper in the same size and draw and cut the wave design onto them. Fix the yellow strips onto the brown and glue them onto the card. When all the areas have been covered, cut pieces to make the eyes and the mouths and glue them into place.

CIRCLE GARLAND

Festoon your room with these simple circular garlands made from vivid tissue paper. Alternate the colours individually or place together in blocks of colour.

YOU WILL NEED
Card
Coloured tissue paper
Glue

1 Cut two circles of card and lots of circles in different colours of tissue paper.

2 Take ten of the tissue paper circles and fold them in half, then half again into a quarter. Do not use any more than ten pieces as they will not fold properly. Now make a cut from the double-folded edge, following the line of the outside of the circle, two thirds down the wedge.

3 Undo the circle and fold again in half the other way. Fold again into a quarter so that you have a new fold line. Make a cut nearer the centre, following the outside line as illustrated. Undo the circle and lay it flat.

4 Glue the first circle onto one of the circular cards and then attach another tissue circle onto it by gluing it at the centre.

5 Glue the next circle to the top and bottom of the first. Continue to glue together alternately gluing them at the centre, and the top and bottom. Finally, glue the other circular card to the last tissue circle. Pull the cards away from each other to reveal the garland.

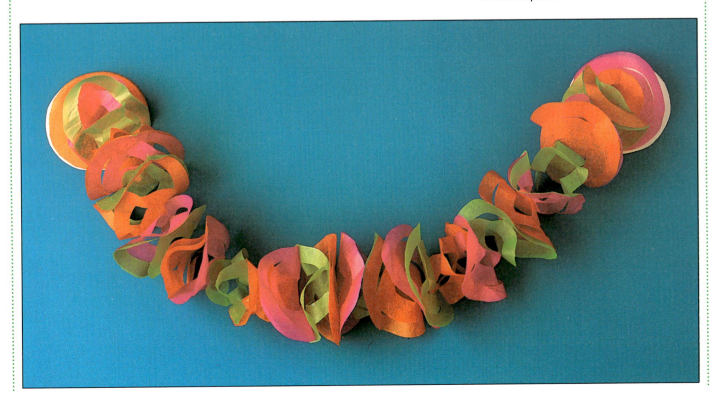

PARTY BOATER

Perfect for a fancy dress party, a theatrical production or a summer picnic, this boater is both elegant and easy to make.

YOU WILL NEED
Coloured card
Glue

1 Measure and draw a 24 cm (10 in) diameter circle on to a piece of coloured card and then draw a second circle with a 19 cm (7 in) diameter inside the first one. Cut out the larger circle.

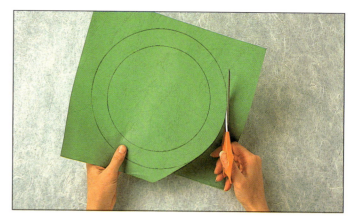

2 Cut darts around the larger circle so that they end at the inner circle. Fold the darts down once they have all been cut. This allows the hat to fit perfectly.

3 Next measure and cut out a strip of card in the same colour measuring 8 × 60 cm (3 × 23½ in). Draw a straight line down the centre of the strip and carefully cut darts down one half. Glue the strip and then fix it to the circle by attaching the darts onto it in order to form the top of the boater.

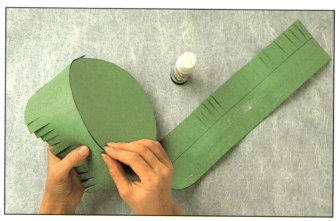

4 Now push the side darts outwards; cut out a ring of coloured card that has an outside diameter of 30 cm (13 in) and an inside diameter of 19 cm (8 in).

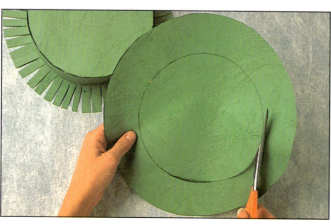

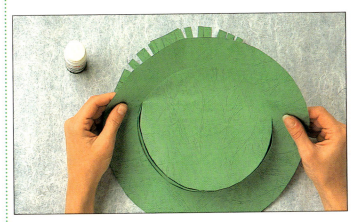

5 Place the card ring over the top and onto the out-turned darts and glue into position.

6 Decorate by putting a band of suitable wrapping paper around it, to create a colourful band. You could make several hats and give each one a different band.

■ BRIGHT BEADS

Papier-mâché can be used to make beads in a huge variety of sizes, shapes and colours, and because of its lightweight nature you can make the most enormous necklaces, bracelets and earrings without being weighed down!

YOU WILL NEED
Newspaper
Diluted PVA glue
Darning needle
White paint
Assortment of poster paints
Non-toxic clear gloss varnish
Thin nylon cord or elastic to string beads

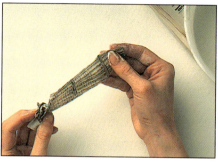

1 Tear the newspaper into long strips about 2½ cm (1 in) wide, and soak them in the diluted PVA glue for a few seconds. Shake off the excess glue, and roll up the paper between your fingers so that it forms round pellets of pulp.

2 Squash each ball of pulp so that it is tightly compacted, and most of the glue is squeezed out. Lay the beads in a warm place to dry for a couple of hours.

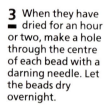

3 When they have dried for an hour or two, make a hole through the centre of each bead with a darning needle. Let the beads dry overnight.

4 When the beads are completely dry, prime each one with two coats of white paint. Let the paint dry, and then decorate the beads with poster paints.

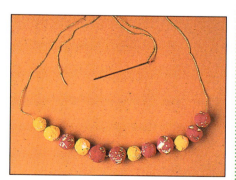

5 Varnish each bead with two coats of clear gloss varnish, and when dry, string them onto thin nylon cord or elastic using a darning needle.

CUT-OUT
ANIMALS

The chicken, frog, and elephant are held together with paper fasteners and have moveable limbs. They are very simple in construction, and many other animals could be attempted using the same process.

YOU WILL NEED
Heavy paper or thin card
Felt-tip pens or coloured pencils
Craft knife
Paper fasteners
Glue

1 Scale up your chosen animal from the template to the required size, and transfer the pieces to paper or card. Cut two bodies for each animal. Remember that one will have to be cut *in reverse* so that the bodies can be stuck together. Next, cut two of each leg, wing, ear and so on. To transfer the pattern in reverse, simply turn it over.

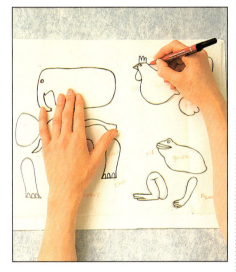

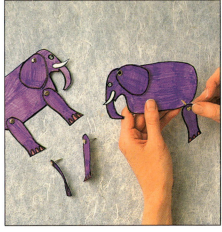

2 Next, colour each piece of animal with felt-tip pen or coloured pencils, and cut them all out, keeping the parts separate.

3 To fix the animal together, make a small incision with a craft knife at the limb positions in each body, and at the top of each body part. Push a paper fastener through the front of each body part, through the body, and open it out on the other side to secure the animal.

4 To join the two halves together, spread a little glue along the top edge of one half of the animal's body, and stick it to the other.

M O N O C H R O M E
D E C O U P A G E

Decoupage is the traditional art of
decorating surfaces with paper cut-outs
of Victorian-style images. This project
has a contemporary feel, however, by
using monochrome cut-outs and a
modern box covered in brown paper.

YOU WILL NEED
Black and white pictures
Card or wooden box
Glue
Varnish (if needed)

1 Start by choosing
your images. The
ones used here are
from a wrapping
paper. Cut them out
carefully following
their outlines.

2 Arrange the
images on a box
and then glue them
into position. A card
gift box is used here
but you could apply
the paper cut-outs to
a wooden box such
as an old cigar box.
However, you would
need to coat the
decorated box with
a layer of varnish.

■ BANGLES AND BEADS

If you want some new accessories and to wear something that nobody else will have, this jewellery that is made from paper could be just what you are looking for.

YOU WILL NEED
Patterned paper
Contrasting coloured card
Pencil or paint brush
Glue
Bead thread
Sticky tape

1 To start, cut 30 cm (12 in) strips of marbled or decorated paper and taper them so that they measure 4 cm (1½ in) at the base and 1 cm (½ in) at the tip. Then cut a small length of contrasting coloured card, wrap it around a pencil or paint brush and fix it with glue.

2 Now apply some more glue to the length of the triangular strip and, beginning with the wider end, start to wrap around the card, so that the strip is kept central. Make several more of these beads, and thread them onto a length of bead thread to form a necklace.

3 To make a matching bangle, cut a long strip of white card and curl it round into a ring, large enough to slip over your hand. Fix by taping it.

4 Now cut long strips of your chosen decorated paper and after gluing them at one end, start to wind them one by one around the bangle shape.

CUT-OUT DOLLS

This charming couple are modern versions of the cut-out dolls that have been popular for several centuries. They have 'casual' and 'smart' outfits, so are ready for any occasion!

YOU WILL NEED
Thick white paper
Felt-tip pens or coloured pencils
Glue
Thin card
Craft knife

1 Start by scaling up the designs from the template to the size required. Next transfer them to white paper.

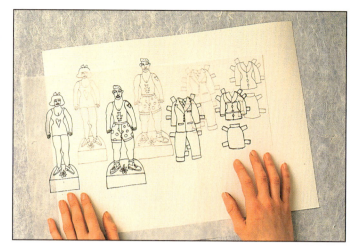

2 Colour in the dolls and their clothes with felt-tip pens or coloured pencils according to your own fashion scheme.

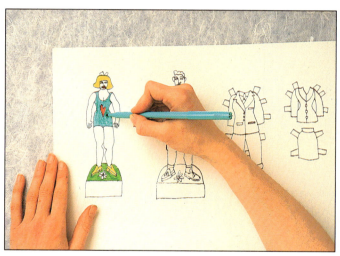

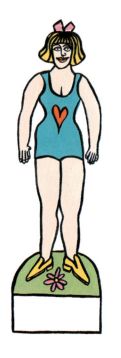
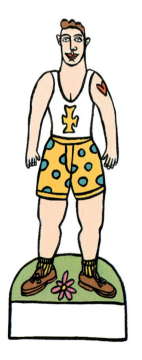

3 Stick the dolls onto the thin card. Cut carefully around the dolls and their clothes with scissors. Using a craft knife, lightly score the fold line of the stand at the bottom of each doll, making sure you do not cut right through. Fold along the scored line to make a prop to help the dolls stand upright. To dress the dolls, simply fold each white tab over to the back of the body.

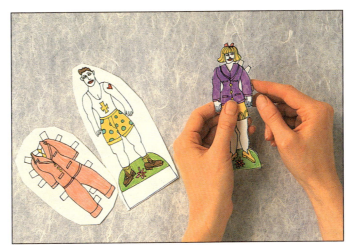

'BAROQUE' CHRISTMAS WREATH

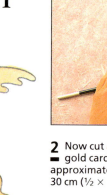

The base for this beautiful wreath is an embroidery hoop. An oval one is used here but a round one would work just as well.

YOU WILL NEED
Gold crêpe paper
Glue
Oval embroidery hoop
Gold card
Paint brush or pencil
Black felt-tip pen

2 Now cut a strip of gold card approximately 1 × 30 cm (½ × 12 in) and wrap it tightly around a paint brush or pencil.

1 First cut a long strip of gold crêpe paper, glue it at one end of the hoop and start to wind it around the hoop until it is completely covered.

3 Attach one end of the curled gold strip half-way up the right-hand side of the hoop, wind round the hoop and fix the other end just beyond the bottom point.

4 Using the template, scaled to the size required, draw the angel playing the trumpet onto the back of some gold card and cut out. Draw on the features in a black felt-tip pen. Make a bow out of gold crêpe paper and stick it on to the top of the wreath.

5 Now fix the angel to the left hand side of the wreath.

FRAME UP

Make your own designer-look photograph frames from thick card and wrapping paper. Choose paper to pick out colours in the photographs or to co-ordinate with furnishings.

YOU WILL NEED
Thick card
Ruler
Craft knife
Wrapping or marbled paper
Glue

1 Cut two pieces of thick card to the required size and cut a window in one of them using a ruler and craft knife. As a guide allow 3 cm (1 in) for the frame but this can be varied depending on the photograph.

2 For the backing card, cut a piece of marbled paper to the same width but slightly longer, then glue and turn the excess length around the top edge.

3 Take the frame front, place it onto another piece of marbled paper and lightly mark and cut out a smaller window so that you have turnings of about 1½ cm (½ in). Glue the turnings on the window to the inside of the frame. Cut across the external corners of the paper and glue the top edge down.

4 Cut spacing strips out of thick card and stick them along the three sides of the back panel.

5 Apply glue to the strips and carefully fix the front frame on top. Glue and turn the edges at the side and base front so that they wrap around the three remaining sides of the back panel.

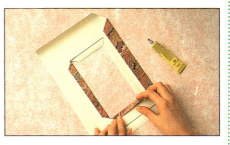

6 Now cut a piece of marbled paper exactly the same size as the frame and stick it onto the back to neaten.

7 To make the support strut cut out a piece of card approximately half the length of frame and cut a pointed end. Cover in paper leaving a long overlap of excess paper at the blunt end.

8 Use the excess paper to glue and attach the strut to the back of the frame.

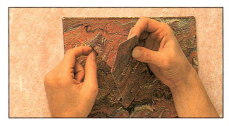

9 Make a support strap from the same paper, and glue it to the back of the frame and the support.

TREE DECORATIONS

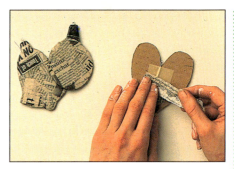

Good, unusual Christmas decorations are often hard to find. If you want an alternative to glittery baubles then you may like to design and make your own decorations in papier-mâché. These are very simple in design and structure, but you could easily make quite ornate, even three-dimensional, decorations to dress your tree.

YOU WILL NEED

Thin card
Craft knife
Small metal jewellery hangers, one for each decoration
Strong clear glue
Masking tape
Newspaper
Diluted PVA glue
Fine sandpaper
White paint
Assortment of poster paints
Black ink (optional)
Non-toxic clear gloss varnish
Cord to hang decorations

1 Trace the decoration shapes from the template, scaling up to the size required, and transfer them to the thin card. Cut out each shape.

Stick a hanger onto the back of each decoration with strong clear glue, and hold it in place with masking tape.

2 Allow the glue to dry for an hour, and then cover each decoration with three layers of small, thin newspaper strips soaked in diluted PVA glue. Let the decorations dry in a warm place overnight.

3 Then, sand the dry decorations lightly with fine sandpaper, and prime each one with two coats of white paint.

4 Draw in any design first with pencil, and then colour your decorations with poster paints. Define details with black ink if required.

Allow the decorations to dry thoroughly, and then seal them with two coats of clear gloss varnish. When they are dry, tie a loop of cord to the top of each decoration.

VICTORIAN BOOKLET

What could be more evocative of the Victorian age than a notebook that has been decorated by decoupage. This little book could be used as a diary, a notebook or a sketch pad.

YOU WILL NEED
Writing paper
Needle and embroidery thread
Victorian-style scraps or magazine pictures
Glue

1 First fold some sheets of writing paper in half to make the booklet, and press down in the centre to create the crease.

2 Now open out the book and, taking a needle and embroidery thread, make three large stitches to bind the booklet.

3 To give the booklet a nostalgic feel use Victorian-style scraps which can be cut out from magazines, or purchased. Arrange and stick them onto the cover of the notebook.

ROYAL CROWN

A regal crown fit for a king, queen, prince or princess! Make your decorations as simple or elaborate as you like, for a right royal celebration.

YOU WILL NEED
Foil card
Silver paper
Glue
Coloured foil paper
Double-sided tape
Foil crêpe paper

1 To make the crown, cut out a length of foil card about 55 cm (22 in) long and 15 cm (6 in) wide. On the back of the card draw out a shaped crown design and cut it out.

2 Now cut out small circles of silver paper and glue them onto the finials. Cut out diamond shapes in different coloured foil paper to make up the 'jewels' and glue them onto the crown.

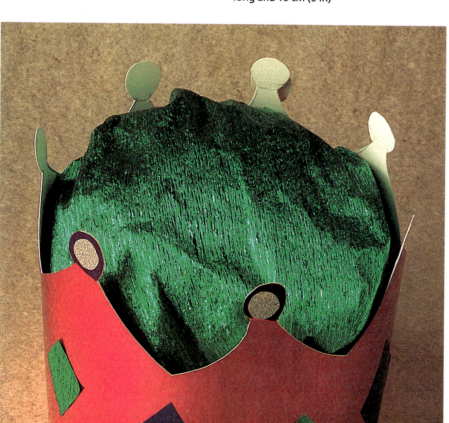

3 Join the ends of the crown together with glue and stick a long piece of double-sided tape all the way around on the inside about halfway down.

4 Take a circle of matching foil crêpe paper, which is just larger than the crown, and carefully place it inside the top so that it is fixed to the tape. Make it billow out by pushing it up from underneath, to represent the velvet in a crown.

CHRISTMAS RING

This is a quick and easy way to make a new collection of Christmas decorations to hang on your tree without spending a fortune. They are made from wooden curtain rings, covered in vivid crêpe paper.

YOU WILL NEED
Crêpe paper
Wooden curtain rings
Glue
Thin ribbon

1 Cut 2 cm (¾ in) wide strips of coloured crêpe paper. Take a wooden curtain ring and wind the strips of crêpe paper around the ring to cover. Glue ends in place.

2 Now take a thin ribbon and secure it at the top of the ring. As before, wind it around the ring leaving gaps to reveal the paper. When you have worked the ribbon back to the top, secure it and then make a loop for hanging.

3 To finish off, make a bow out of the crêpe paper and stick it on at the top of the ring.

BUTTERFLY MOBILE

Mobiles can drift gently in the slightest breeze or draught, entertaining young and old alike. Here the pretty butterfly wings are particularly eye-catching as they sparkle in the light.

YOU WILL NEED
Brightly coloured card in different
*   shades*
Sequins or glitter (optional)
Glue
Cotton thread
Sewing needle
Sticky tape
Three mobile wires, or three thin
*   lengths of thin wooden rod*

1 Scale up the template to the required size and trace four butterflies onto different coloured cards and then cut them out. Then cut out a fifth butterfly, using a smaller scale so that it is approximately half the size of the other four.

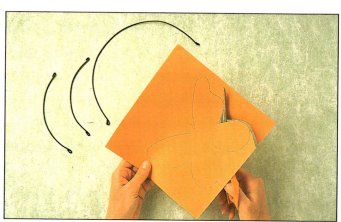

2 Next start to decorate the butterflies by sticking on small pieces of card, making sure that the colours are strong and bright. You could use other materials such as sequins or glitter to add extra sparkle.

3 Thread a long length of cotton through the top of each of the large butterflies, knotting the end securely and fixing it with sticky tape. Attach the other end of each piece of thread to the mobile wires. Each piece of thread should be a different length to add variety to the positions of the butterflies.

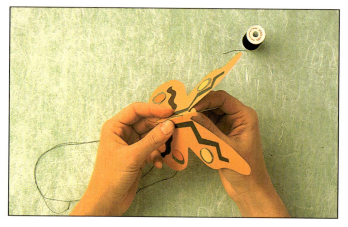

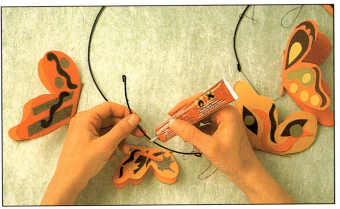

4 Last, but not least, decorate the smallest butterfly and stick it onto the top wire of the mobile, to make it look as if it is having a rest from flying around!

B A U B L E
B O X

This box can be made in a variety of sizes, and could be filled with handmade sweets as a gift on a special occasion. It may be decorated in a variety of ways, perhaps with small pieces of brightly coloured pottery to emulate mosaic, or glass 'gems' from a theatrical costumiers.

YOU WILL NEED
Heavy and thin corrugated cardboard
Craft knife
Strong clear glue
Masking tape
Newspaper
Diluted PVA glue
Fine sandpaper
White paint
Assorted poster paints
Non-toxic clear gloss varnish

Box wall

1 Scale up the box pieces from the template to the size required and, apart from the lid handle, transfer to heavy corrugated cardboard. Cut out using a craft knife. Place the box wall pattern so that the corrugations run vertically along its width. Cut the lid handle from thin corrugated card.

Base and lid Cut 2

Handle Cut 1

2 Next, assemble the body of the box and the lid. Bend the box wall at each corrugation so that it forms a circle. Glue and tape it in position on the box base. Then glue and tape the lip to the underside of the lid, and fix the handle in position.

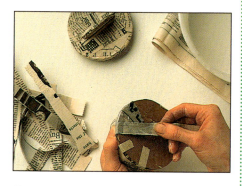

3 Tear newspaper into thin strips and soak in diluted PVA glue. Cover the body of the box and the lid with four layers of papier-mâché. Make sure the strips of paper are thin enough to ensure a smooth surface, especially around the curved edges.

4 Leave the box to dry overnight in a warm place. When quite dry, lightly smooth the surface of the box with fine sandpaper, and prime it with two coats of white paint. Leave to dry thoroughly in a warm place.

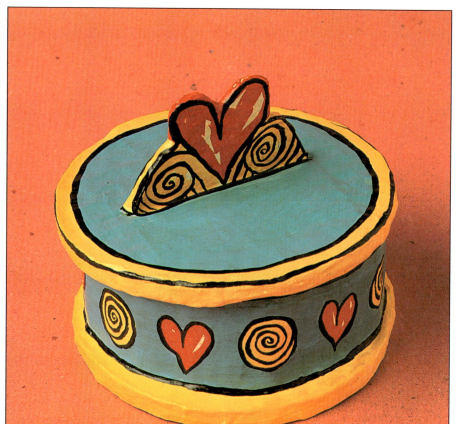

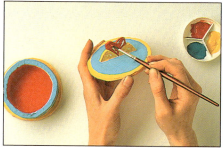

5 Decorate the box and its lid, both inside and out, using poster paints. When the paint is completely dry, apply a coat of clear gloss varnish.

▪ DOLL

This doll is formed from tightly taped and compacted newspaper twists. The resulting structure is very sturdy and quite large dolls or other toys could be constructed using this method.

YOU WILL NEED
Newspaper
Masking tape
Diluted PVA glue
Fine sandpaper
White paint
Selection of poster paints
Black ink (optional)
Non-toxic clear gloss varnish

1 First, twist a double sheet of newspaper together to form a 'rope' and tape the top, about 5 cm (2 in) down, to form the doll's head. Cut the remaining paper 'rope' to the desired length to form the body, and secure it with masking tape.

2 Cover the body and head with strips of masking tape to add extra strength. Next, make the arms and legs by the same process, twisting smaller pieces of paper and taping them along their length. Cut the resulting 'ropes' to the right length, and tape them firmly in place on the doll's body.

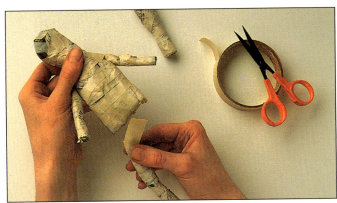

3 Tear some newspaper into thin strips and soak in diluted PVA glue. Then cover the doll with four layers of papier-mâché. To make the doll's hair, hands and feet, roll up small strips of glue-soaked paper between finger and thumb to form pellets of pulp and stick them in place on the head. Paper over the pulp hair with short, thin strips of paper.

4 Let the doll dry overnight in a warm place. When completely dry, lightly smooth the surface with fine sandpaper and prime it with two coats of white paint.

5 When the paint has dried thoroughly, draw in the features of the doll with pencil and fill in the design with poster paints. Define the decoration with black ink if more detail is needed. Seal the doll with two coats of non-toxic clear gloss varnish and allow to dry.

Origami

∎ INTRODUCTION

It is not difficult to understand why origami is the most popular of all papercrafts: the art is very inexpensive, can be done anywhere at anytime and requires no equipment or facilities other than a sheet of paper and a firm surface to work on. Moreover, the transformation of an ordinary piece of paper into a pleasing origami design is a kind of alchemy, perhaps even more so in today's increasingly push-button, computer-controlled, battery-operated culture, than ever before.

The history of origami is rather obscure, but clearly cannot pre-date the invention of paper in China about two thousand years ago. The word 'origami' is not Chinese but Japanese, and is used worldwide out of respect for the ancestral home of the art. When China invaded Japan in AD 610, the secret of papermaking travelled with them and was immediately assimilated into Japanese culture, not just as origami, but more practically as screens, mats, bags, umbrellas, woven clothes and many other objects. As an indication of the importance of paper to the Japanese, the word 'origami' is formed from 'ori' (to fold) and 'kami'

meaning paper and also God ('kami' becomes 'gami' when combined with 'ori'). Indeed, many of the early origami designs were created for symbolic or ceremonial purposes, not for recreation.

The growth of creative origami in the West began in the 1950s, though it was a minor Spanish tradition and practised by the occasional creative individual before that time. Curiously, since that same decade, the art has also undergone a major creative revival in Japan, so much so that there are now several hundred Japanese language books currently in print, most containing new creative work. A great amount of new work is also coming from the West, in all manner of styles ranging from the charmingly simple to the astonishingly complex and from the expressive to the geometric.

If you are new to origami the next few pages will introduce the basics. Readers who have folded before will find these pages a useful refresher. The designs which follow have been graded according to their level of difficulty and you are encouraged not to be too ambitious too soon.

ORIGAMI PAPER

Although origami is defined as 'the art of *paper* folding', most paper folders spend little time thinking about paper, preferring to get straight down to the business of folding, frequently with whatever paper happens to be to hand, however inappropriate it may be. A little consideration for paper, though, can significantly improve the look of what you make and increase your pleasure in folding it.

The easiest and cheapest source of good quality practice paper is photocopy (Xerox) paper. The photocopy and quick print shops now found in most shopping centres sell reams (packets of 500 sheets) of white or coloured photocopy paper, either A4 size or American Letter Size (both about the same size as a page in this book). The shop will trim a ream to square on a power guillotine for a nominal sum. Two or three reams can usually be purchased for a very

reasonable price. Part-reams may also be purchased.

For two-tone models, origami paper bought in packets is ideal. However, it can be difficult to find and is relatively expensive. Also, the bright colours can make some designs look rather childish, so it should be used with care. Patterned gift-wrap paper is a good alternative if origami paper cannot be found. Other good practice papers include computer paper, typing paper, writing paper and even brown wrapping paper.

For displaying origami, perhaps at home or at a place of work, quality papers appropriate to the design should be used. A surprising range of interesting papers can be found in art, craft and graphic equipment supplies shops. It is also worth starting a collection of unusual papers such as old posters, discarded wrapping paper, wallpaper and telephone note blocks.

TIPS

In many ways, nothing could be more basic than folding a sheet of paper. Yet, despite this wonderful simplicity, there are a few guidelines to follow that will make the process of folding easier and very satisfying. Please follow them.

- Check that the paper you are folding is *exactly* square. The best method for making a square is described in the following pages. Nothing is more frustrating than trying to fold paper which is not quite square!

- Do not fold against a soft surface, such as a carpet, your lap or bedsheets. Fold against a hard surface such as a large hardback book or a table.

- Crease slowly, firmly and accurately. Form the early creases with particular care – if they are incorrectly placed, all the later, smaller creases will be difficult to place accurately and will look messy.

- Read the instructions and follow the symbols on each step. Many a mistake is made by ignoring written instructions or by not following all the written instructions on a step, particularly during complex manoeuvres.

- The instructions and symbols on one step will create a shape which looks like the next step but stripped of its symbols. So, you must always *look ahead* to the next step to see what shape you are trying to make. Never look at steps in isolation, but see them as being interconnected, like links in a chain.

ORIGAMI SOCIETIES

If you would like to know more about origami, here are addresses for two well-organized societies. Both accept overseas members and welcome beginners. Also, both publish regular magazines, hold conventions and regional meetings, sell a wide variety of books and paper, and publish booklets on specialist origami topics. The British Origami Society has a postal library service.

British Origami Society,
253 Park Lane,
Poynton,
Stockport,
Cheshire,
SK12 1RH,
England.

The Friends of the Origami Centre of America,
15 West 77th Street,
New York,
NY 10024,
USA.

The Japanese Paper Place,
966 Queen Street West,
Toronto M6J 1G8,
Canada.

The Australian Origami Society,
2/5 Broome Street,
Highgate,
Perth 6000,
Australia.

The New Zealand Origami Society,
79 Dunbar Road,
Christchurch 3,
New Zealand.

HOW TO MAKE A SQUARE

Most papers are bought as rectangular sheets that need to be trimmed square before being folded. Here, then, is a quick and simple way to accurately trim a large sheet to a smaller square, ensuring that the edges are kept straight and clean.

1 Fold over an edge of the sheet, lining up the edges at the sides to ensure square corners.

2 Carefully cut along the crease with a series of large, smooth slicing movements, made with a non-serrated kitchen knife (one with a 15 cm [6 in] blade is best). Set aside the unwanted portion of the sheet.

3 Fold over the short edge to make a triangle.

4 Bend the sheet backwards and make a crease underneath the bottom edge of the triangle.

5 Cut along the crease.

6 Unfold the triangle.

7 The square complete.

OTHER METHODS

Scissors
Duplicate the method shown in the photographs, but use scissors instead of a non-serrated knife. Be careful to control the cutting to ensure a straight edge.

Craft knife
Duplicate the method shown in the photographs, but unfold each crease and cut along them with a craft knife held against a metal rule. Before cutting, place thick card beneath the paper so that the knife does not damage your work surface.

Guillotine
Paper bought in bulk from photocopy print shops and cut on the premises on a power guillotine will be perfectly square, but paper cut by hand on a manually-operated guillotine has the annoying habit of never quite being square, whatever safeguards are taken. So, hand guillotining is not recommended if it is important that your paper is perfectly proportioned.

Tearing
Tearing is not recommended, but is acceptable if there is no other way to trim paper. Before tearing, crease the folded edge backwards and forwards several times, pressing firmly. This will weaken the crease and make tearing easier and neater.

▮ S Y M B O L S

No sequence of origami diagrams can be followed without an understanding of the symbols they use. The meaning of most symbols is obvious and it is not necessary to learn them all now, but it would be very helpful to at least learn the difference between the mountain and valley fold symbols. The other symbols can be learnt as they appear by referring back to this page.

The same symbols can be found in most origami books, whatever language they are written in, be it English, Spanish or even Japanese. This standardization means that the language of origami is truly universal, and that enthusiasts can fold from almost any book, East or West.

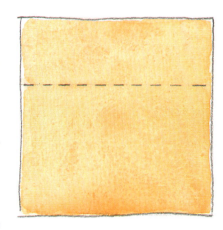

▮ valley

▮ mountain

▮ existing creases

▮ turn over

■ fold dot to dot

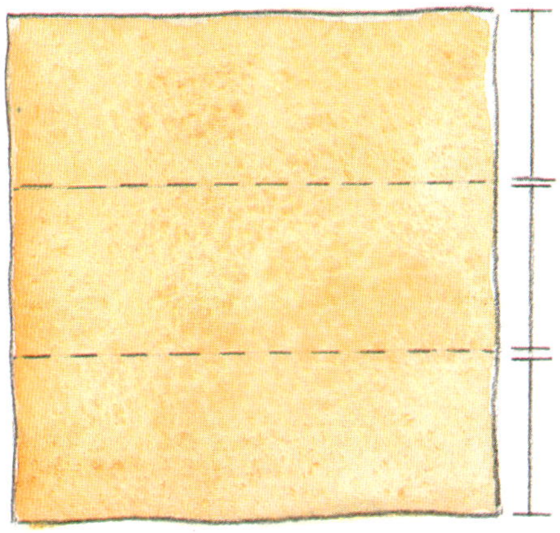

■ these distances are equal

■ unfold or pull out

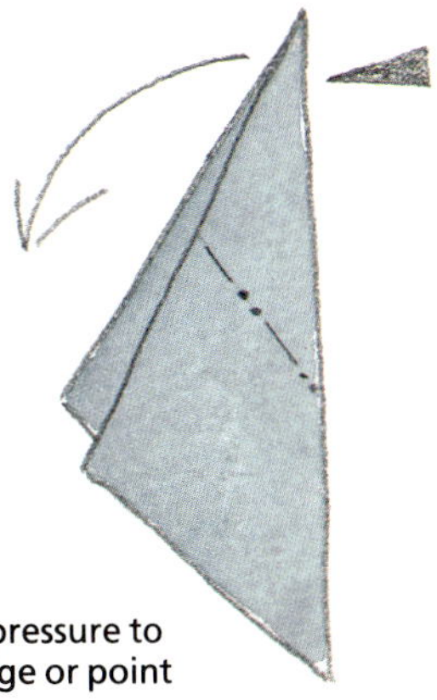

■ apply pressure to this edge or point

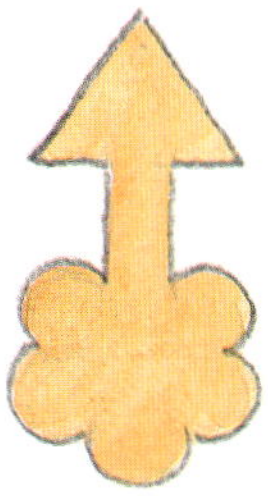

■ inflate

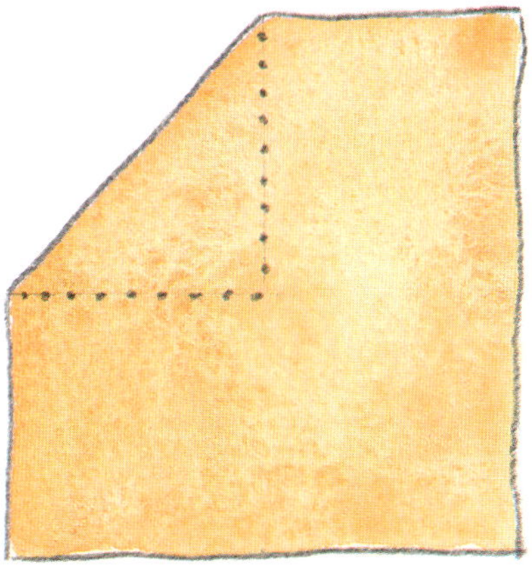

■ x-ray view

■ cut

■ ORIGAMI TECHNIQUES

Apart from the basic mountain and valley creases from which all origami designs are folded, there are four advanced techniques found in the designs that follow. These techniques are used in combination and are: the squash fold, the sink fold and the inside and outside reverse folds. However, not all designs use these advanced techniques, and only the Elephant uses them all together.

Squash and sink folds are the least common. To save space, a detailed explanation of each is given once in the book within a particular design. For an explanation of the squash fold see the Multiform House, Steps 4–6 for an explanation of the sink fold see the Star, Steps 8–12. When you come across a squash or sink fold in another design, refer to these designs for a step-by-step guide.

Inside and outside reverse folds are not more complex than squash or sink folds, but are more common and come in a greater variety. So, to simplify cross referencing, here are the basic forms of each. Refer to this page whenever you need to be reminded how to make them.

INSIDE REVERSE

Pull-through version

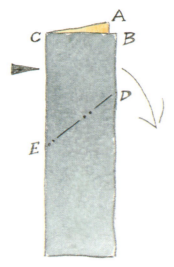

1 This is how the manoeuvre is illustrated in the book.

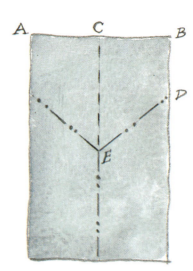

2 This is the crease pattern.

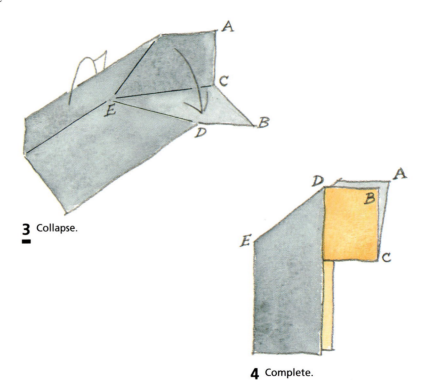

3 Collapse.

4 Complete.

Push-in version

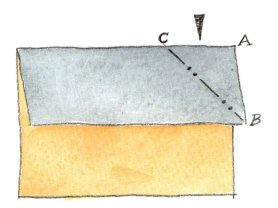

1 This is how the manoeuvre is illustrated in the book.

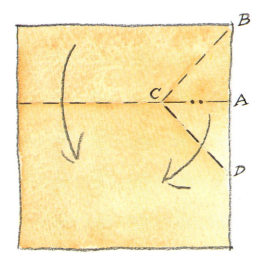

2 This is the crease pattern.

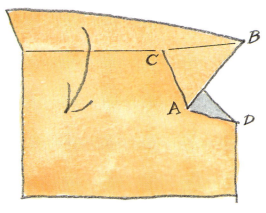

3 Collapse.

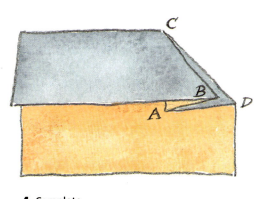

4 Complete.

OUTSIDE REVERSE

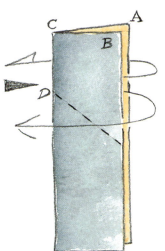

1 This is how the manoeuvre is illustrated in the book.

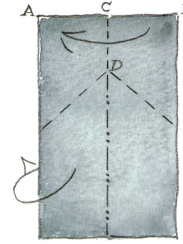

2 This is the crease pattern.

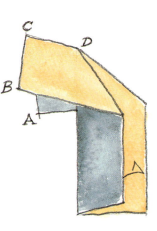

3 Collapse.

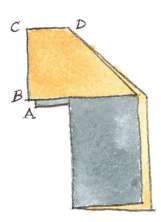

4 Complete.

SIMPLE PROJECTS

G L I D E R

This design is one of a number of similar gliders of Chinese origin, all of which fly extremely well. The secret of good paper plane making is to fold with great accuracy and to practise a variety of launching actions – a carefully-made plane will not fly well if launched wrongly. Use an A4 or American Letter Size sheet of paper.

Traditional design.

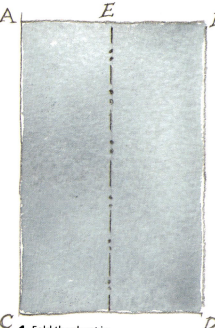

1 Fold the sheet in half down the middle, as a mountain fold (it is easier to make a valley fold, then to turn the sheet over). Unfold.

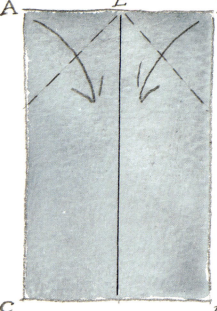

2 Fold in corners A & B to the centre crease.

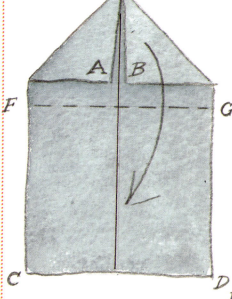

3 Fold down E along crease FG. Note that FG is a little below the level of AB.

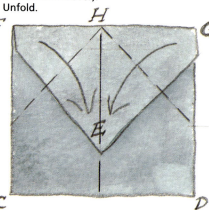

4 Fold in corners F & G, leaving E exposed.

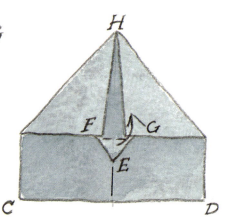

5 Fold up E over F & G.

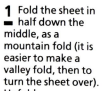

6 Mountain fold D to C.

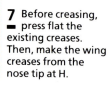

7 Before creasing, press flat the existing creases. Then, make the wing creases from the nose tip at H.

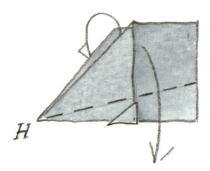

8 The Glider complete. Hold as shown at the point of balance, the wings forming a slight 'V' shape. Release smoothly but firmly.

▪ C A N D Y B A G

If folded from greaseproof paper, this practical design will hold fries and other oily or sticky foods. For extra strength, fold two squares together. For sweets or candies, use any paper, not too thin. Use a 15–25 cm (6–10 in) square. If using origami paper, start coloured side up.

Designed by Paul Jackson.

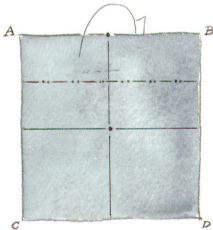

1 Fold and unfold the paper in half horizontally and vertically. Mountain fold edge AB to the centre crease.

2 Fold in the top corners to the centre crease.

3 Similarly, fold in bottom corners C & D, but tucking them beneath A & B, to lock them flat.

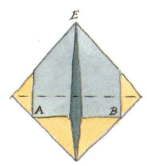

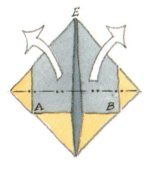

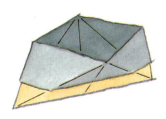

4 Valley fold in half across the middle, then . . .

5 . . . mountain fold in half, to create a flexible crease. Open out the bag.

6 The Candy Bag complete.

■BUTTERFLY

There are a great many origami butterflies in all manner of styles, some very complex. This is one of the simplest. It is important to use origami paper, so that white triangles appear at the edges between the coloured wings, to visually separate them. Cut a square of origami paper in half to create a 2 × 1 rectangle. Start coloured side up.

Designed by Paul Jackson.

1 Fold corners A & B behind to the centre.

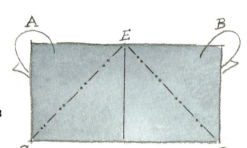

2 Fold EC & ED to the centre crease, allowing corners A & B to flip outwards . . .

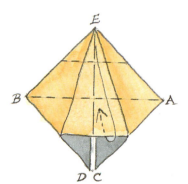

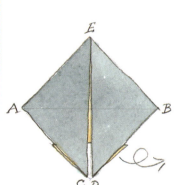

3 . . . like this. Compare the position of the lettered corners with their position in Step 2. Turn over.

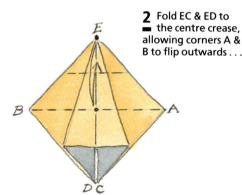

4 First, crease from B to A, across the middle. Then, fold E to the centre point.

5 Re-form the Step 4 creases, but tucking E up under the horizontal edge.

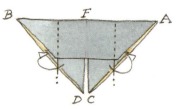

6 With vertical creases that run inside up to edge BA, mountain fold the loose corners behind as far as they will go.

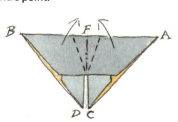

7 Make a mountain and two valley creases where shown, to create the body and to swivel D & C apart.

8 The Butterfly complete.

■ S A M P A N

This is a simplified version of a sampan with a canopy over each end of the boat. Both designs feature an extraordinary move, here shown in Steps 7–9, in which the entire shape is turned inside out. With a little extra folding, one end of the sampan can be blunted to create a rowing boat. Use a square of paper. If using origami paper, start coloured side up.

Traditional design.

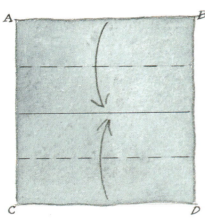

1 Crease and
■ unfold across the
centre. Fold the top
and bottom edges to
the crease.

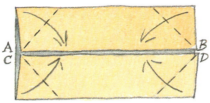

2 Fold in the
■ corners.

3 Narrow the
■ corner at the
right, as though
making the familiar
paper dart.

4 Repeat at the left,
■ overlapping the
Step 4 creases. .

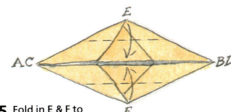

5 Fold in E & F to
■ the centre crease.
The paper is thick, so
press firmly.

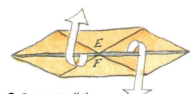

6 Open out all the
■ layers revealing
the coloured base
. . .

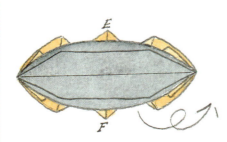

7 . . . like this, to
■ form a loose boat
shape. Turn over.

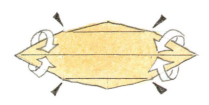

8 To lock the
■ sampan, push
down on the four
arrowed corners, so
that the whole of
the structure inverts
and turns inside out!

9 The Sampan
■ complete.

NAPKIN FOLDS

Napkin folds always create a point of interest on a dining table. The Duck Step is a basic form from which other varieties of napkin fold can be made. The Cable Buffet server allows guests at a buffet or picnic to help themselves to food, a napkin and cutlery all at once, while the Bishop's elegant curves and free-standing structure create a strong impact on any table.

Designed by Paul Jackson.

DUCK STEP

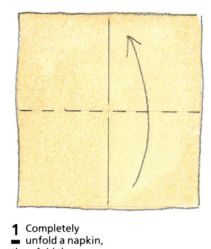

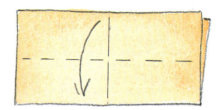

2 Fold the top edge down to the crease.

1 Completely unfold a napkin, then fold the bottom edge up to the top.

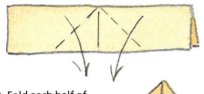

3 Fold each half of the top edge down the centre crease . . .

4 . . . like this. Turn the napkin over.

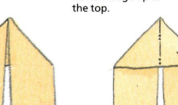

5 Mountain fold the right side behind the left.

6 Valley fold the front square up over the triangle. Repeat behind.

7 The Duck Step napkin complete.

CABLE BUFFET

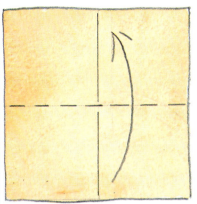

1 Completely unfold a napkin, then fold the bottom edge up to the top.

2 Fold the top layer down to the crease.

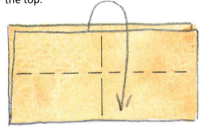

3 Fold the top layer back up a little way . . .

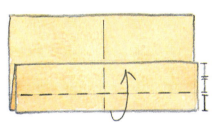

4 . . . like this. Turn the napkin over.

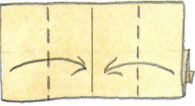

5 Fold the sides to the middle.

6 Tuck one half deep into the other, locking the napkin flat.

7 The Cable Buffet server complete. Insert cutlery into the pocket ready for the meal.

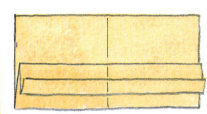

(Continued . . .)

BISHOP

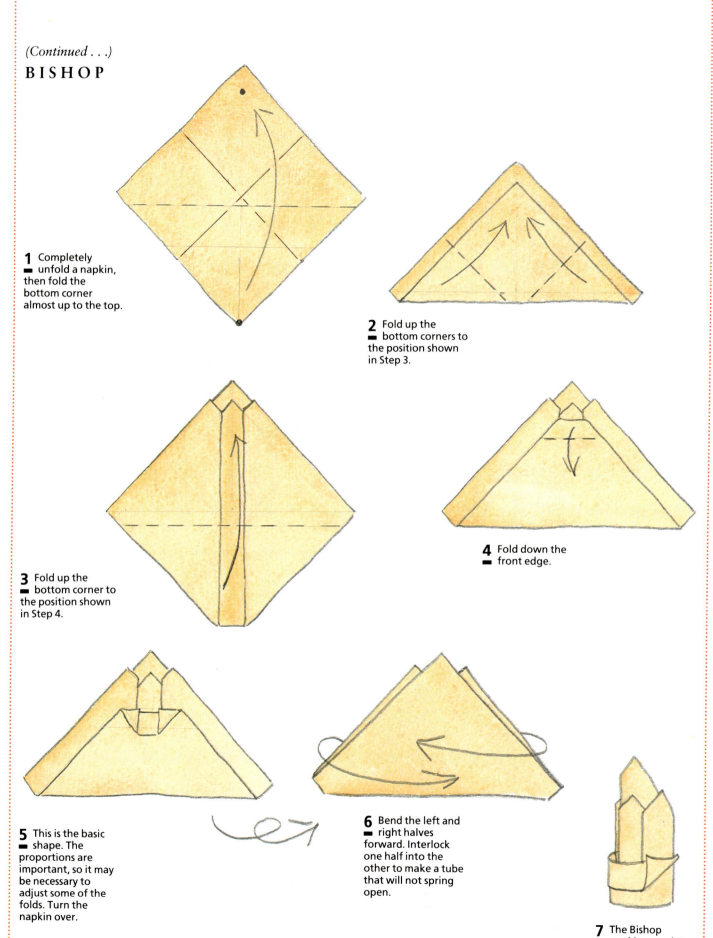

1 Completely unfold a napkin, then fold the bottom corner almost up to the top.

2 Fold up the bottom corners to the position shown in Step 3.

3 Fold up the bottom corner to the position shown in Step 4.

4 Fold down the front edge.

5 This is the basic shape. The proportions are important, so it may be necessary to adjust some of the folds. Turn the napkin over.

6 Bend the left and right halves forward. Interlock one half into the other to make a tube that will not spring open.

7 The Bishop napkin complete.

∎ F I S H

The creator of this fish is known for designs which are pre-creased and collapsed into shape. When pre-creasing, it is important to fold accurately (here, up to Step 5), otherwise the creases will not fall into place to achieve Step 6. For extra flatness, a speck of glue inside the mouth will close the layers. Use a square of origami paper, coloured side up, or a square with the same colour on both sides.

Designed by Jeff Beynon, UK.

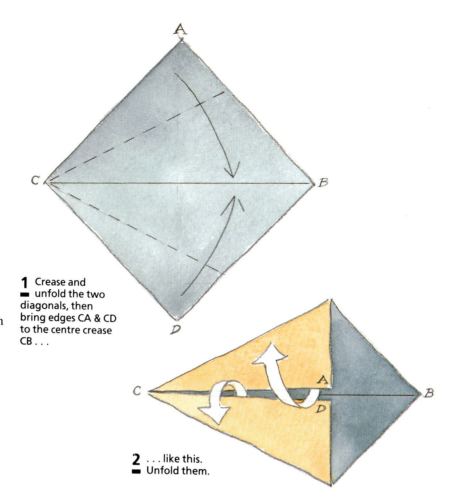

1 Crease and unfold the two diagonals, then bring edges CA & CD to the centre crease CB . . .

2 . . . like this. Unfold them.

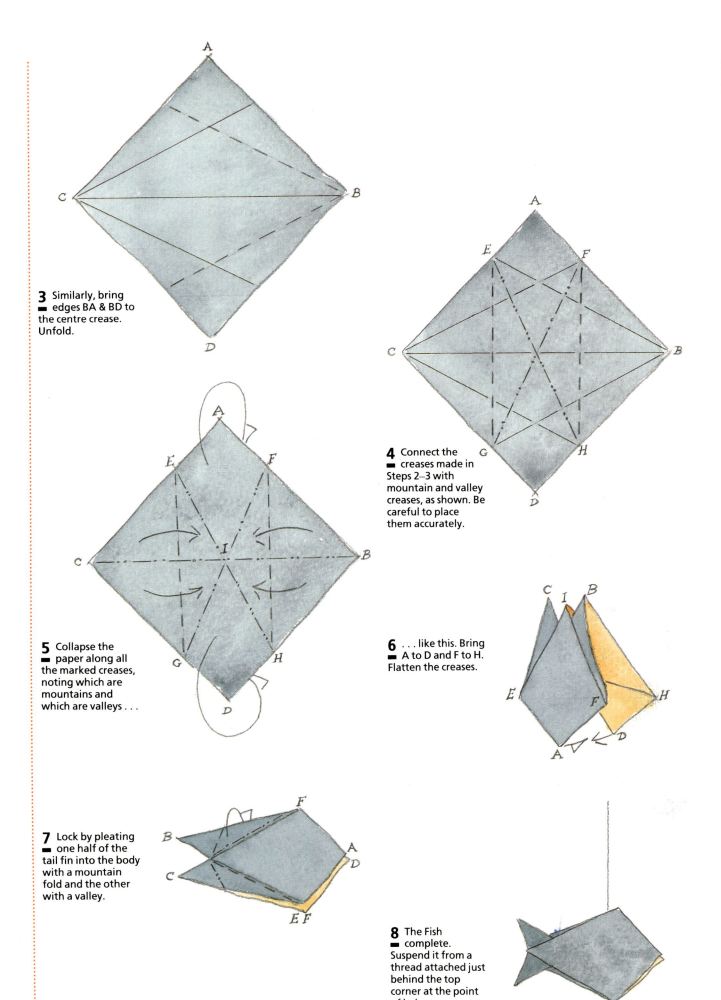

3 Similarly, bring edges BA & BD to the centre crease. Unfold.

4 Connect the creases made in Steps 2–3 with mountain and valley creases, as shown. Be careful to place them accurately.

5 Collapse the paper along all the marked creases, noting which are mountains and which are valleys . . .

6 . . . like this. Bring A to D and F to H. Flatten the creases.

7 Lock by pleating one half of the tail fin into the body with a mountain fold and the other with a valley.

8 The Fish complete. Suspend it from a thread attached just behind the top corner at the point of balance.

▮ SLEEPY DOG

The design is simple to make, but it is
important to place C accurately in
Steps 1 & 2. Once Step 3 has been
achieved, the remaining folds fall
naturally into place. Note the way in
which the eyes are suggested. Use a
square of origami paper, coloured
side up.

Designed by Paul Jackson.

1 Crease and unfold the two diagonals, then fold in corner C to the point described in Step 2.

2 Note the position of C. Fold C back out, adding an extra crease as marked.

3 Mountain fold B behind, along the AD diagonal.

4 Mountain fold A behind to touch D.

5 Fold back points D & A to the outside.

6 With a reverse fold, swing B through the middle. Note the position of the crease.

7 Mountain fold E behind. Repeat at F behind. Turn D, A & C inside out. Fold B forward. Curve the edge at the eye. Repeat for other eye.

8 The Sleepy Dog complete.

MODULAR DECORATION I

A modular design is one in which a number of identical units are folded, then locked together without glue to create a decoration or geometric form. Other modular designs are included and appear later. In recent years, it has become a very popular branch of origami, East and West. Method 1 begins with a rectangle, Method 2 with a small square.

Designed by Paul Jackson.

METHOD 1

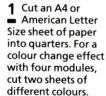

1 Cut an A4 or American Letter Size sheet of paper into quarters. For a colour change effect with four modules, cut two sheets of different colours.

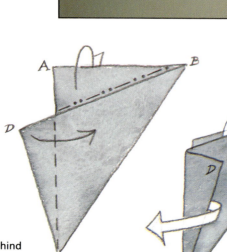

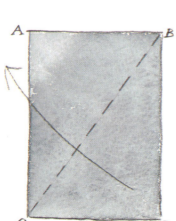

2 Take one quarter sheet of paper and fold diagonal BC.

3 Fold A behind and D to the front.

4 Unfold a little, but do not flatten the sheet.

5 The Module complete. Make four: two of one colour and two of another.

METHOD 2

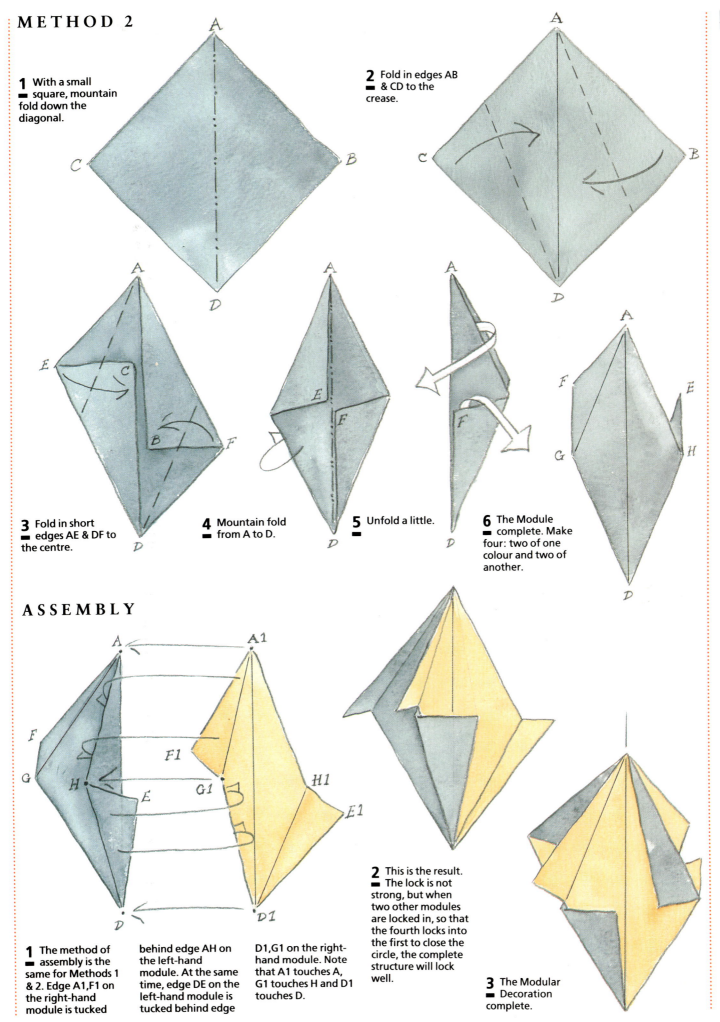

1 With a small square, mountain fold down the diagonal.

2 Fold in edges AB & CD to the crease.

3 Fold in short edges AE & DF to the centre.

4 Mountain fold from A to D.

5 Unfold a little.

6 The Module complete. Make four: two of one colour and two of another.

ASSEMBLY

1 The method of assembly is the same for Methods 1 & 2. Edge A1,F1 on the right-hand module is tucked behind edge AH on the left-hand module. At the same time, edge DE on the left-hand module is tucked behind edge D1,G1 on the right-hand module. Note that A1 touches A, G1 touches H and D1 touches D.

2 This is the result. The lock is not strong, but when two other modules are locked in, so that the fourth locks into the first to close the circle, the complete structure will lock well.

3 The Modular Decoration complete.

COLOUR-CHANGE BIRD

This design is included because it is a particular favourite. The simple shape of the completed bird and the effectiveness of the colour contrasts are achieved by a fluent and concise sequence of folds. Perhaps it is too stylized for some readers, but less can sometimes be more. Use a square of origami paper, white side up.

Designed by Paul Jackson.

1 Crease and unfold the two diagonals, then fold corner A to the centre point.

2 Roll the triangle downwards, along crease CB.

3 Fold C & B dot to dot, as shown.

4 Unfold C & B.

5 Turn over.

6 Fold dot to dot, aligning edges DC & DB with the tops of the creases made in Step 3.

7 Pull out corner A.

8 Fold down A, level with the folded edge.

9 Fold B behind.

10 Fold up B & C along existing internal (hidden) creases made in Step 3.

11 Reverse fold D to create the head. Fold out the feet to create a stable base for the bird.

12 The Colour Change Bird complete.

MODULAR DECORATION II

The basic modules are very simple to make, but some thought must be given to assembling them correctly. Once locked, they will hold together very well. For re-use – perhaps from one Christmas to the next – the decoration may be flattened for easy storage. Use two 10–15 cm (4–6 in) squares of paper. If using origami paper, start with the white side up.

Designed by Paul Jackson.

METHOD

1 Crease and fold a vertical diagonal, then fold D up to A.

2 Fold edge AD,B forward to the vertical crease (valley fold) and edge AD,C behind to that crease (mountain fold).

3 This is the completed module. Make another.

ASSEMBLY

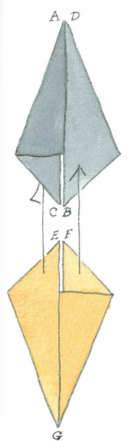

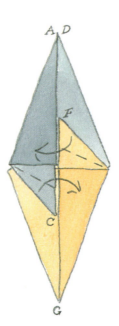

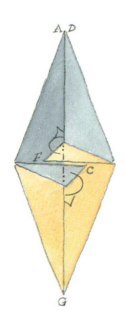

1 Take careful note of the lettered corners. Bring the two modules together, so that F is on top of B, and C is on top of E . . .

2 . . . like this. Fold F across to the horizontal. Repeat with C, then with E & B behind.

3 Lock the modules together by tucking F & C behind the vertical edges. Repeat behind with E & B.

4 Separate the modules by twisting one away from the other, so that they lie perpendicular to each other.

5 The Modular Decoration complete. Suspend from a thread.

MULTIFORM

Here is a remarkable sequence of designs which are all made from the same basic shape, the House. The designs shown here are not the full set: it is also possible to fold a dustpan, purse, fox puppet, crown . . . and very probably many others! Experiment by folding the paper this way and that to see what you can discover. Use a square of origami paper, white side up.

Traditional design.

HOUSE

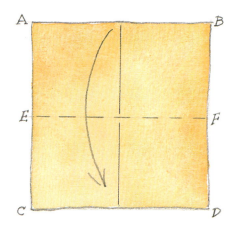

1 Crease and unfold down the middle of a square, then fold AB down to CD.

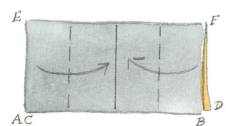

2 Fold the edges to the centre.

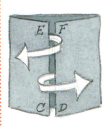

3 Unfold.

4 Lift up the edge BD,F. Separate B from D, applying pressure on the edges below F . . .

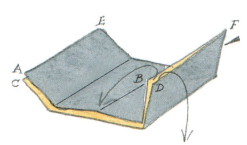

5 . . . like this. Pull B & D right apart and squash F flat.

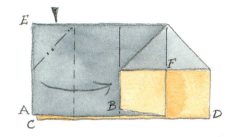

6 Repeat Steps 4–5 on the left, separating A from C and squashing E flat. Let A touch B.

7 The House complete. Children like to draw windows and a door to finish the design.

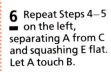

3D HOUSE

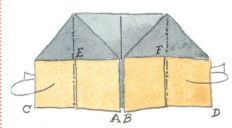

1 Begin with Step 6 of the House. Fold C & D behind.

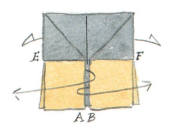

2 Unfold AC & BD.

3 The 3D House complete.

(Continued . . .)

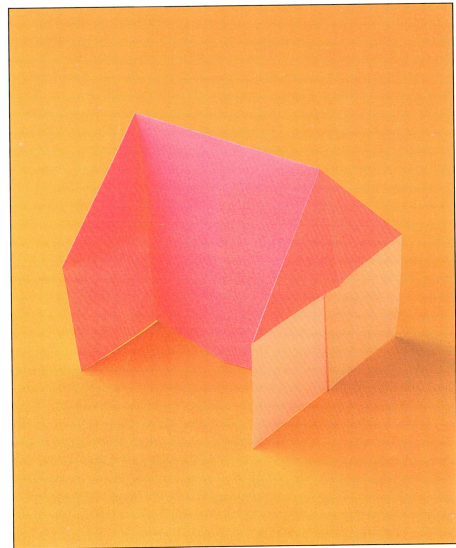

SEAT

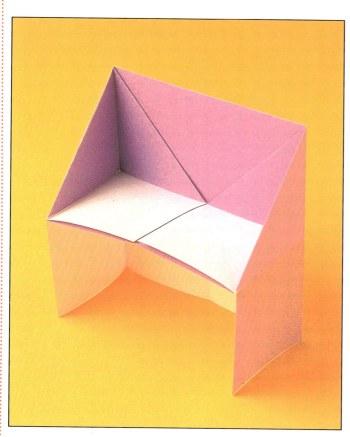

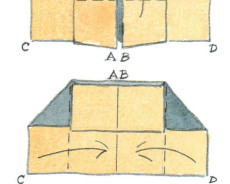

1 Begin with Step 6 of the House. Fold AB up to the top edge.

2 Fold in C & D.

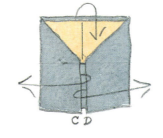

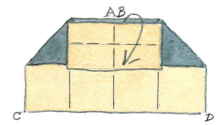

3 Swing open C & D and pull down AB.

4 The Seat complete.

ORGAN

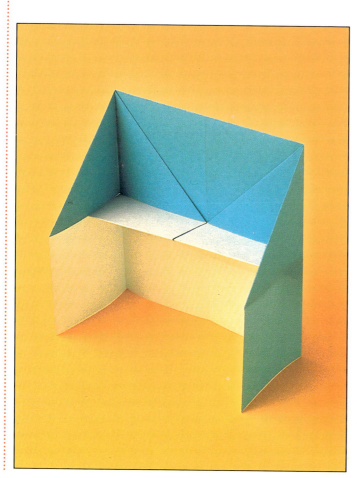

1 Begin with Step 2 of the Seat. Fold edge AB back down to the folded edge across the middle of the paper.

2 Fold in C & D.

3 Swing open C & D and pull down the ledge.

4 The Organ complete.

G.I. CAP

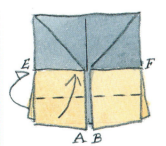

1 Begin with Step 2
of the 3D House.
Fold AB up to EF.
Repeat behind.

2 Fold up the
bottom section
along crease EF.
Repeat behind.

3 Open out the cap.

4 The G.I. Cap
complete. To
make a full-sized
cap, use a square
trimmed from a
large format
newspaper.

SIMPLE PROJECTS

201

STAR

The shape made in Step 7 is known in origami as the Preliminary Base, so called because other, more advanced bases can be developed from it, including the Bird and Frog bases and their stretched variants. Use a square of paper or perhaps paper-backed foil, coloured side up.

Designed by Florence Temko, USA.

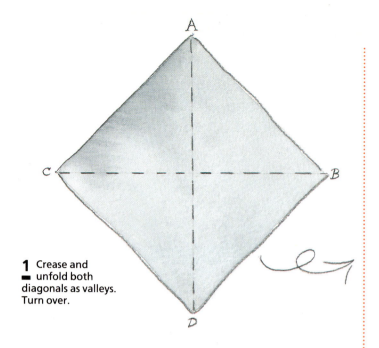

1 Crease and unfold both diagonals as valleys. Turn over.

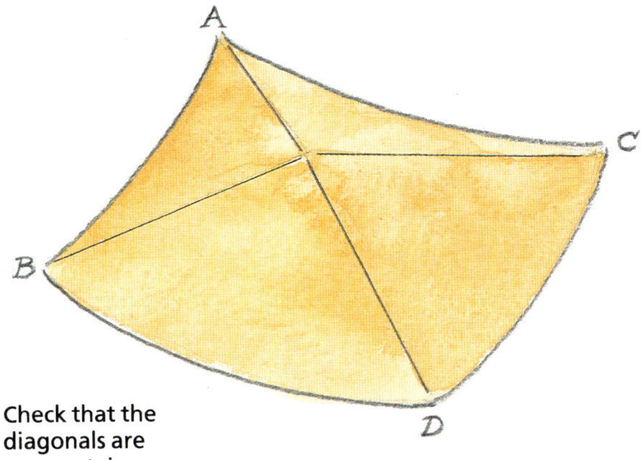

2 Check that the
diagonals are
now mountain
creases.

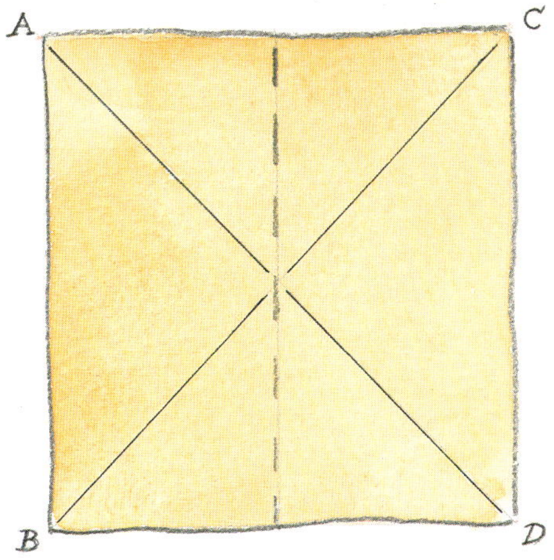

3 Fold and unfold
in half down the
middle, then . . .

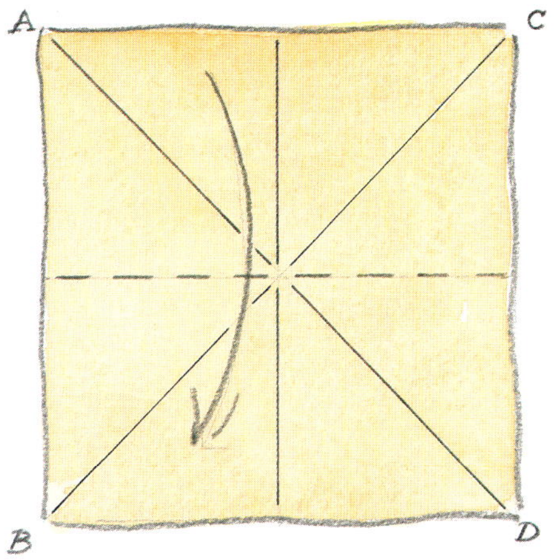

4 . . . fold in half
across the middle.

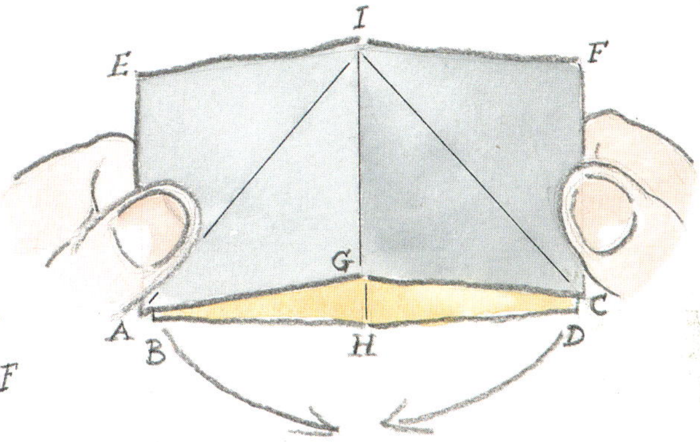

5 Hold as shown. If
the mountain and
valley creases have
been placed
correctly, a 3D
diamond shape will
emerge when the
hands are swung
towards each other
. . .

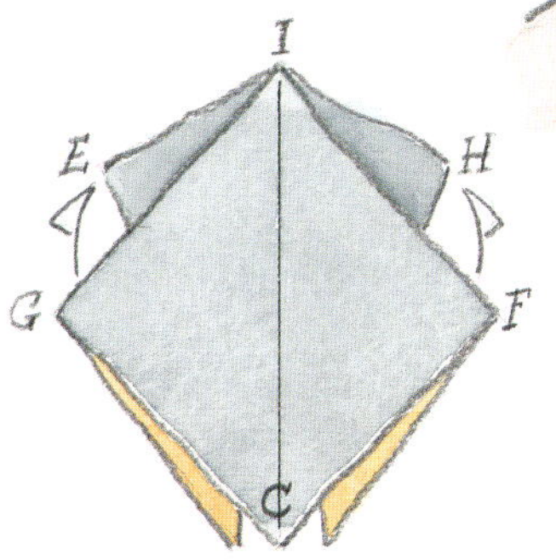

6 . . . like this.
Flatten G against
E and F against H.

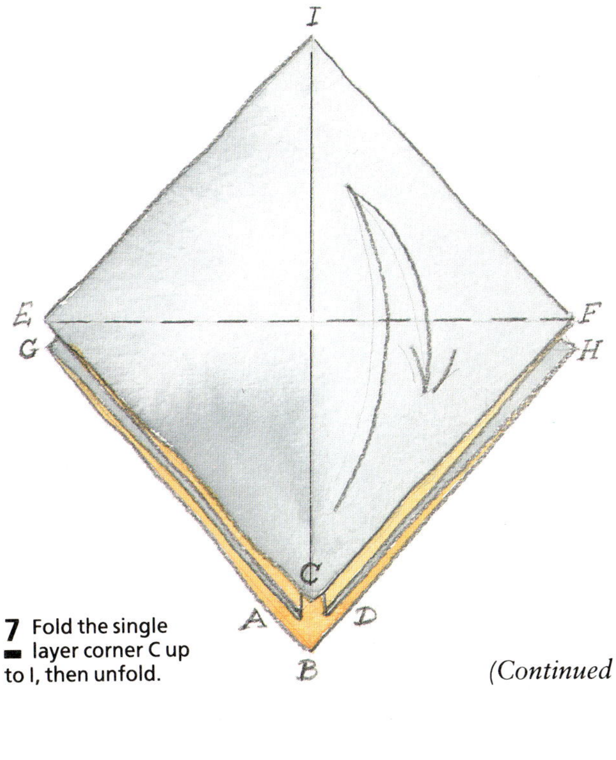

7 Fold the single
layer corner C up
to I, then unfold.

(Continued . . .)

9 The crease formed in Step 8 makes a square. Crease the four sides of the square as mountains . . .

8 Fold I down to the centre point. Unfold. Open the paper a little.

10 . . . like this. Flatten the centre square, then push it downwards into the paper . . .

11 . . . like this. Reform the Step 8 shape, but with I now sunk inside the paper.

12 Fold up C again.

13 Swing C down to corner G, whilst also bringing corner F across to touch G. Note that the crease from G is a mountain, not a valley.

14 Halfway.

15 Complete. Note how F,C,G & E lie one behind the other.

16 Similarly, fold up D along line FH . . .

17 . . . and swing towards corner F, bringing H across to touch corner F. Repeat this sequence with A then B, turning the paper over and around each time, to keep the same number of layers on each side of the paper. Fan out the points in a symmetrical pattern.

18 The Star complete. Suspend from a thread.

INTERMEDIATE PROJECTS

■ WATERBOMB

Many people – particularly mischievous children – have learnt how to make a waterbomb, but without practice, it is very easy to forget how to lock it. Without a good lock, it cannot contain the water it is designed to hold! More peaceably, it makes an excellent Christmas decoration if folded from a patterned paper. Use a square of paper. If using origami paper, start with the white side uppermost.

Traditional design.

1 Mountain fold horizontally and vertically across the paper. Unfold each time.

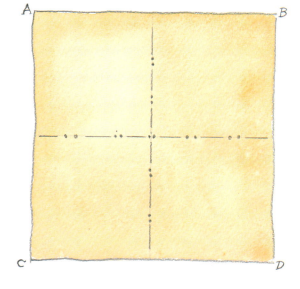

2 Form a vertical valley diagonal (the other creases are mountains). Unfold.

3 Fold A down to D.

4 Hold as shown. If the mountains and valleys have been placed correctly, the paper will form a 3D pyramid when the hands are swung towards each other . . .

5 . . . like this. Flatten A against B, and D against C.

6 Fold A & C up to E. Repeat behind with B & D. (Note: to increase the size of the hole through which air is blown to inflate the Waterbomb, fold the corners *short* of E. A hole that is too small is difficult to blow through.)

7 Fold G & H to the centre. Repeat behind.

8 Fold A & C into the centre at G & H.

9 Valley fold the small triangle above A into the pocket made by separating the layers above G. Repeat with C on the right and twice more behind with B and D.

10 The Waterbomb is now locked, front and back. Blow into the hole at the bottom to make it 3D. If the hole is too small, enlarge it.

11 The Waterbomb complete.

TRADITIONAL BOX

This is perhaps *the* classic origami box. It is quick and simple to make, and locks strongly. A box made from a slightly larger square will form a lid. In Step 3, if the creases are not placed at the quarter points, but elsewhere, taller or squatter boxes can be made. Use a square of strong paper. If using origami paper, start white side up.

Traditional design.

1 Mountain fold horizontally and vertically across the centre, unfolding each time.

2 Fold the corners to the centre. (The existing creases are mountains.)

3 Fold each edge in turn to the centre point, unfolding each crease before making the next.

4 Pull open corners A & D.

5 Re-crease valleys where shown.

6 Make the paper 3D by bringing F & E to the centre dot . . .

7 . . . like this. Lock the end of the box by folding A over the top and into the middle.

8 Repeat Steps 6–7 with H & G, folding D over the top to lock.

9 The Traditional Box complete.

NESTING BIRD

The design features a peculiar and little-used manoeuvre at Steps 4–5, when one spike is pulled out from inside another that envelops it. The move is very satisfying! What was a closed and rather unpromising shape in Step 4 becomes much more useful by Step 6, yet no new creases are made. Begin with a square of paper, same colour both sides.

Designed by Paul Jackson.

1 Crease and unfold a vertical diagonal, then fold D up to A.

2 Fold edges AD,B and AD,C to the centre crease.

3 Fold out corners B & C.

4 Note the shape of the paper. Pull out D from inside A . . .

5 . . . like this. Flatten D on top of A.

6 Turn over.

7 Collapse the paper as shown, separating A from D and bringing C to touch B.

8 Lift up corner C, squashing the paper flat at the left.

9 Fold B behind.

10 Reverse fold D. Fold out the bottom corners to stay away from the wings and so create a stable base for the bird to balance on.

11 The Nesting Bird complete.

◾ B E A K

This is a variation on a well-known origami 'action' theme. The mechanism will be familiar to knowledgeable paper folders, but here the eyes are made differently. It is important to use origami paper, to achieve a contrast of colour for the eyes and the inside of the mouth. The colour should be on the outside in Step 1.

Designed by Paul Jackson.

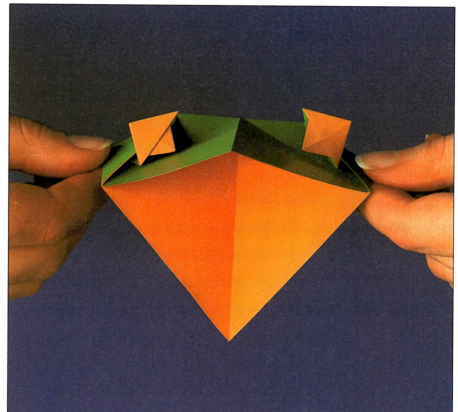

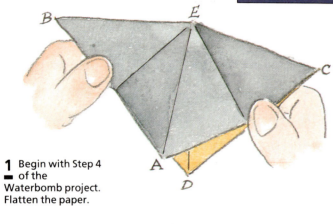

1 Begin with Step 4
▬ of the
Waterbomb project.
Flatten the paper.

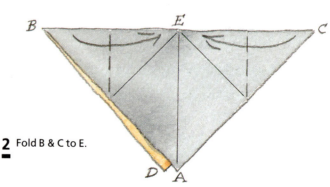

2 Fold B & C to E.
▬

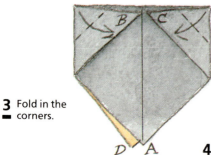

3 Fold in the
▬ corners.

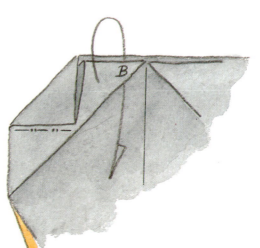

4 (The instructions
▬ now refer to B
only, but repeat all
Steps with C.) Swivel
B behind and
downwards . . .

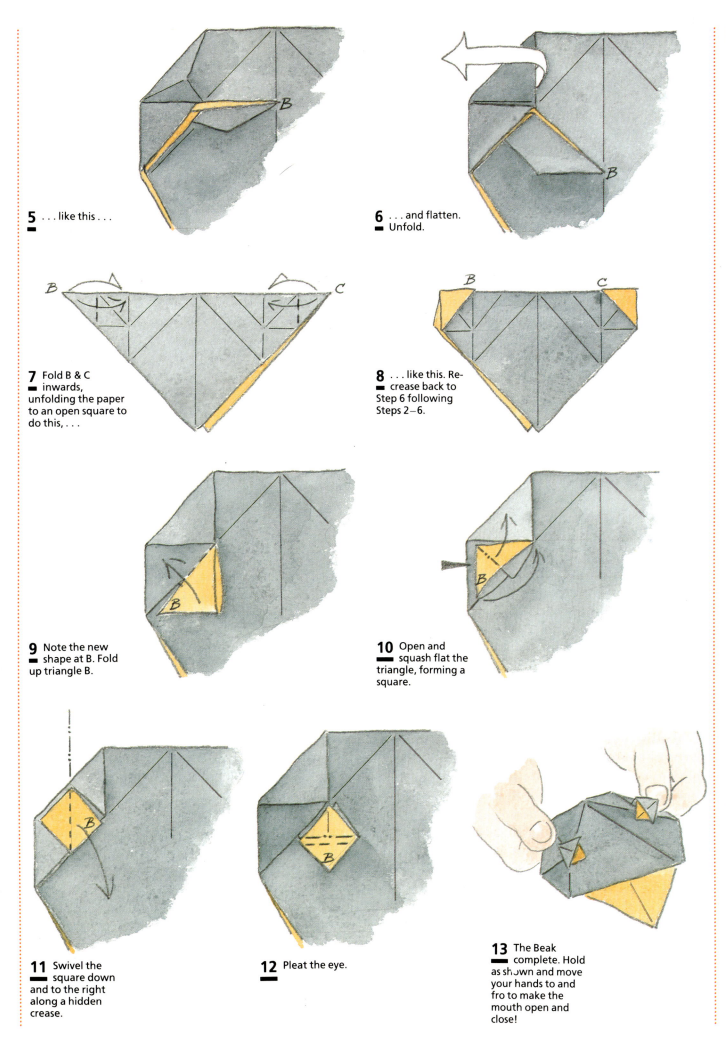

5 . . . like this . . .

6 . . . and flatten. Unfold.

7 Fold B & C inwards, unfolding the paper to an open square to do this, . . .

8 . . . like this. Re-crease back to Step 6 following Steps 2−6.

9 Note the new shape at B. Fold up triangle B.

10 Open and squash flat the triangle, forming a square.

11 Swivel the square down and to the right along a hidden crease.

12 Pleat the eye.

13 The Beak complete. Hold as shown and move your hands to and fro to make the mouth open and close!

▊ L I G H T H E A R T E D

Original concepts are rare in origami. Most designs, however good, are created within relatively predictable themes, so it is pleasing to occasionally find a fresh approach. In this design, the final shape is unimpressive, but reveals a translucent heart when held against the light! Fold the paper carefully, particularly at Steps 2–3, or the heart will be poorly proportioned. Use a square of thin paper; thicker papers will not reveal the heart.

Designed by Wayne Brown, UK.

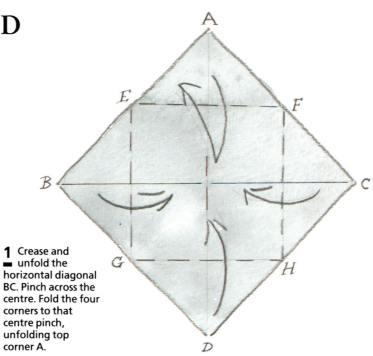

1 Crease and unfold the horizontal diagonal BC. Pinch across the centre. Fold the four corners to that centre pinch, unfolding top corner A.

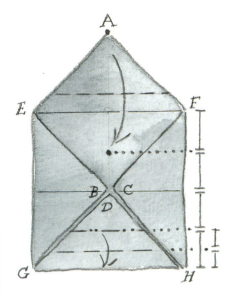

2 Fold down corner A as shown. Pleat triangle DGH as shown.

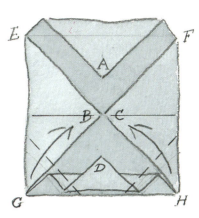

3 Fold in corners G & H. Note the very small intrusion of the crease into the D triangle. This is important, as it affects the proportion of the heart.

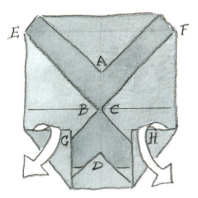

4 Unfold Step 3.

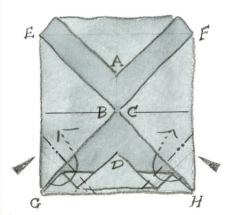

5 Re-crease Step 3, but reverse folding the top part of each crease to push G under B, and H under C.

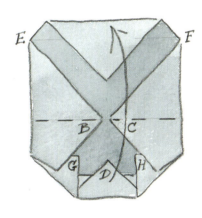

6 Fold in half.

7 Fold in E & F just a little way.

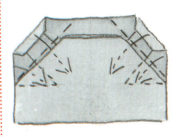

8 Fold over as shown, locking the edges into the pockets made in Step 5.

9 Fold the excess paper into the top pocket.

10 Note that the shape is locked flat.

11 To see the heart, hold the paper up to a window or other diffuse light source (but not the sun).

This is one of the simpler decorative origami boxes. It is relatively easy to make a square, straight-sided box, such as the Traditional Box project, but the technical complexities increase as the final shape becomes less plain. Here though, the design is pleasingly bold. Use a square of origami paper, with the coloured side outwards.

Traditional design.

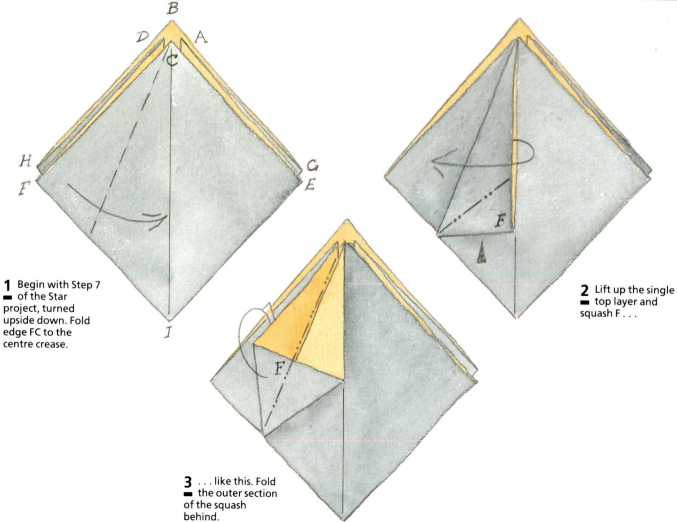

1 Begin with Step 7 of the Star project, turned upside down. Fold edge FC to the centre crease.

2 Lift up the single top layer and squash F . . .

3 . . . like this. Fold the outer section of the squash behind.

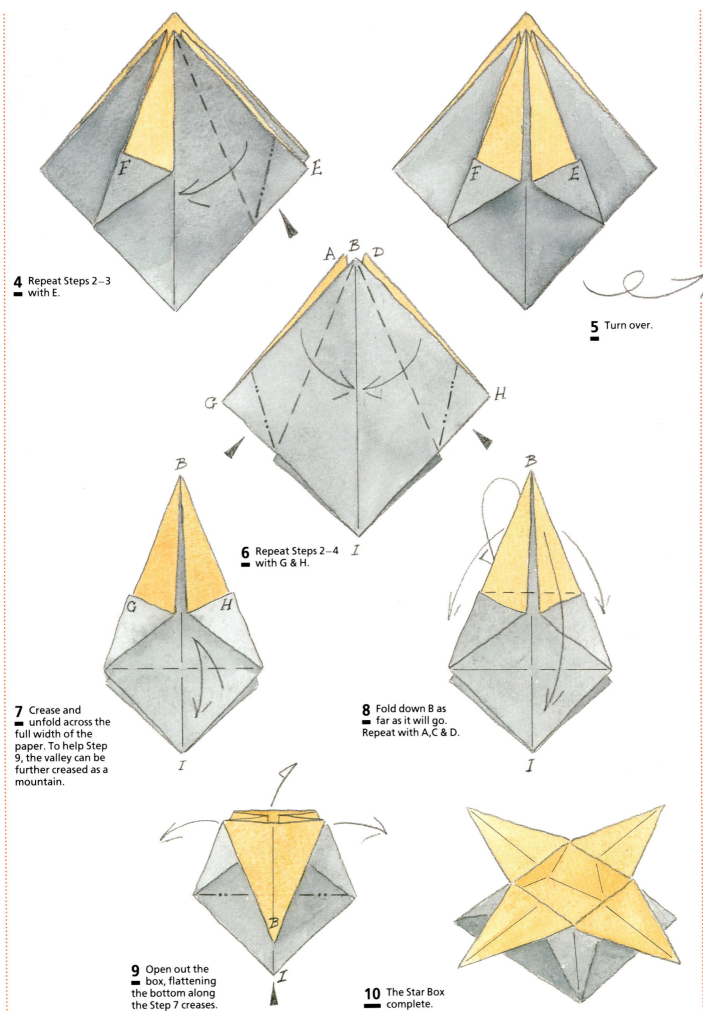

4 Repeat Steps 2-3 with E.

F E

A B D

5 Turn over.

G H

B

I

6 Repeat Steps 2-4 with G & H.

G H

B

I

7 Crease and unfold across the full width of the paper. To help Step 9, the valley can be further creased as a mountain.

I

8 Fold down B as far as it will go. Repeat with A,C & D.

B

I

B

9 Open out the box, flattening the bottom along the Step 7 creases.

I

10 The Star Box complete.

There are many origami jumping frogs, most – like this one – made by creating a frog shape, then pleating across the body to create the spring. This version is a particularly athletic jumper. Use a 20 cm (8 in) square of paper. A 2 × 1 rectangle of thick paper may also be used, starting at Step 2.

Traditional design.

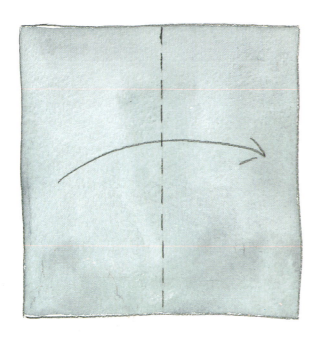

1 Fold a square in half down the middle.

2 The paper is now two layers thick, but will be referred to as though it was a single layer. Collapse AB to make the shape seen in Step 6 of the Waterbomb project.

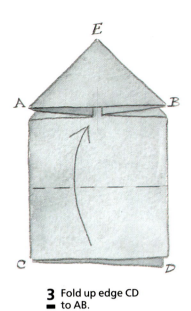

3 Fold up edge CD to AB.

4 Swing out A & B. Note that they do not touch E, but protrude to the side.

5 Fold in the sides.

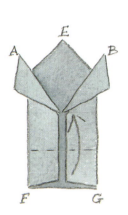

6 Fold edge FG to the centre point.

7 Fold down corners F & G . . .

8 . . . like this.

9 Hold tightly as shown. Slide F & G away from H . . .

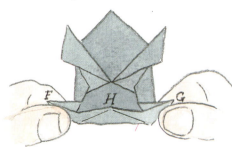

10 . . . like this, keeping firm hold of F & G. When F & G have been pulled out as far to the side as they will go, flatten the paper . . .

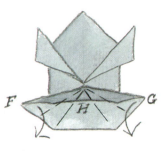

11 . . . like this. Fold down F & G.

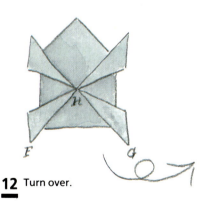

12 Turn over.

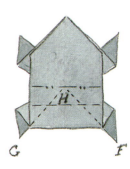

13 Make a pleat, with the mountain crease passing through H. The paper is very thick, so use considerable pressure.

14 The Jumping Frog complete.

15 To make it jump, put your finger on its back. Flatten the pleat and slide your finger off! With practice, it will jump quite a distance.

■ BIRD

This design is straightforward until Step 9, when the difficult 3D crimp transforms an ordinary flat bird into a 3D bird with a pleasingly rounded shape. Some origami creators argue that such '3D-ing' at the end of the folding sequence is a cheat, and that a *truly* 3D design is folded as such from the start. Use a 15–20 cm (6–8 in) square of paper, coloured the same on both sides.

Designed by Paul Jackson.

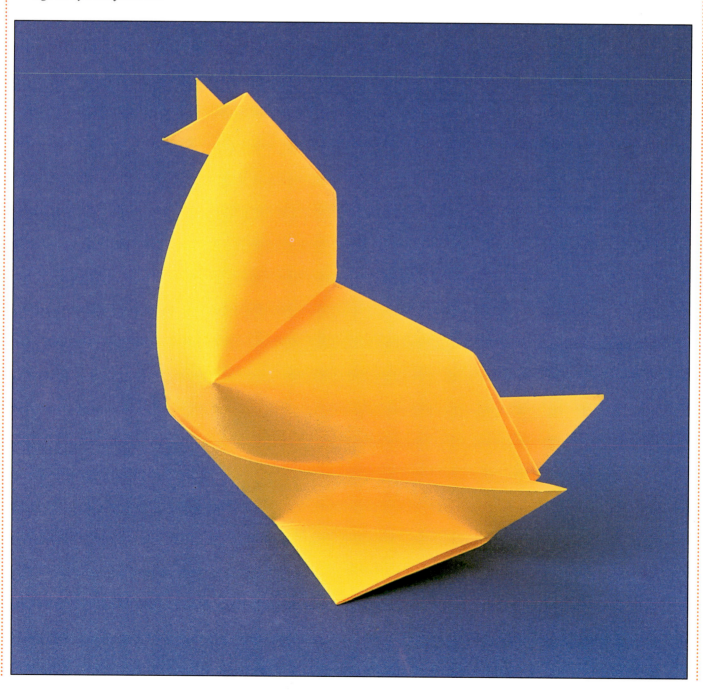

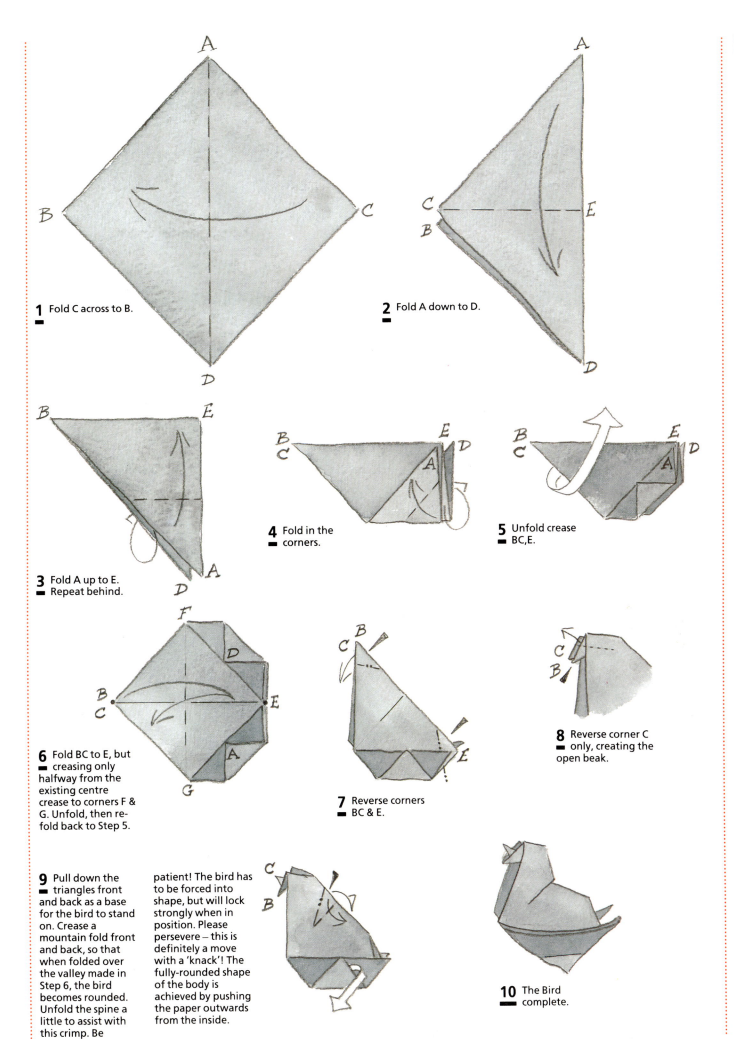

1 Fold C across to B.

2 Fold A down to D.

3 Fold A up to E. Repeat behind.

4 Fold in the corners.

5 Unfold crease BC,E.

6 Fold BC to E, but creasing only halfway from the existing centre crease to corners F & G. Unfold, then re-fold back to Step 5.

7 Reverse corners BC & E.

8 Reverse corner C only, creating the open beak.

9 Pull down the triangles front and back as a base for the bird to stand on. Crease a mountain fold front and back, so that when folded over the valley made in Step 6, the bird becomes rounded. Unfold the spine a little to assist with this crimp. Be patient! The bird has to be forced into shape, but will lock strongly when in position. Please persevere – this is definitely a move with a 'knack'! The fully-rounded shape of the body is achieved by pushing the paper outwards from the inside.

10 The Bird complete.

BUILDING

The design is included in the book to show how the rectangles and triangles that are created naturally by folding a square along halves and quarters, can be articulated to create a form such as this semi-abstract building, complete with colour-change roofs. Often, allowing the paper to do what it wants to do without contrivance is the best way to create. Use a square of origami paper, white side up.

Designed by Paul Jackson.

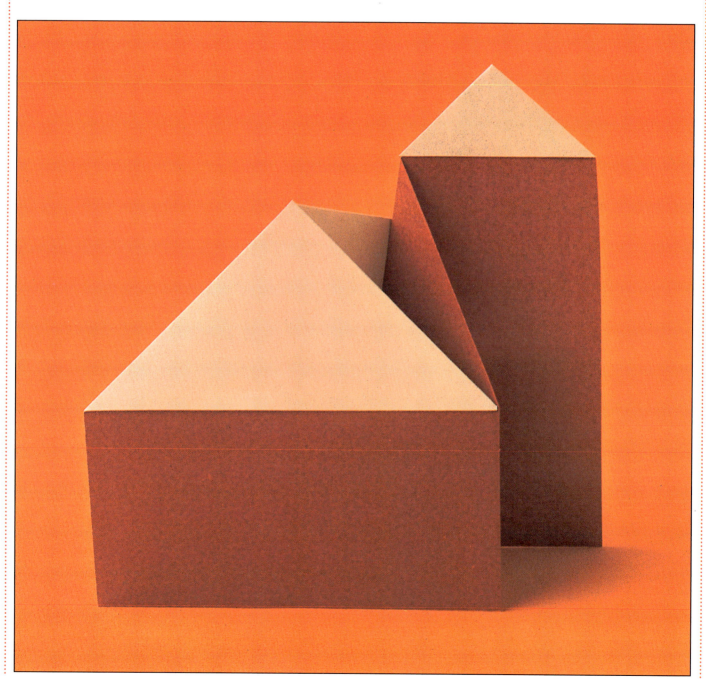

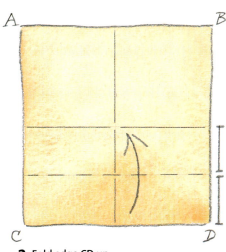

1 Crease as shown.
■ Note the short
crease at the right.

2 Fold edge CD up
■ to the centre
crease, then fold in
half down the
middle.

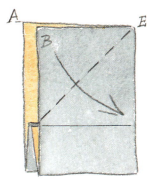

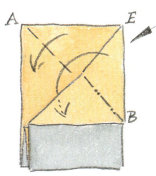

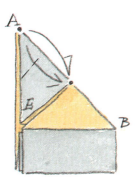

3 Fold down corner
■ B.

4 Reverse fold
■ corner E behind B.

5 Fold corner A as
■ shown, opening
the paper to do this.

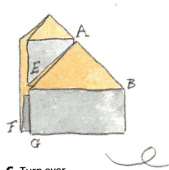

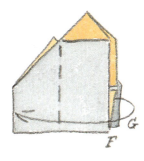

6 Turn over.

7 Swing F over to
■ the left.

8 Hold as shown
■ and move your
hands apart. Corner
H will lift. Crease and
flatten H as shown . . .

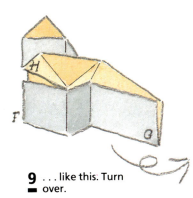

9 . . . like this. Turn
■ over.

10 The Building
■ complete.

PIG

The Pig, although a fairly complex project, is rewarding to construct, especially as the finished animal emerges in the final steps. Take time over the snout folds – they may appear complicated but do give a realistic result. Choose a 'pig'-coloured paper and use a 2 × 1 rectangle, the same colour on both sides. It is easy to create a whole 'family' of origami pigs: simply vary the size of the initial 2 × 1 rectangle.

Designed by Paul Jackson.

1 Crease and unfold the long horizontal centre crease, then crease and unfold down the shorter axis.

2 Fold edge AC behind.

3 Fold edge BD behind to the crease made in Step 2.

4 Unfold.

5 Pleat along existing creases EF & GH.

6 Turn in corners G & H.

7 Swivel B & D behind, along horizontal mountain creases. Note the shape of Step 8.

8 Fold in corners A & C.

(continued . . .)

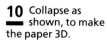

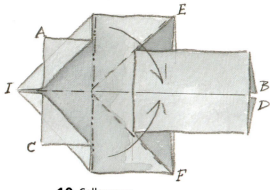

9 Fold A & C back out, the creases tapering towards I.

10 Collapse as shown, to make the paper 3D.

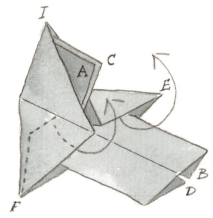

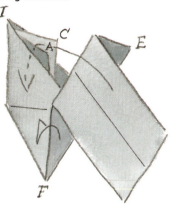

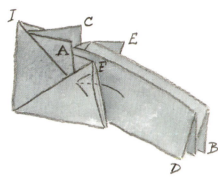

11 Pull out the hidden ledge . . .

12 . . . and feed it back into the pig between A & C . . .

13 . . . like this, bringing F & E back together again.

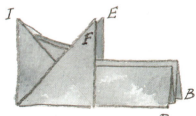

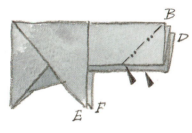

14 The manoeuvre is complete – its purpose is to stop the pig from splaying its front legs. Turn the paper the right way up.

15 Reverse fold at B & D.

16 Fold B & D towards the neck.

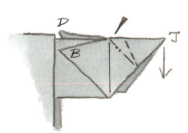

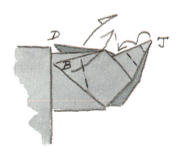

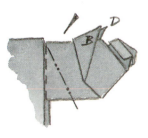

17 Create two reverse folds near the snout, forming a crimp.

18 Fold the snout over and over. Fold the ears forward.

19 Crimp the neck, lowering the head.

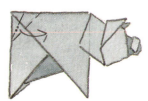

20 Pleat the tail.

21 The Pig complete.

■ STANDING HEART

Hearts are a favourite origami theme, particularly when combined with another element, such as a heart pierced by an arrow, twin hearts or a heart on a finger ring. Here is a conventional single heart, but one which could make an attractive standing ornament for a mantelpiece or desk top. Use a square of red/white origami paper, red side up.

Designed by Paul Jackson.

(Continued . . .)

1 Crease and unfold across the middle, then fold AC across to BD.

2 Mountain fold corners C & D inside.

3 Squash fold corner E.

4 Fold the outer section of the squash fold behind.

5 Open the paper between G & H. Turn over to see . . .

6 . . . a pyramid. Corner I is the apex (the corner nearest to you). Push on I so that it inverts and the paper pops inside out. Corner I is now the furthest point from you, not the nearest.

7 This is the shape. Note I.

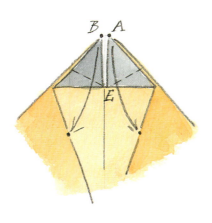

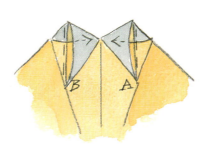

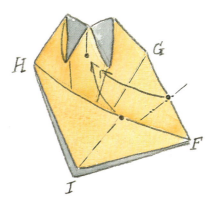

8 Fold down B & A, dot to dot.

9 Tuck the excess paper into the pockets at B & A.

10 Collapse as shown, folding the two outer dots onto the inner one.

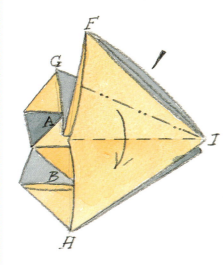

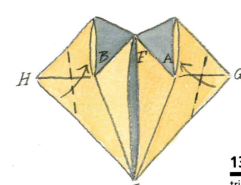

11 Squash F, presently standing upright.

12 Fold in H & G.

13 Fold over G to lock the triangle to the edge behind.

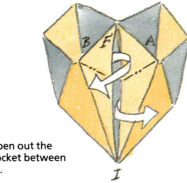

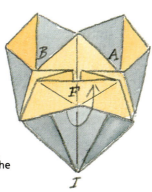

14 Open out the pocket between F & I . . .

15 . . . like this, flattening the paper.

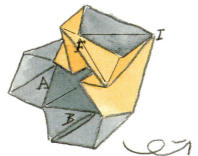

16 Partly close the pocket again. Turn over.

17 The Standing Heart complete.

FIGHTER JET

There are purists who may cry 'cheat' at this design, because it is made from two pieces of paper. A near-identical one-piece version from a 3 × 2 rectangle post-dated this original design, but is messy to make and lacks the simplicity of the original. Use two identical squares of paper of the same size and colour, coloured the same on both sides.

Designed by Paul Jackson.

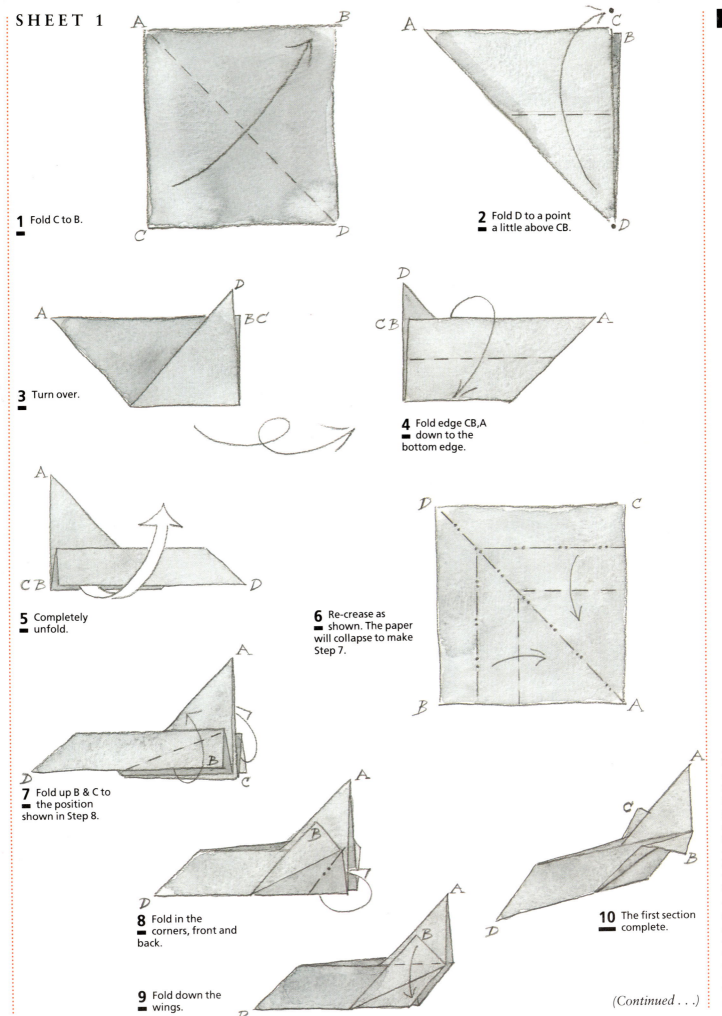

1 Fold C to B.

2 Fold D to a point a little above CB.

3 Turn over.

4 Fold edge CB,A down to the bottom edge.

5 Completely unfold.

6 Re-crease as shown. The paper will collapse to make Step 7.

7 Fold up B & C to the position shown in Step 8.

8 Fold in the corners, front and back.

9 Fold down the wings.

10 The first section complete.

(Continued . . .)

SHEET 2

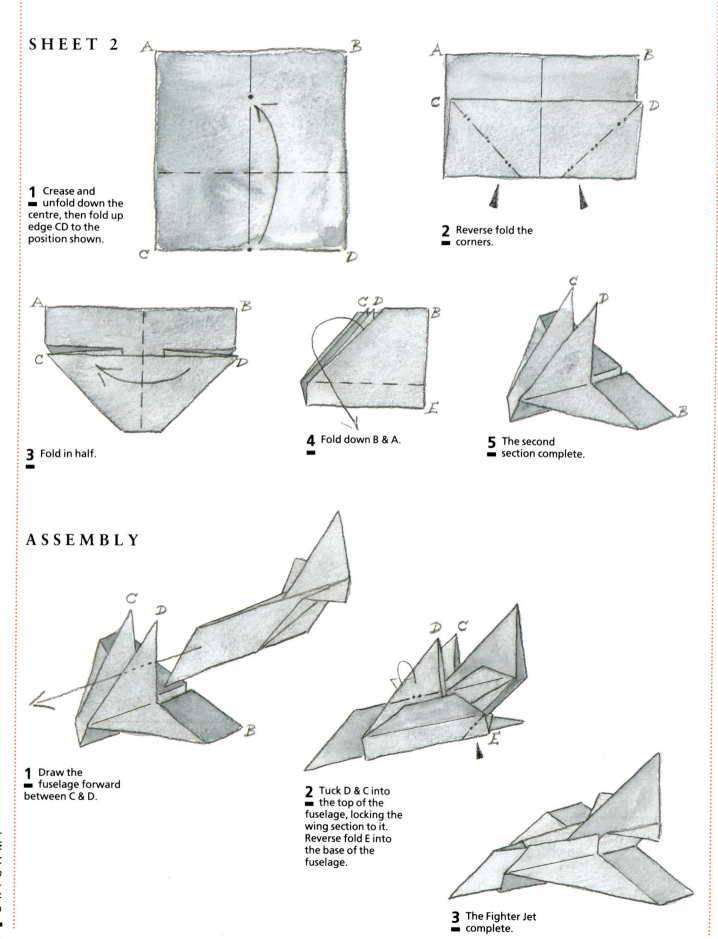

1 Crease and unfold down the centre, then fold up edge CD to the position shown.

2 Reverse fold the corners.

3 Fold in half.

4 Fold down B & A.

5 The second section complete.

ASSEMBLY

1 Draw the fuselage forward between C & D.

2 Tuck D & C into the top of the fuselage, locking the wing section to it. Reverse fold E into the base of the fuselage.

3 The Fighter Jet complete.

ADVANCED PROJECTS

CAMEL

The shape formed in Step 5 is commonly known in origami as the Fish base, and for obvious reasons. Apart from fishes (and a camel), the base at Step 6 is ideally shaped to create many different birds – the blunt points make wings and the sharp points form a head and tail. Use a 15–20 cm (6–8 in) square of paper, same colour both sides.

Designed by Paul Jackson.

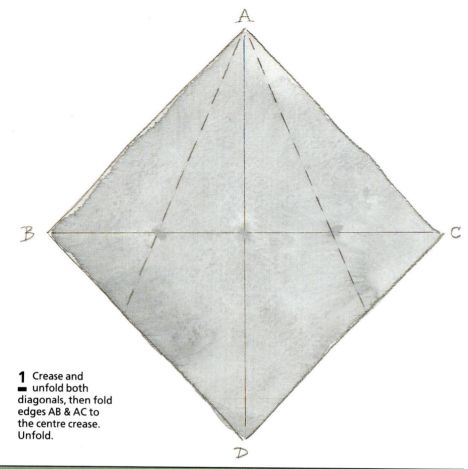

1 Crease and unfold both diagonals, then fold edges AB & AC to the centre crease. Unfold.

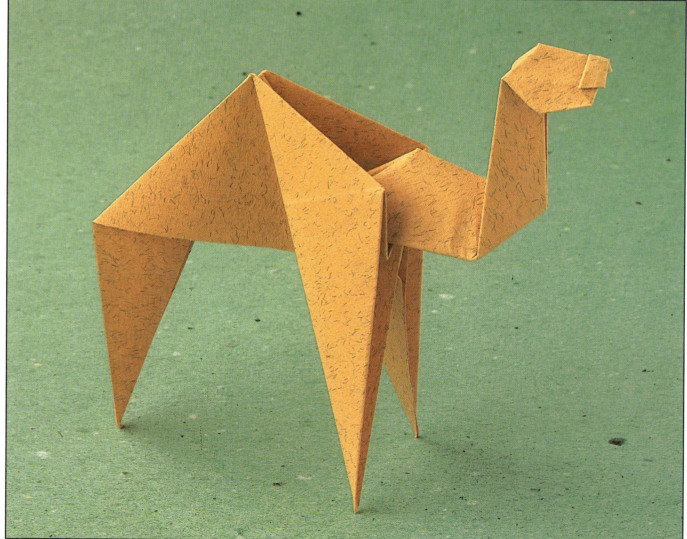

2 Similarly, fold edges DB & DC to the centre crease. Unfold.

3 Collapse the paper as shown, making it 3D.

4 Mountain fold across the middle, so that D swings up and back to lie behind A . . .

5 . . . like this. Fold in half.

6 Reverse fold A out to the left.

(Continued . . .)

7 Crease and unfold three creases which bisect the angles of the large triangle. The creases should all meet at a common point. Repeat behind.

8 Re-crease front and back, collapsing the paper . . .

9 . . . to this shape. Outside reverse fold D.

10 Outside reverse fold A & D.

11 Release the layers at A & D. At A, fold the released layers back over the legs. At D, allow the layers to remain visible, increasing the width of the head.

12 Fold the central layer in half to lock the hump shut.

13 This is the shape at the back.

14 Reverse fold D inside.

15 Turn the muzzle inside out.

16 The Camel complete.

∎ CHINESE VASE

This wonderful design was first
introduced to the West by Dr Philip
Shen (whose bowl appears earlier) and
popularized in the USA by the late
Verdi Adams. It has a beautifully direct
sequence of folds, climaxed by the
extraordinary opening out from 2D to
3D. Use a square of paper, not too
small. If using origami paper, start
white side up.

Traditional design.

(Continued . . .)

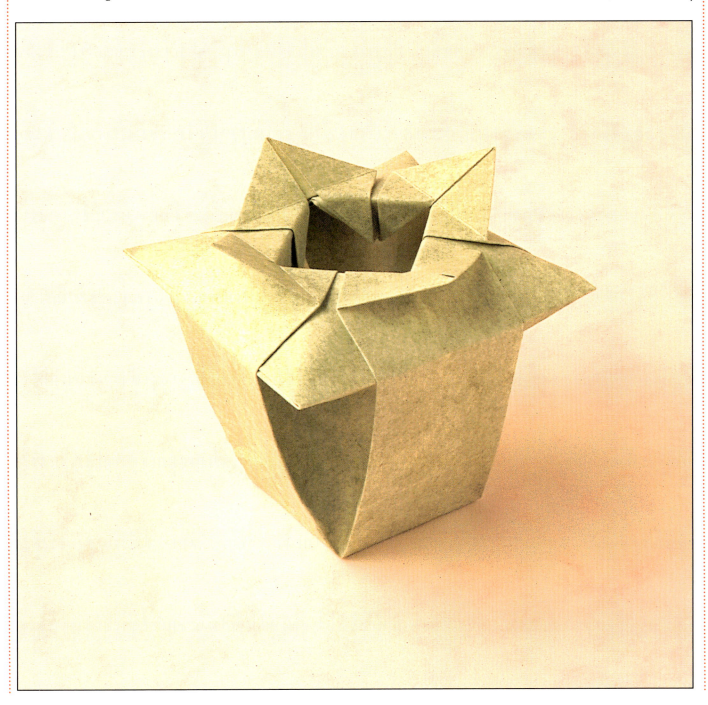

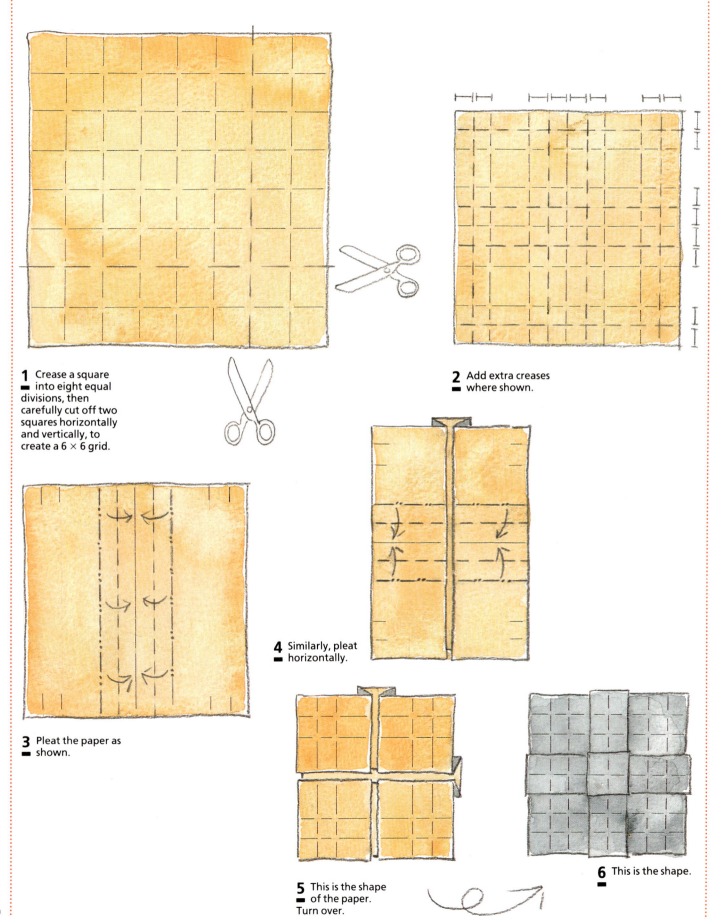

1 Crease a square into eight equal divisions, then carefully cut off two squares horizontally and vertically, to create a 6 × 6 grid.

2 Add extra creases where shown.

3 Pleat the paper as shown.

4 Similarly, pleat horizontally.

5 This is the shape of the paper. Turn over.

6 This is the shape.

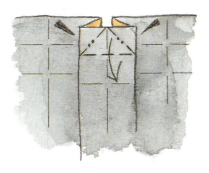

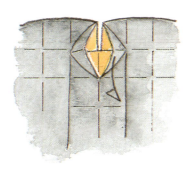

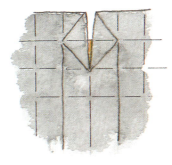

7 Lift and squash the end of each pleat . . .

8 . . . like this.

9 Repeat along each edge.

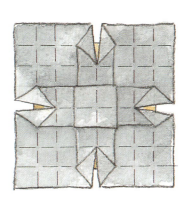

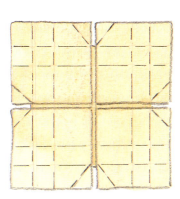

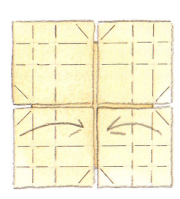

10 Here are the squashed pleats. Turn over.

11 Crease and unfold each loose corner at the pleats. This is to prepare for Step 14.

12 Fold the sides to the middle.

13 Fold the top and bottom edges to the middle, tucking the corners deep into the pockets.

14 Fold the loose corners inside, to create a square opening . . .

15 . . . like this. Turn over.

16 This is the fun part! Carefully tease out the trapped layers inside the pleats to make the vase 3D. Do this by rotating the paper frequently, so that all four sides are developed equally.

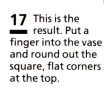

17 This is the result. Put a finger into the vase and round out the square, flat corners at the top.

18 The Chinese Vase complete.

SEATED FIGURE

One of the delights of origami is its ability to conjure complex subjects from relatively simple folds, to create not a detailed representation, but a stylized abstraction. When successful, the result is poetic, both in concept and form. Use a square of origami paper, coloured side up.

Designed by Paul Jackson.

A

B — — — — C

1 Crease and
■ unfold both
diagonals as
mountains.

D

A

B
C

D

2 Fold edges AB &
■ AC to the centre
crease.

A

B C

D

3 Fold A down to
■ BC and pinch
across the middle.
Unfold.

A

B
C

D

4 Fold C behind.
■

A

B C

D

5 Using the Step 3
■ pinch as a guide,
reverse fold A. Note
the angle in Step 6.

A

A

6 Reverse fold A
■ again. Note the
angle in Step 7.

A

7 Unfold back to
■ Step 4.

A

8 Fold A down to
■ the reverse fold
made in Step 6.
Pinch across the
middle. Refold to
Step 7.

(Continued . . .)

9 Reverse fold A, using the Step 8 pinch as a guide. Note the angle in Step 10.

10 Reverse fold A again. Note the angle in Step 11.

11 Completely unfold.

12 Mountain fold D behind.

13 Collapse as shown. Note that the reverse folds made in Steps 6 & 7 are here reformed through both layers, but the latter pair of reverse folds are not formed at all.

14 Fold back B & C.

15 Open the head.

16 Fold back the tip.

17 Fold in B & C.

18 Tuck C into B to lock the chair. Turn over.

19 The Seated Figure complete.

ELECTRA

An appeal of modular folding is that spectacular structures can be made from simple units, so that the whole is very much more than the sum of its parts. Thirty modules are needed for this design, which will take about an hour to make. Fold them all very carefully, then slot them together, with diligent regard for the '5 and 3' (pentagons and triangles) interlocking pattern. The result is a pierced structure of great beauty and strength. Use 30 10 cm (4 in) squares. If using origami paper, start with the coloured side up.

Designed by David Mitchell, UK.

(Continued . . .)

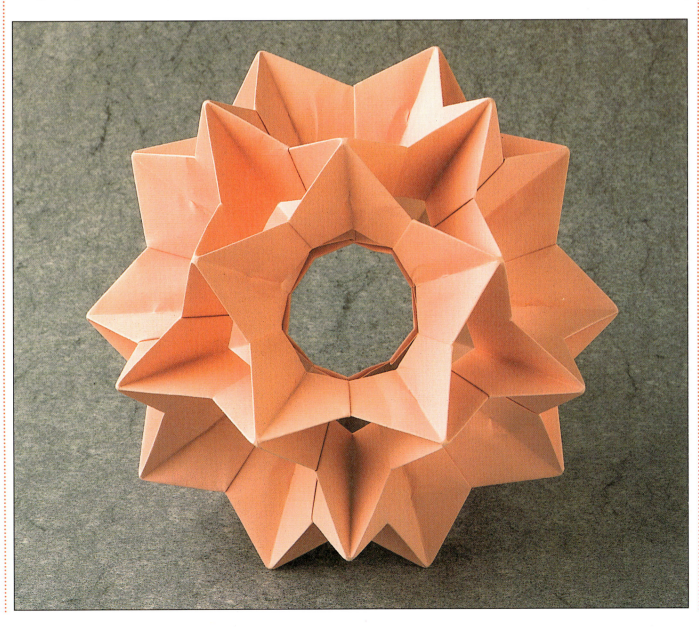

METHOD

1 Crease and unfold both diagonals as valleys. Turn over.

2 Crease and unfold horizontally and vertically. (The diagonals are mountains.)

3 Pinch the quarter points along crease EH.

4 Fold corners B & C to the middle.

5 Fold and unfold corners A & D.

6 Collapse all the creases.

7 Form a crease between A and the pinch made in Step 3, folding E across to the left side. Unfold.

8 Reform the crease, but reverse fold E inside.

9 This is the result. Turn over.

10 Repeat Steps 7–9 with H.

11 Fold K across to the left, allowing the triangle above D to swivel inside and across to the right. Repeat behind with J.

12 Mountain fold D inside, creating a pocket below K. Repeat with A.

13 This is the completed module. Note the closed pockets below J & K and the extended flaps at F & G.

ASSEMBLY

1 Tuck the extended flap on one module (F1), deep inside the pocket of another. To lock them together, fold F or G (depending on which one flap F1 has been tucked into) towards G1.

2 Repeat with the nearside flaps and pockets.

3 Lock 5 modules together, leaving no excess flaps in the centre of the pentagon. A sixth module is shown at the very bottom of the drawing connecting two neighbouring pentagon modules, thereby creating a triangle with no loose flaps in its centre. The completed Electra is thus a combination of pentagons and triangles. Interlock the remaining modules following this pattern.

4 The completed Electra.

SEAL ON A ROCK

So called 'double subjects' or 'combination folds' are common in complex origami, where two subjects or objects are folded from a single sheet. Examples might include a mother pushing a pram, a man playing an instrument or, as in this case, a seal basking on a rock. Some creative folders have combined even more subjects, such as several birds in a nest. Use a square of origami paper coloured side up, or for a better effect, two differently coloured or textured sheets folded back to back.

Designed by Dr Martin Wall, UK.

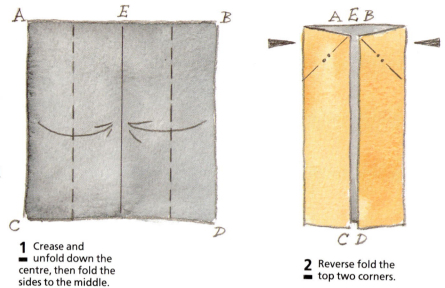

1 Crease and unfold down the centre, then fold the sides to the middle.

2 Reverse fold the top two corners.

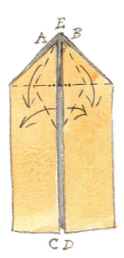
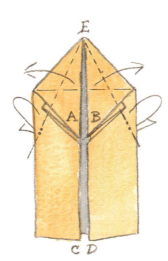
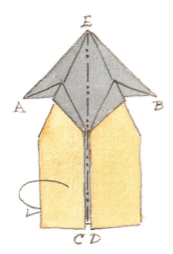
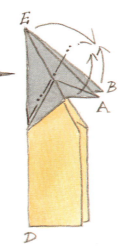

3 Collapse, folding A & B downwards and adding the reverse folds.

4 Fold as shown, allowing A & B to swivel outwards.

5 Mountain fold A behind.

6 Reverse fold E, allowing A & B to pivot upwards to touch E.

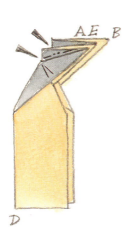
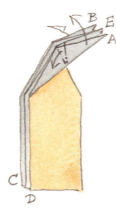

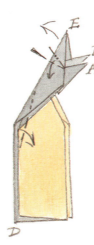
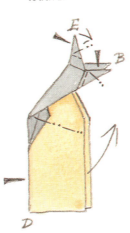

7 Narrow the paper with two reverse folds.

8 Pleat A & B.

9 Turn E inside out, lowering A & B.

10 Crimp the neck upwards. Release paper for the tail. Repeat behind.

11 Crimp the head. Squash the flippers. Reverse fold the rock.

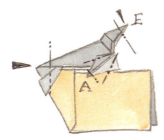

12 Reverse fold the snout. Round off the flippers. Sink the excess paper inside at the tail.

13 Crimp the rock to make it 3D.

14 The Seal on a Rock complete.

BOWL

Dr Shen is renowned for his geometric and abstract forms which collapse dramatically into shape from an apparently unpromising pattern of pre-creases. In this example, note how the soft, cushion-like base makes an effective contrast to the straight-sided walls. The locking mechanism in Steps 13–14 is also pleasing. Use a square of origami paper, white side up, or paper the same colour both sides.

Designed by Dr Philip Shen, Hong Kong.

1 Crease mountains and valleys as shown.

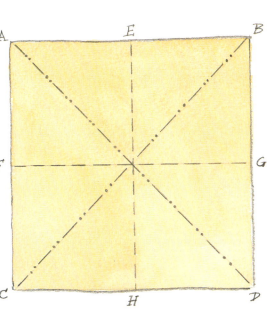

2 Lightly lay corner B onto crease HE, in such a position that if the paper were flattened to make a crease, the crease would run exactly to corner A. However, flatten to make a crease *only* in the two short sections shown. Be precise.

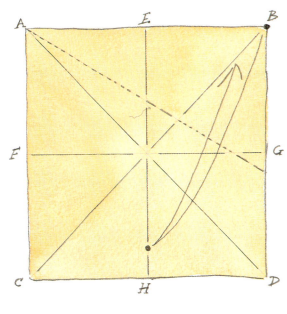

3 Repeat, laying corner C onto crease GF.

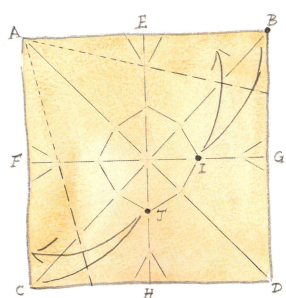

4 Note the crease pattern, both pairs of creases pointing to corner A. Repeat the pattern, so that pairs of creases point to corners B, C, & D.

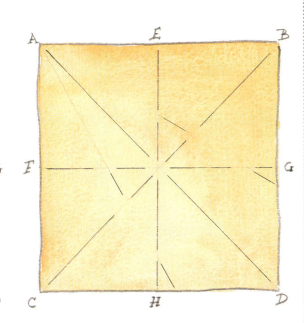

5 Note the octagon of creases in the centre and the 'V's' at E, F, G, & H. Fold B to point I, but crease only where shown. Similarly, fold C to J. Note that if extended, both creases would meet at corner A.

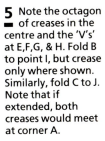

6 This is the crease pattern. Repeat Step 5, creating creases which if extended, would meet at corners B, C, & D.

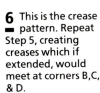

(Continued . . .)

BOWL

(continued)

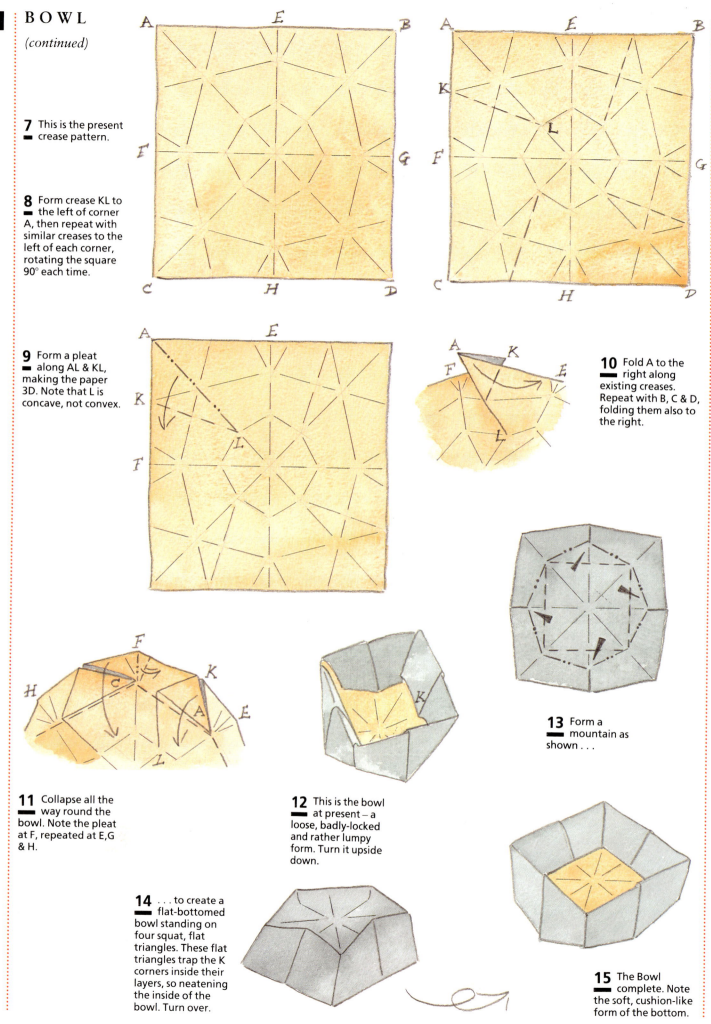

7 This is the present crease pattern.

8 Form crease KL to the left of corner A, then repeat with similar creases to the left of each corner, rotating the square 90° each time.

9 Form a pleat along AL & KL, making the paper 3D. Note that L is concave, not convex.

10 Fold A to the right along existing creases. Repeat with B, C & D, folding them also to the right.

11 Collapse all the way round the bowl. Note the pleat at F, repeated at E,G & H.

12 This is the bowl at present – a loose, badly-locked and rather lumpy form. Turn it upside down.

13 Form a mountain as shown . . .

14 . . . to create a flat-bottomed bowl standing on four squat, flat triangles. These flat triangles trap the K corners inside their layers, so neatening the inside of the bowl. Turn over.

15 The Bowl complete. Note the soft, cushion-like form of the bottom.

■ E L E P H A N T

This final design in the advanced origami section is appropriately the most difficult. Step 7 contains a fiendish closed sink, which will have even the most experienced folders fumbling a little. The Step 11 half-closed sink is little better. It is puzzling to wonder why a design which looks so little like a real elephant should be so immediately recognizable as one! Use a square of paper, same colour both sides. If using origami paper, the coloured side should be outside at Step 1.

Designed by Paul Jackson.

(Continued . . .)

1 Begin with Step 6 of the Waterbomb project. Fold A across to the right.

2 Fold A & D across to edge EC . . .

3 . . . like this, so that when the crease is made, it is precisely horizontal. Unfold it.

4 Unfold A & D, then swivel B upwards to create the Step 5 shape.

5 Squash, separating F from G.

6 Fold G behind.

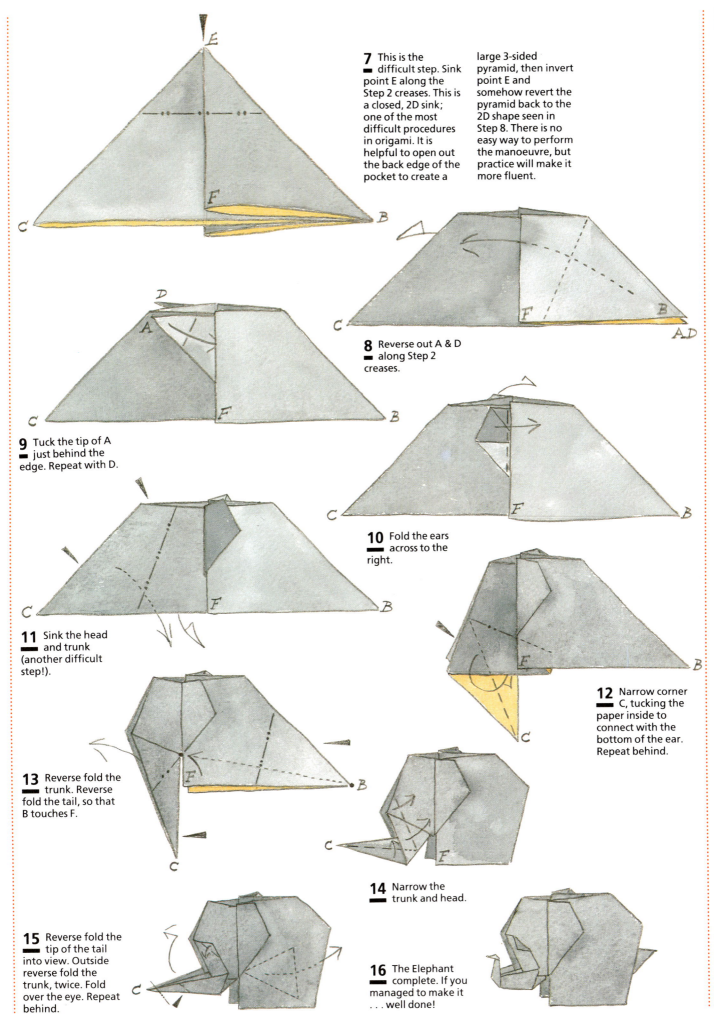

7 This is the difficult step. Sink point E along the Step 2 creases. This is a closed, 2D sink; one of the most difficult procedures in origami. It is helpful to open out the back edge of the pocket to create a large 3-sided pyramid, then invert point E and somehow revert the pyramid back to the 2D shape seen in Step 8. There is no easy way to perform the manoeuvre, but practice will make it more fluent.

8 Reverse out A & D along Step 2 creases.

9 Tuck the tip of A just behind the edge. Repeat with D.

10 Fold the ears across to the right.

11 Sink the head and trunk (another difficult step!).

12 Narrow corner C, tucking the paper inside to connect with the bottom of the ear. Repeat behind.

13 Reverse fold the trunk. Reverse fold the tail, so that B touches F.

14 Narrow the trunk and head.

15 Reverse fold the tip of the tail into view. Outside reverse fold the trunk, twice. Fold over the eye. Repeat behind.

16 The Elephant complete. If you managed to make it . . . well done!

SUPPLIERS

SUPPLIERS

The author and publishers would like to thank the following suppliers for their generous help and advice in providing materials used to create the projects in this book. These suppliers specialize in selling papers and card direct to the public and can be contacted at the addresses shown below.

UK

Mara Amats
ADAE Associates
c/o 8 Wendover Court
Chiltern Street
London W1M 1PB
(*Specialist in handmade Nepalese papers*)

Falkiner Fine Papers Ltd.
76 Southampton Row
London WC1B 4AR

Robert Horne Paper Company
Huntsman House
Mansion Close
Moulton Park
Northampton NN3 1LA

Neal Street East
5 Neal Street
London WC2H 9PU
(*Stockists of a wide range of origami papers*)

One Four Nine Paper Supplies
PO Box A13
Huddersfield
West Yorkshire HD3 4LW
(*Mail order specialists*)

Paperchase
213 Tottenham Court Road
London W1A 4US

Paperpoint
130 Long Acre
London WC2E 9AL

Paperpoint
26 Calthorpe Road
Edgbaston
Birmingham B15 1RP

USA

Kate's Paperie
8 West 13th Street
New York
NY 10001

Papersource Inc.
730 N Franklin Suite 111
Chicago
Il 60610

Australia

ACT Papers Pty Ltd.
10 McGlone Street
Micham
Victoria 3132